"What a ground-breaking and courageous critique of contemporary social work as a profession and practice! *Abolish Social Work (As We Know It)* is an inspiring collection that offers compelling arguments for abolishing the current incarnation of social work, advocating instead for a radical reimagining that includes transformative models rooted in community care and solidarity. It is essential reading for social work scholars, practitioners, and activists committed to dismantling oppressive systems and fostering genuine liberation for those most affected by intersecting forms of oppression."

CAMISHA SIBBLIS, director, Black Studies Institute; assistant professor, Sociology and Criminology, University of Windsor

"*Abolish Social Work (As We Know It)* is a cutting-edge collection that joins the growing canon of abolitionist, anti-carceral, and decolonial social work literature calling for a fresh, new, liberatory approach to social work theory and practice. Centring communities that are marginalized and heavily policed, the editors and authors provide a complex and compelling update to the care, coercion, and control nexus underlying contemporary social work. This collection provides an important and decisive contribution to this pressing and important debate and the potential for an emancipatory future for social work."

DONNA BAINES, professor and former director, School of Social Work, University of British Columbia

"*Abolish Social Work (As We Know It)* is a transformative collection of essays by a range of critical social work scholars and practitioners, community-based advocates and activists, and people who have been directly harmed by social work institutions and agencies. Together, the chapters advance an important critique of carceral social work practice, emphasizing the need for resistance to penality and policing within the field and the necessity of decolonization, anti-racism, mutual aid, and community politics of care. It is a must-read for professional social workers and anyone engaged in informal social work!"

EMILY VAN DER MEULEN, professor, Department of Criminology, Toronto Metropolitan University

"*Abolish Social Work (As We Know It)* is an essential collection, which challenges the long-held assumption that social work is the 'helping profession' applied equitably to those in need. The collection calls us to reflect upon the principles of abolitionist social work, which challenge the carceral-entangled, power-over nature of the profession, and to evolve social work into a profession that is congruent with the values of integrity, solidarity, and care that it espouses."

RAVEN SINCLAIR, professor (retired), University of Regina, CEO Raven Sinclair Consulting

ABOLISH SOCIAL WORK
(AS WE KNOW IT)

ABOLISH SOCIAL WORK
(As We Know It)

EDITED BY
Craig Fortier
Edward Hon-Sing Wong
MJ Rwigema

Between the Lines
Toronto

Abolish Social Work (As We Know It)
© 2024 Craig Fortier, Edward Hon-Sing Wong, and MJ Rwigema

First published in 2024 by
Between the Lines
401 Richmond Street West, Studio 281
Toronto, Ontario · M5V 3A8 · Canada
1-800-718-7201 · www.btlbooks.com

All rights reserved. No part of this publication may be photocopied, reproduced, stored in a retrieval system, or transmitted in any form or by any means, electronic, mechanical, recording, or otherwise, without the written permission of Between the Lines, or (for copying in Canada only) Access Copyright, 69 Yonge Street, Suite 1100, Toronto, ON M5E 1K3.

Every reasonable effort has been made to identify copyright holders. Between the Lines would be pleased to have any errors or omissions brought to its attention.

Library and Archives Canada Cataloguing in Publication
Title: Abolish social work (as we know it) / edited by Craig Fortier, Edward Hon-Sing
    Wong, and MJ Rwigema.
Names: Fortier, Craig, editor. | Hon-Sing Wong, Edward, editor. | Rwigema, MJ, editor.
Description: Includes bibliographical references and index.
Identifiers: Canadiana (print) 20240285778 | Canadiana (ebook) 20240286251 |
    ISBN 9781771136556 (softcover) | ISBN 9781771136563 (EPUB)
Subjects: LCSH: Community-based social services. | LCSH: Social service. |
    LCSH: Social problems. | LCSH: Police abolition movement.
Classification: LCC HV66 .A26 2024 | DDC 361—dc23

Cover design by Jenny Chan
Text design by DEEVE
Printed in Canada

We acknowledge for their financial support of our publishing activities: the Government of Canada; the Canada Council for the Arts; and the Government of Ontario through the Ontario Arts Council, the Ontario Book Publishers Tax Credit program, and Ontario Creates.

MOON/WATER SONG

Catherine Tammaro
Taǫmę̨ʔšreʔ ~ date:ž.tǫ ⁿgyaʔwiš hatiyerunǫʔ

aʔyatráʔskwah ~ (*I dream*)

sawatę:ⁿdišrihšę̨ʔ ~ (*the moon becomes complete*)

aʔyeyę́ʔ aʔwažaʔtihša: ~ (*I see, she looks for me*)

ǫmahšutáʔah yaáʔkwahstih ~ (*Grandmother Moon—She is beautiful!*)

yǫtarawáhstih (*good lake*) ~ *imę̨nǫ́:tę̨ʔ* (*they have life*)

aʔyarǫ́h awáteʔyę̨ʔáhaʔ yayunǫrǫhkwanyǫh ~ (*I hear my siblings thank them*)

iyátǫʔ yǫtarawáhstih ~ (*I say beautiful waters!*)

uⁿdatrę̨ⁿdút awáteʔyę̨ʔáhaʔ ~ (*they are standing songs up, we are siblings*)

yǫtarawáhstih ~ (*the waters—lake—beautiful*)

ǫmahšutáʔah yaákwahstih ~ (*beautiful Grandmother Moon*)

yatuyę̨h yaⁿgwę̨ʔnyahkwih (*it is so/certain, by way of the blood*)

ⁿdutahsehtih kwaaʔtayǫh (*that which is hidden inside our bodies*)

aʔyatéʔskuh (*I go into the water*)

THE ORIGINAL POEM/SONG

> *I dream the moon becomes full. I see She looks for me—Grandmother Moon is so beautiful!*
>
> *The waters are alive! I hear my sisters thanking them; they are offering up songs.*
>
> *I feel how beautiful they are . . . (The Waters, my Sisters and Grandmother Moon!)*
>
> *The water is beautiful . . . and the Moon—It is certain (that we are all connected) through our blood—The mystery that is hidden inside of us . . . I walk into the water . . .*

AN OPENING POEM/SONG

We begin this volume with a poem/song offering from Elder Catherine Tammaro in the hopes that it will guide the work we intend to take on. In the spirit of the moon/water song, we seek to ground our discussion in connections, in recognizing the need to be rooted in community, and in a spirit of fluidity and adaptation.

CATHERINE TAMMARO

Elder Tammaro is a multidisciplinary artist whose practice spans decades. She is an enrolled member of the Wyandot of Anderdon Nation, part of the Wendat Confederacy, and served as their Communications Officer for many years. Elder Tammaro is a "Utrihont" or "seated" Spotted Turtle Clan Tradition Keeper and is active throughout the city and beyond in many organizations as Elder in Residence, Mentor, and Cultural Advisor.

She is an alumna of the Ontario College of Art and has had a diverse career, with multiple exhibits and installations, published written and musical works, and public artworks. Elder Tammaro is in demand as a public speaker and continues her extensive practice while also providing ongoing support for the work and development of other artists. She is the Indigenous Arts Program Manager at Toronto Arts Council and their first Elder in Residence. She is grateful to serve the Indigenous communities that make up our vast urban landscape.

CONTENTS

Introduction
Craig Fortier, Edward Hon-Sing Wong, and MJ Rwigema / 1

PART ONE
ABOLITION SOCIAL WORK

Chapter 1. Towards Abolitionist Social Work
Building Praxis
Cameron Rasmussen / 17

Chapter 2. Mental Health Workers Have Never Been the Solution to Racial Violence by Police
Edward Hon-Sing Wong / 32

Chapter 3. For Black Women, Health Care Is an Abolition Issue
Renée Nichole Ferguson / 44

Chapter 4. "Keep This Up and They'll Be Pulling You from the Red"
Young People Are Dying to Survive Winnipeg's Child Welfare System
Juvie / 55

Chapter 5. Not Criminally Responsible
The Fatal Intersection of the Mental Health and Justice Systems
Carly Seltzer, Lue Palmer, and Golta Shahidi / 70

Chapter 6. Shifting Praxis
Social Work and Community-Based Approaches to Abolition
Krystle Skeete and Heather Bergen / 82

Chapter 7. The Antitrafficking Movement Is Not Abolitionist
How Carceral Feminists and Social Workers Harm Migrant Sex Workers
Elene Lam / 92

Chapter 8. A Masterpiece We Can Call Abolition
Reflections from the Pages of *Cell Count*
Sena Hussain, Nolan Turcotte, and Zakaria Amara / 103

PART TWO
SOCIAL WORK ABOLITION

Chapter 9. Social Work Abolition in Unsettling Times
Craig Fortier and Edward Hon-Sing Wong / 115

Chapter 10. The Only Good Social Worker Is a Criminal Social Worker
Chanelle Gallant / 124

Chapter 11. Conversations on Decolonizing Justice
With Members of It Starts With Us and No More Silence
Audrey Huntley and Carol Lynne D'Arcangelis / 134

Chapter 12. Baby Bundle Project and Community Birth Work Journeys
Krysta Williams / 154

Chapter 13. Social Work's Very Complicated Relationship with Indigenous Languages
Rochelle Allan / 165

Chapter 14. Toronto Indigenous Harm Reduction
Solidarity with Indigenous Encampment Residents
Brianna Olson Pitawanakwat / 179

Chapter 15. Black Creek Community Farm
Mutual Aid, Abolition, and Food Justice in Jane and Finch
Suzanne Narain, Sabrina "Butterfly" Gopaul, Sam Tecle, Zakisha Brown, Rosie Mishaiel, Anan Lololi, and Leticia Ama Deawuo / 182

Notes / 193

Index / 221

INTRODUCTION

Craig Fortier,
Edward Hon-Sing Wong,
and MJ Rwigema

This book intervenes in conversations about the nature and purpose of social work as a profession at a critical historical juncture and moment of reckoning. The COVID-19 pandemic alerted us to the limits of institutional frameworks of care.[1] Black Lives Matter mobilizations laid bare the complicity of social work in the carceral apparatus of the state just as social workers were being proposed as an alternative to racist policing.[2] The Truth and Reconciliation of Canada's *Calls to Action* specifically identified the need for reparation from professional social workers who have been complicit in maintaining the system of segregation, assimilation, and family separation formalized during the era of residential schools.[3] The questions that confront us are many: How do we practice forms of social work that aren't steeped in carcerality, containment, and control? Can or should social work as a profession survive a social transformation that seeks to reimagine how we relate to and care for one another? How can social workers and social work scholars play a meaningful role in emerging mutual aid projects? Who *actually* does social working in our community and which functions of social work practice are *actually* policing by another name?

We have titled this book *Abolish Social Work (As We Know It)* to give name and form to these questions and to open a space of reflection about what responding to calls for abolition and decolonization might look like for social workers and social work institutions. This edited volume began in 2018 when three of the original editors, Craig Fortier, Edward Hon-Sing Wong, and Nicole Penak, met to discuss a potential panel on social work for the Abolition Convergence that was to be held in Toronto in May 2020. Nicole brought MJ Rwigema into the fold in 2019.[4] COVID-19 forced the organizers of the Abolition Convergence to postpone the event indefinitely and we decided to turn towards a book that might capture some of the conversations and practices floating within the social work spaces we operate within. The four of us all had experience as front-line social workers (Edward and Nicole predominantly as clinical social workers; Craig and MJ predominantly as community social workers), as activists and political organizers, and as social work educators. These overlapping experiences, as well as some of our own encounters with professional social workers in our personal lives, strongly influenced our decisions regarding who we invited to contribute to this book. The contributors to this book are diverse in their experiences of and relationships to social work as a profession. They include frontline social workers, social work scholars, sex workers and sex work advocates, Indigenous Elders and language learners, community health practitioners, community farm organizers, incarcerated people, birth workers, and people who have survived carceral social work institutions. They are also predominantly Black, Indigenous, People of Colour (BIPOC) and white working class—many of them are queer/trans, some are Muslim, and many others are disabled, and their positionalities are reflected in the themes, contributions, and discussions that emerge in their chapters. While this volume is not exclusively Canadian in content, most of our contributors are situated in Toronto and other parts of Canada and provide a nuanced analysis of the politics of abolition and decolonization within social work circles in this country.

HOW SOCIAL WORKING BECAME SOCIAL WORK

Social work is an assemblage of practices. We have become accustomed to thinking about social work through the myopic lens of its professionalized identity, but the practices we can define as "social working" are broad, disparate, and at times contradictory—someone who practices social working is not necessarily a social worker. In this book we take a broad and inclusive approach to the study of social work. We attempt to differentiate social work in its professional sense (an organized set of institutional relationships and organizations that educates, registers, regulates, and licenses who can and cannot be employed as a social worker) and social working in its community sense (a series of actions, groups, events, and practices of care and mutual aid that can overlap or conflict in their intents and purposes with professional social work). Professional social workers may be engaged in informal forms of social working, may overlap with such initiatives in their paid employment, or may see such groups as a nuisance or as competition with their more established organizations.

Many, if not all, of the practices we call "social work" existed well before the formalization of the profession in the twentieth century. Often these practices were forms of survival work and mutual aid among people in families, small communities, or neighbourhoods, relational types of work that ensured that everyone was fed, housed, loved, and cared for—community practices of care.[5] These types of work were organized by religious groups, ethnocultural associations, trade unions, neighbourhood associations, groups of friends or relatives, and municipal governments (among numerous others). Such practices laid the foundation for parts of the social work profession that are concerned with community welfare, public health, and individual well-being. Alongside these early forms of care practice, there also existed a number of informal social practices of coercion and containment that have also influenced the social work profession. Temperance societies, friendly visiting, Indian agents, and other religious and social institutions sought to dictate socially acceptable behaviour, campaigned against "social idling" to force people into oppressive work conditions, and worked to exclude, surveil, and monitor various racialized, queer, migrant, and disabled groups.[6] To understand social work today, we need to see it as part of a lineage of these reinforcing and contradictory practices of care, extraction, support, coercion, collaboration, punishment, healing, gaslighting, help, and policing.

Professional social work exists in multiple spheres in our society, some formal and others much less so. The spaces where social workers have a significant impact in our community are vast and diverse—they may work in the areas of child and family services, clinical mental health practice, community health, occupational therapy, legal clinics, penal institutions, housing, nonprofit administration, street outreach, harm reduction, LGBTQ+ programming, Indigenous services, policing, community work, sex worker outreach, arts programs, alternative medicine, hospitals, courts, violence against women shelters, and a wide array of grassroots community-based organizations—to name but a few such areas.

However, the practice of informal social working often exists within and outside these formal social work areas through projects of mutual aid and social solidarity: practices that often emerge through friend or family support groups, neighbourhood collectives, workplace group chats, and social movement mobilizing (among many other spaces). These practices often seek to meet our own needs and the needs of others in our communities without the institutional supports we generally consider to be the realm of "social work." These include, but are not limited to, street medics, needle and syringe distribution, disaster relief, care collectives, community pantries, food deliveries, community gardens, sex worker unions—actions and activities that often lie outside the charitable model and assert a more horizontal (rather than vertical) form of power.[7]

In the early twentieth century, social work lacked general acceptance as a profession, given the gendered discourse of social workers as "well-intentioned, committed volunteers who would soon get married."[8] Social workers embarked on professionalization to "help legitimize members in provision of programs and services that helped buffer most extreme poverty."[9] Professional status was also thought to provide social workers with a competitive advantage in the labour market through the establishment of a collective identity.[10]

But as Edward Said argues, professionalization establishes the authority to dictate acceptable practices and, ultimately, an "inevitable drift towards power and authority in its adherents, towards the requirements and prerogatives of power, and towards being directly employed by it."[11] This professionalization leads to specialization, introducing a narrow bound on legitimate knowledge. While Said's analysis was explicitly in relation to intellectuals and writers, this is a helpful starting point for understanding social work professionalization and its distinction from social working practices.[12] Consistent with Said's description of professionalization, social work scholars Richard Edwards, Wes Shera, P. Nelson Reid, and Reginald York explain that, for social work to qualify as a profession, it must be distinguishable based on the work involved and an associated body of knowledge; it must involve education and training to "expand and refine that body of knowledge and to disseminate it to future and current practitioners of the profession";

and it must involve credentialization, controlling how professional practice is undertaken and who can participate in the practice.[13]

In Canada, an important step in this process of acquiring these elements was the establishment of the Canadian Association of Social Workers (CASW) in 1926.[14] An announcement of the launch described how the establishment of the CASW marked the maturation of social work, "a profession with a technique all its own, demanding a rigorous training, and a code of ethics and standards to be lived up to."[15] As a sign of future credentialization, CASW restricted membership to those with social work training "who have been professionally occupied with the work of social work education, organization or adjustment, and whose professional standards of behaviour are in conformity with those of the association."[16]

Professionalization, especially as embodied by the advocacy of CASW, was partly sought out as an alternative to unionization to secure better work conditions. While several CASW committees conducted studies that concluded unions were the most effective means of improving labour conditions and protecting social workers as employees, CASW ultimately avoided that approach, given the "red scare" and the association of union organizing with communism. CASW did not want to associate with blue-collar workers and risk diminishing social work's social status. According to a report by the Montreal branch of CASW, many social workers held concerns about "unions being dominated by communists, and unions being 'beneath our dignity.'"[17] Unlike unionization, professionalization directs critiques away from the sector and social structures and towards individual "bad apple" social workers. Collective action and direct action are discouraged in favour of working with policymakers, funders, and other institutional authorities.

In a broader context, Bonnie Burstow describes the development of social work, and professionalized mental health care in particular, as part of the ongoing enclosure of the commons.[18] Nandita Sharma and Cynthia Wright follow Silvia Federici's definition of the commons as being inclusive of practices that nurture "relationships of mutuality with fellow commoners and developing the framework for new ways of organizing society."[19] Practices associated with the commons are seen as a threat to professional social work because the field would lose its raisons d'être if communities had the resources and freedom to address their issues on their own terms.

Patricia Johnston and Frank Tester explain, "In order to be seen as a profession, social work has to lay claim to skills and forms of practice that distinguish it from other professions, and relationships and practices that occur in the 'everyday world.'"[20] This monopolization of power and responsibility is not simply ideological, professional social work bodies have often actively worked to position themselves as better equipped to deal with social issues that communities are seeking to address themselves. Social work, like other professions, also dominates appeals for funds and resources to address social issues through a politic of respectability—an ethic that often aligns the profession's accountability to funders and power brokers rather than the communities in which they work.

Chris Chapman and A. J. Withers describe the presumption of care practices and social provisioning being the exclusive domain of white professionals as a form of displacement, rendering informal work conducted by racialized people to support others in their own communities invisible.[21] Even when social work institutions publicly express their commitment to racial equity and social justice, they often leave "whiteness intact through a variety of mechanisms, including sentimentalism, colorblindness, and transhistoricism."[22] We can trace these processes historically. In 1946, when the Canadian government sought to transition away from the use of Indian agents on Indigenous reservations, a joint submission from the Canadian Welfare Council (CWC) and the CASW successfully argued that they were the logical replacements for enacting the social welfare functions of the Indian agent, rather than allowing communities themselves to re-institute their own practices of care.[23] The results of these forms of monopolization came with the effects and impacts of normative whiteness and settler colonial mentality among social workers sent into Indigenous communities.

For instance, while Mi'kmaw society did not stigmatize hearing voices or seeing things that others did not, the active role of social workers in their communities often meant that Western medical approaches that understood these behaviours as pathological and requiring professional intervention were foisted onto Mi'kmaw and other Indigenous communities.[24] Similarly, Johnston and Tester write about how Inuit Qaujimajatuqangit (Traditional Knowledge) has also become marginalized through social work encroachment into their lives. Inuit beliefs around the need for collective remedies to address harm were replaced by punitive approaches that blame individuals for maladaptation. Similarly, the 1953 attempt by the Canadian settler state to apply the *Northwest Territories Child Welfare Ordinance* to Inuit people meant that professional social workers from southern Canada were sent to assess the welfare of Inuit children and in doing so intervened in how the community had collectively supported themselves through their own spiritual, intellectual, and social practices.[25]

Displacement of community social working also came in the form of criminalization and state violence. While Canadians often seek to evade complicity in the legacy of slavery, Robyn Maynard's *Policing Black Lives* reaffirms the ways anti-Black racism is foundational to the modern Canadian state and its institutions (including social work).[26] As Maynard argues, Black women in particular face state antagonism and repression in their attempts to parent, migrate, and make a living, often due to the perceptions, reports, and beliefs held and produced by social workers they encounter.[27] While there are distinct difference between the historical relationship faced by Black and Indigenous communities in Canada in relation to social welfare agents, Maynard shows that "both communities face high rates of child apprehension from state-funded child welfare agents, and both communities' children suffer the consequences of the systemic racism that tears them from their families 'for their own good.'"[28]

In Saidiya Hartman's *Wayward Lives, Beautiful Experiments*, she shows how, in its earliest incarnations, social work functioned as a technology of control and containment, all under the guise of "care" within Black communities in urban centres in the United States.[29] Hartman, however, takes great care to show the ways young Black women and gender nonconforming folks were audaciously asserting their liberation *despite* the matronly care of wealthy white women and social workers. The community "social working" practices among these young women were rejected by professional social workers as inferior or lay knowledges and practices. This distinguishment is consistent with Said's claim that the pressure of specialization in relation to professionalism causes a narrowing of one's scope of knowledge and a disconnect from experience and context through an "increasing technical formalism."[30] This was why social work leaders argued for a more systematic, science-based process in how charity was dispensed during the early days of social work and how discipline and punishment were meted out to those who were presumed wayward or maladapted.[31]

This specialized knowledge was partly disseminated through social work education. Graduates, as recognized holders of this specialized knowledge, become professional social workers.[32] Through this training process, social workers are taught to exalt the specialized knowledge associated with the profession and invalidate the perspectives of service users.[33] Even W. E. B. Du Bois, the founder of the concept of abolitionist democracy, first encountered this form of community social working as a young sociologist sent to study the problem of poverty in Black ghettos—what we may understand today as a form of policy-oriented social work.[34] Witnessing the radical liberatory values and practices of community care among the poor Black families he interviewed fundamentally transformed Du Bois' views on Black empowerment. These interactions transformed his political analysis and precipitated his radical turn away from identifying the interpersonal traits and qualities that caused Black people to be maladaptive to the economic system and towards abolitionism as a principle of democracy and Black liberation.[35] For Du Bois, the witnessing of deep and complex systems of relational support, neighbourliness, and collective resistance to institutional interlopers helped him to articulate and reject the forms of control and containment that "professional care" brought to Black neighbourhoods.[36]

ABOLITION SOCIAL WORK AND SOCIAL WORK ABOLITION

Contemporary abolitionist politics in social work can be traced to feminist of colour organizing work in Canada and the United States over the past thirty years. For instance, INCITE! Women of Color Against Violence produced two seminal anthologies in the mid 2000s, *Color of Violence* (2006) and *The Revolution Will Not Be Funded* (2007), that critiqued the ability of institutionalized social work and other "helping" professions to address the needs of marginalized communities and transform society in any meaningful way.[37] In problematizing these helping professions (and our own complicity working within them), INCITE! proposed pathways to liberation guided by the principles of abolition, transformative justice, and community-led and noninstitutional programming. In proposing and modelling practices to address the root structures of interpersonal violence through intersectional and collaborative movements working across differences in power and social position, INCITE! radicalized an emerging generation of community-based activists seeking to develop new approaches to dealing with violence, trauma, poverty, and precarity outside of the logics of the nonprofit industrial complex. It also pushed a subsection of radical social workers to turn the lens inward on their profession and identify the ways the profession is tethered to the violence of settler colonialism, white supremacy, heteropatriarchy, and carceral capitalism (among many other structures of power).[38] This radical turn has coalesced into a politics of "abolition social work"; however, it has also given rise to questions about whether social work as a professional association itself needs to be abolished—or at the very least transformed beyond recognition.

Abolitionism has its roots in Black liberation struggles against enslavement and the criminal justice system. Angela Davis understands these institutions as intrinsically linked, contesting the idea that slavery was abolished by the Thirteenth Amendment of the United States Constitution.[39] Instead, Davis argues, enslavement was simply transformed and its function fulfilled by institutions like lynching, segregation, policing, and incarceration. She further argues that parallels remain with today's "wide-ranging corporatization of punishment that has produced a prison industrial complex."[40] It is within the context of criminalization and marginalization in the 1960s that Angela Davis further developed the idea of abolition democracy: "The creation of an array of social institutions that would begin to solve the social problems that set people on the track to prison, thereby helping to render the prison obsolete."[41] Underlying this proposal to address social problems is the notion that abolition is not only about eliminating carceral institutions but also about challenging the social conditions that allow for the existence of carceral institutions. To do so requires naming the entanglements of current social service provision with the goals of carceral capitalism. As Jackie Wang argues, the "evolution in the social function of the state from *provider of social services to provider of security* also represent[s] an evolution in how racialized populations in the United States [are] managed."[42] The social work profession continues to work closely with law enforcement authorities (i.e., police, immigration enforcement, courts, etc.) to uphold and expand carceral institutions targeting Indigenous, poor, queer/trans, disabled, and racialized communities.[43] Thus, as radical social work scholars Leah Jacobs and colleagues suggest in their widely read article "Defund the Police: Moving Towards an Anti-Carceral Social Work," "the suggestion that social workers provide an ameliorative softening of police powers or a more pronounced *alternative* to the police has complicated calls for police funding to be redistributed to social work organizations.[44] Similarly, in our (Fortier and Wong) article, "The Settler Colonialism of Social Work and the Social Work of Settler Colonialism," we argue that social workers continue to help facilitate the dispossession of Indigenous peoples from their territories and (re)produce the settler state under the guise of being "helpful."[45]

So, what is abolitionist social work and how does it overlap and differ from calls for social work abolition? The chapters in this book speak to and advance a politics of abolitionist social work that affirms the following four broad principles:

> **Resistance to Collaboration with Carceral Institutions:** Social work practice must problematize carceral institutions and be wary about, refuse, or reject collaboration with police and other carceral agents.
> **Kill the Cop Inside Us:** Social work practice must seek to identify, limit, and disinvest from forms of policing within social work institutions and organizations, including the rules, regulations, and conflict resolution policies of agencies.
> **Disinvest from Our Own Power:** Social work practice must work to decentralize its own power, collaborate with community-based initiatives, and support anti-authoritarian, decolonizing, and abolitionist social movements.
> **Weapons of the Weak:**[46] When placed in a compromised political position in which one's precarious employment is at risk, social workers should attempt to practice noncooperation and/or contravention of professional policies and protocols that put people at risk of incarceration, migrant detention or deportation, removal from community, and refusal of service to the best of their ability.

The politics of abolition social work are multiple and scaffolded. For instance, Beth Richie and Kayla Martensen call on social workers to reconsider programs, practices, organizations, and institutional forms that help build up carceral society.[47] Sparrow Preston writes about what abolitionist politics looks like in day-to-day social work practice and offers key scripts for harm reduction in the event of police being called to respond to an issue at an agency you work for.[48] Autumn Asher BlackDeer and Maria Gandarilla Ocampo explain the importance of rejecting explicit and implicit forms of curriculum that reinforce commitments to professionalism in social work education over critical thinking, movement building, and social action.[49] Similarly, this book, and in particular chapters in the first half of the book, seeks to highlight how carceralism is prevalent within social work spaces, offers theoretical and practical means to address this carceralism, and contributes to a growing body of literature on abolitionist social work.

The concept of social work abolition is less written about or studied, but it too plays a large part in the conversations happening on front lines and within communities about the role, power, and purpose of professional social work in people's lives. While social work scholar Daphne Jeyapal provides an important reminder that "social work is still the only profession with a critical concern over the fundamental role of social justice," she implores those who work in the field to "respond to racialized communities' anticolonial movements with a politics and ethics that engages with 'marginality as a site of resistance' and recognizes that resistance itself can, in a white settler society, be marginalizing."[50] Resistance to carceral politics and practices within social work organizations is coming from clients/participants, front-line workers, students and scholars, and even some managers—and inevitably, without collective power, these folks are often marginalized and ostracized in their workplaces, schools, or other institutions. A full-scale transformation of social work that divests from its carceral functions is an enormous challenge and one that requires serious consideration of whether it is possible to achieve this goal while also maintaining the professional apparatus. Social work abolition emerges, thus, not as a rejection of the essential social justice and community-based practices that social workers continue to do, often being an essential service of survival for people on the margins of society, but rather as a means of envisioning a future space of social working that exists outside the profession's carceral, colonial, and capitalist confines. The chapters in the latter half of this book seek to enrich our conversations about what social work abolition might look like in theory and practice. There are five broad principles that weave through these chapters:

- **Disinvestment from Our Own Mystique:** Recognize the limits of professional social work as an institutional force for social justice and work to limit, decentre, and dissolve its power from within and outside of institutions and organizations in which we operate.
- **Recentre Community as the Site of Leadership:** Emphasize work that supports and resources community-based transformative justice, harm reduction, resurgence, and mutual aid initiatives that exist within, against, and beyond official social work-type organizations.
- **Stop Teaching the Same Things:** Transform pedagogy in social work classrooms to educate students on the limits of professionalized social work within a neoliberal capitalist nonprofit industrial complex apparatus.
- **Find Alternatives to Institutional Funding:** Develop ways to find financial resources for grassroots initiatives that do not tie them to trusteeships, accountability to "funders," and 501(c)(3) and charitable organization status that limit their political work.
- **Be Humble, Create as Much as You Take Down:** Collectively construct radical alternative spaces of care, accountability, action, and humility that are antagonistic toward carceral social work organizations and structures *and also* productive in laying the foundation for abolitionist and decolonizing futures.

THE ORGANIZATION AND FRAMEWORK FOR THIS BOOK

Abolish Social Work (As We Know It) is organized into two distinct parts: (1) Abolition Social Work; (2) Social Work Abolition. These parts are meant to balance the tensions between critique and possibility, between care and carcerality, between professionalism and survivalism. These parts are preceded by a song and gift offering from Elder Catherine Tammaro (Wyandot of Anderdon Nation, Spotted Turtle Clan), "Moon/Water Song," that reminds us of our relationships and responsibilities to these territories, the waters, and the cosmos. Elder Tammaro also offers a piece of artwork, "Honouring Our Sisters," which further reminds us of our responsibilities and accountability to women and in particular Indigenous women who are confronted by the issues and themes that we discuss in this volume.

In the first part (Abolition Social Work), the contributors speak to the contours, histories, theories, and practices of abolition within, against, and beyond social work as it exists today. We begin with Cameron Rasmussen's chapter, "Towards an Abolitionist Social Work: Building Praxis," which historicizes both carceral and abolitionist politics within social services and offers practical frameworks for how we might begin to engage in abolitionism inside (and outside) the state. This chapter is one of the few that bridges the Canadian and US contexts with respect to abolitionist social work and works to connect the political shifts taking place in both countries. In chapter 2, Edward Hon-Sing Wong's "Mental Health Workers Have Never Been the Solution to Racial Violence by Police" exposes the eugenicist and xenophobic beliefs that have animated mental health social work in the past and today—arguing that the call to replace police officers with social workers does not inherently solve the problem of carceralism and the punishment of those who need support and care. Chapter 3, Renée Nichole Ferguson's "For Black Women, Health Care is an Abolition Issue," focuses on the experiences of Black women patients, health care workers, and social workers within the medical system in Ontario and reflects on abolitionist approaches within these fields. In chapter 4 "'Keep This Up and They'll Be Pulling You from the Red': Young People Are Dying to Survive Winnipeg's Child Welfare System," Juvie reflects on their lived experience of racism, violence, and control couched in a rhetoric of care and protection by Child and Family Services in Manitoba. In chapter 5, "Not Criminally Responsible: The Fatal Intersection of the Mental Health and Justice Systems," Carly Seltzer (a social worker), Lue Palmer (a caregiver with lived experience), and Golta Shahidi (a criminal defence lawyer) walk us through the ways the mental health and criminal justice systems in Canada mutually reinforce processes of containment, control, and surveillance instead of supporting people struggling with mental health issues. In chapter 6, "Shifting Praxis: Social Work and Community-Based Approaches to Abolition," Krystle Skeete (Freedom Fridayz) and Heather Bergen (Community Action for Families) reflect on abolitionist social work practice through their involvement with two projects that seek to engage in mutual aid and solidarity among Black and racialized youth and single mothers experiencing the child welfare system, respectively. In chapter 7, "The Antitrafficking Movement Is Not Abolitionist: How Carceral Feminists and Social Workers Harm Migrant Sex Workers," Elene Lam argues that the recent wave of "anti-trafficking" activism by carceral social workers and feminists has more to do with the moral goal of eliminating the selling of sex than ensuring women's safety. And finally, in chapter 8, "A Masterpiece We Can Call Abolition," Sena Hussain, the current editor of *Cell Count*, a news publication circulated inside prisons in Ontario, collaborates with two incarcerated contributors serving life sentences, Nolan Turcotte and Zakaria Amara, to reflect on how abolition and social work are conceptualized by people who are currently incarcerated.

Part two of the book, "Social Work Abolition," grapples with the challenges and possibilities of trying to bring about the worlds we wish to see—including the real possibility that turning towards an abolitionist and decolonizing social work might mean transforming the social work profession beyond recognition. This section asks hard questions about the failures, missteps, and learnings that have emerged from some of the prefigurative practices that have been attempted—ones that move alongside and outside the realm of social work. It explores both the possibilities and risks of transforming social work beyond its current professional boundaries. It begins with chapter 9, "Social Work Abolition in Unsettling Times," where Craig Fortier and Edward Hon-Sing Wong grapple with what it might mean to see social work abolition as a potential necessary step for social workers to respond to calls for decolonization. Chapter 10, Chanelle Gallant's "The Only Good Social Worker Is a Criminal Social Worker," provocatively pushes us to think about social work outside the confines of regulatory bodies and legalistic frameworks and to enact the types of care and solidarity people need when confronted with the violence of our social and political realities. Chapter 11, "Conversations on Decolonizing Justice with Members of It Starts With Us and No

More Silence," by Audrey Huntley and Carol Lynne D'Arcangelis weaves in reflections, hopes, and desires from Elders, aunties, and organizers from the movement in support of missing and murdered Indigenous women, girls, Two-Spirit people, and their families. In chapter 12, "Baby Bundle Project and Community Birth Work Journeys," Krysta Williams shares experiences and lessons learned as an Indigenous full spectrum doula and longtime sexual health educator in Tkaronto's urban Indigenous community. Chapter 13, Rochelle Allan's "Social Work's Very Complicated Relationship with Indigenous Languages" explores the author's frustrations and successes in trying to develop an active Anishinaabemowin learning community within and outside current institutional programs. In chapter 14, Brianna Olson Pitawanakwat contributes a short piece titled "Toronto Indigenous Harm Reduction: Solidarity with Indigenous Encampment Residents" that explains how this grassroots mutual aid initiative started amidst the COVID-19 pandemic. And finally, in chapter 15, "Black Creek Community Farm: Mutual Aid, Abolition, and Food Justice in Jane and Finch," Suzanne Narain draws on a roundtable discussion with organizers and participants of the Black-led Black Creek Community Farm to reflect on the possibilities and potentialities that arose out of a community effort to take control of an urban farm that was not meeting its mandate of serving the community.

CONCLUSION

We are grateful that you've decided to engage in this conversation and want to acknowledge the multitudes of whispers, foot dragging, covert resistance, and open defiance that many people working in the formal social work field have engaged in as part of a growing movement towards abolitionist social work and the eventual abolition of carceral social work and its professional bodies. If we begin to understand social work as a series of assemblages of practices and relationships, we are much more likely to see how easy it is to work together to undo its carceral logics, to sever our relationships with the structures of power that seek to contain us, and to build long-standing and sustainable projects of mutual aid as members of and in relation to communities seeking liberation. We offer these chapters as seeds that will hopefully sprout through the small cracks in history.

PART ONE
ABOLITION SOCIAL WORK

CHAPTER 1
TOWARDS ABOLITIONIST SOCIAL WORK
Building Praxis

Cameron Rasmussen

In Canada and the United States, social work has long been complicit and at times an active partner in the making and sustaining of the prison industrial complex (PIC).[1] Its troubled history as an accomplice to what Ruth Wilson Gilmore calls organized violence and organized abandonment is reflected in both principle and practice. At the same time, there is a legacy of those within the social work sphere who have challenged the existence of the PIC and its underlying forces of oppression and domination.[2] They have, instead, worked to cultivate life affirming institutions and liberatory responses to harm. More recent iterations of radical social work have surfaced the concept of an abolitionist social work, situating social work within efforts for PIC abolition, and providing a horizon from which to realize more emancipatory formations and relations within the world of social work.[3]

This chapter offers scaffolding for the thinking and practice of an abolitionist social work, including pillars and frameworks for identifying where and how abolitionist social work can happen, and highlights concrete efforts that have helped realize abolitionist possibilities within social work. In exploring the liberatory possibilities of social work, this piece builds on the work of Ruth Wilson Gilmore, Mariame Kaba, Dean Spade, Mimi Kim, Beth Richie, and others to situate abolitionist praxis within the context of social work.

RECKONING WITH CARCERAL SOCIAL WORK

Professional social work in most of its manifestation has always been proximate to capitalism, whiteness, ableism, cisheteropatriarchy, and carceral notions of power, justice, and human development.[4] In the United States, while this proximity has always existed, social work's relationship with the carceral state began to increase significantly in the 1970s. This increased entanglement between social work and the carceral state was part and parcel of the rise of neoliberalism and its influence to move social work towards professionalization and "fixing" individuals and away from organizing and structural change.[5]

Several social work scholar-activists have charted some of the historic relationships between social work and the PIC. Mimi Kim has written about social work's reliance on law enforcement in its relationship with antiviolence work, specifically intimate partner violence.[6] This is part of the broader and growing literature on carceral feminism that has theorized and documented the ways some feminist efforts have contributed to the growth and maintenance of the carceral state.[7] Kim's work provides a useful window into how justifications for safety for some come at a cost to marginalized groups. More specifically, how the supposed protection of white women can create more precarity for those at the margins of our society, including people of colour, undocumented people, people experiencing poverty, people with disabilities, and trans and queer people. This framework grounds our analysis of social work's relationship with the PIC and how social works' interventions of "protection" can reinforce criminalization and strengthen the power of the state to harm the most vulnerable communities.

Similarly, for more than twenty years, Dorothy Roberts has written about the harms of the child welfare system, now referred to by abolitionists as the "family regulation system." Roberts's seminal work *Shattered Bonds* not only reveals how the family regulation system was set up to oppress Black women and Black families, but how the intersections of criminalization, carcerality, and racial domination have always been central to social work.[8] The study of social works' efforts in the spheres of antiviolence and family regulation offer clear root cause analysis regarding carceral collaboration and complicity, which allows practitioners to better understand how and why social work became even more embedded in the carceral state in the last twenty years.

With the rise of mass incarceration, so too came the precipitous rise in social work engagement in all the tentacles of the PIC. Social workers were called in to meet increasing demands for mental health care in incarcerated settings, treatment programs, probation, diversion, and alternative to incarceration programs and electronic monitoring, leading to the development of the formalized field of forensic social work. This was apart from and in addition to the countless ways social work and social workers were already engaging with people affected by criminalization and incarceration—whether in schools, shelters, clinics, health care settings, or elsewhere. While the justification for social work's engagement included a range of commitments to social justice, journalists and activists Maya Schenwar and Vikki Law demonstrate in their recently published book *Prison By Any Other Name* that these reforms, which represent "kinder, gentler" approaches to social problems, have actually expanded the carceral state rather than reduced its power and reach.[9] In short, the growth in social work's efforts in and around the carceral state have furthered its power, size, and harm.

These realities, this scholarship, and the work of many others, have led to the concept of carceral social work, defined by Jacobs et al. as

> a form of social work that relies on logics of social control and white supremacy and that uses coercive and punitive practices to manage BIPOC and poor communities. Carceral social work enacts these logics and practices in tandem with the penal arm of the state, condoning and in many cases collaborating or integrating with police, prosecutors, jails, prisons, juvenile and criminal courts. Therefore, we understand carceral social work as two interlocking components—the deployment of tactics, within social work, dependent on the same white supremacist and coercive foundations as policing, as well as direct partnership with law enforcement itself.[10]

Beth Richie and Kayla Martensen offer the framework of "carceral services," which "replicate the control, surveillance, and punishment of the Prison Nation, and thus, punitive and social services can become indistinguishable."[11] Where Jacobs, Kim, and their colleagues differentiate two intersecting expressions of carceral social work—the alignment of social work and the carceral state and how social workers directly partner with carceral systems like the police—Richie and Martinsen's more localized definition describes the ways the practice of social work can and does replicate the logics of the carceral state.

Carceral social work is built upon the mythological hierarchies of humanity: the deserving and undeserving, the good and bad, the criminal and innocent. In the context of entrenched neoliberalism, these ideological pillars of individualism, domination, and criminality have become central to professional social work, legitimating and entrenching the participation of social workers in the PIC. In writing about social works' relationship to policing and its pursuit of legitimacy and professionalization, my friend and colleague Dr. Kirk "Jae" James and I recently wrote:

> This has meant aligning social work with systems and structures of power, conceding much of its capacity to address deeply rooted oppression and racialized injustices. A key neoliberal manifestation of these concessions has been to locate the roots of social problems and "crime" in the individual. This harmful idea—that society is endangered not by systems and institutions of the state but by individual behavior—has been foundational to the prison-industrial complex and much of social work. It is then not surprising that social work is so readily accepted as a palatable alternative to police.[12]

Carceral social work has legitimized its existence in social work research, education, and practice, in part by expanding on social work's legacy of individualizing social problems, maintaining hierarchies of humanity, and prioritizing capital over people. Abolitionist social work must include an ongoing reckoning with carceral social work; naming and memorializing the harms of its history and presence, making reparations for these harms, and transforming social work to one that no longer harms but instead shifts power and transforms.

PIC ABOLITION AND ITS INFLUENCES ON SOCIAL WORK

Just as social work and social workers have become increasingly entangled in the carceral state, over the last twenty years, the movement for PIC abolition has steadily become an undeniable force in the organizing and activism around prisons, police, punishment, and surveillance. While the legacy of carceral social work looms large, anticarceral factions within the profession have increased in size and influence, especially in the last decade.

The dramatic escalation of social work's proximity to the carceral state has led some in social work to critically examine this relationship. This growing consciousness of the participation and partnership of social workers with the carceral state has likely played a key role in radicalizing some in the profession towards abolition.[13] And while a full telling of the rise towards abolitionist social work requires more attention, there is no doubt of the considerable impact of organizations/formations that moved towards building entirely different paradigms and practices, namely INCITE!, Generation 5, Creative Interventions, the Bay Area Transformative Justice Collective, and Project Nia.

Building upon movement convenings like the first Critical Resistance conference in 1998 and the 2010 release of Michelle Alexander's *The New Jim Crow*, the tide really began to turn in the popular consciousness about prisons in the US. As people took to the streets following the police murder of Michael Brown in August of 2014, transforming Black Lives Matter into the Movement for Black Lives, now the largest social movement in the US since the civil rights era, we began seeing the explicit convergence of the fight for Black liberation and the dismantling of PIC. New formations like Black Youth Project 100, Survived and Punished, the Abolitionist Law Center, the Community Justice Exchange, to name but a few, picked up the mantle of PIC abolition praxis first formulated and championed by Black women leaders like Angela Davis, Ruth Wilson Gilmore, Mariame Kaba, and their comrades in Critical Resistance. These same public intellectuals, organizations, and the political movements from which they emerge have also compelled at least some social work schools and organizations in the United States and Canada to confront colonization, anti-Black racism, white supremacy, patriarchy, ableism, transphobia, and to some degree, the manifestations of neoliberalism in social work.

TOWARDS AN ABOLITIONIST SOCIAL WORK

The meaning and value of abolitionism as a concept is intricately woven into the context in which it is developed and resides. In offering what I view as some of the defining foundations of an abolitionist social work, I am not attempting to draw boundaries around what is and is not abolitionist social work; rather, I hope to open up more discourse, theorizing, and practice and to get closer to the paradoxes and contradictions that arise along the way. It is also important to make clear that what is offered below is an amalgamation of the work of many organizers, scholars, activists, strung together for discussion and practice.

As the title of this book implies, discussions of an abolitionist social work raise the question of the abolition of social work. Within my own organizing in the social work community, this is a familiar question and generative tension we hold. On the one hand, I can see an abolitionist future of social work rooted in solidarity over charity, one that is decolonized, deprofessionalized, anticapitalist, and committed to repair, accountability, and continual transformation. Borrowing from Mariame Kaba, I would describe this as the abolitionist social work horizon. And yet, social work as a profession, with its history of facilitating and maintaining white domination and its partnership with the carceral state, has given us countless reasons to wish for and even work towards its abolition, and this may yet be where I arrive. For now, I hold this tension as a truth to attend to in the work of theorizing and practicing an abolitionist social work.

NAMING HORIZONS AND PILLARS

Social works' long-standing de facto commitment to a carceral society makes it all the more important that, as a starting point, abolitionist social work explicitly names the world we seek, including, if it is to exist, the form and function of the social work we can commit our energies and lives to. As my friend and colleague Sethu Nair, a restorative justice and conflict resolution practitioner, has observed, we are too often forced to fit the needs of people into existing structures and ways of being instead of building the structures around peoples' existing needs. Abolitionist social work must root its work in the material needs of people and build from there.

An abolitionist social work must be explicitly and fundamentally anticarceral, meaning against the existence of police and policing, incarceration, punishment, and surveillance. An abolitionist social work must also work towards a world in which these violent forms of domination and control are no longer the guideposts for the structure of society. As Ruth Wilson Gilmore has made clear, "Abolition is about presence, not absence, it's about building life affirming institutions."[14] If, as Jacobs, Kim, and colleagues have argued, carceral social work is about both the direct partnership with law enforcement and the ways carceral and domination logics permeate throughout social work more broadly,[15] an abolitionist social work requires ending all partnerships with the PIC as well as dismantling and uprooting the countless carceral and punitive frameworks that guide the practice of social work.

For social workers to be co-conspirators in moving towards a society centred on affirming life, we must be anticapitalist, decolonialist, and positioned squarely against white supremacy, patriarchy, ableism, and oppression and domination in all forms. Abolitionist social work should be working for and towards a society centred around care, support, solidarity, self-determination, and collective wellness. In contrast to organized abandonment and violence, the horizon should be one of organized care and support, within our communities and, where possible, from the state. While state governance may always remain something that warrants distrust, it is my belief that the state should and must provide for the peoples' welfare and human rights. Fully funded, accessible, and high-quality public education, health care, and housing must be central to an abolitionist social work. Abolitionist social work should be one that understands the inextricable relationship between ideologies, structures, and people—making central the structural drivers of harm and wellness while also holding and attending to the complexity of lived realities and the urgency of human needs today. Said differently, abolitionist social work is simultaneously working to dismantle structures of harm and death while imagining and building life affirming structures anew and transforming people's materials conditions today.

PRINCIPLES AND FRAMEWORKS FOR MOVING TOWARDS ABOLITIONIST HORIZONS

The road to abolition, and to abolitionist social work, is filled with borders, blockades, decoys, and seductions of domination. Yet, movements, organizers, activists, and scholars have practiced, theorized, and documented their work, which provides us with scaffolding as we work towards these horizons. What is offered below is far from exhaustive, but it is one collection of principles and frameworks that might further abolitionist social work. They are categorized loosely under four themes: people, power, justice, and reform.

People

Perhaps most fundamental is the centrality of people and relationships, both their primacy and the values and lenses through which we view them. While professional social work has long named the importance of people and relationships, the de facto values, lenses, and practices have often fallen short of advancing human flourishing. There are countless values and frameworks that have helped inform the centrality of people in abolitionist practice. The several named here may be of particular importance to an abolitionist social work. Black feminist thought and organizing has shown that liberatory work must focus on freedom for people at the margins of society, and that by making this central, everyone is more likely to be free.[16] Disability justice organizing and theorizing has made clear that everyone is deserving of care, joy, pleasure, and a society that makes access a fundamental value and practice for everyone, starting with those who have been the least cared for.[17] The work of trans liberation has been particularly influential in disrupting gender binaries and binary and hierarchical ways of understanding people and relationships. And finally, the work of antiviolence movements, led largely by women of colour survivors, have shown us the complexity of survivorship violence and that the binaries of perpetrator and survivor and good and bad survivor do more to perpetuate violence than to reduce it.[18]

Power

As a profession, social work is far more aligned with an ideology of charity than solidarity, which can also be described as an ideological allegiance to exercising power *over* rather than power *with*. Thus, solidarity must be a core principle and practice of abolitionist social work, shifting power away from the powerful minority and towards the majority. The work of Black feminists and formerly incarcerated organizers, among others, have taught us that shifting and building power must be rooted in the leadership of people at the margins—that abolitionist social work must be rooted in the leadership of those most impacted by the carceral state and by carceral social work. This is not just a goal but an everyday practice, in relationships, in organizing, and in healing.

The primacy of relationships should be central to the work of building power that centres our care for one another, and thus, mutual aid should be of particular importance to abolitionist social work. The practice of mutual aid is deprofessionalized and politicized survival work rooted in an ethos of collective care. While some of the best of what social work has to offer has been related to the work of healing and care, so much of it has been harmful, individual-centric, and often inaccessible—steeped in normative whiteness, ableism, and capitalist logics. This is not to say we should do away with individualized healing, but that, rather than being a footnote in social work textbooks, an ethic and practice of mutual aid should permeate an abolitionist social work. Mutual aid prioritizes dignity, self-determination, agency, and a shared governance that centres those at the margins, all of which should be core tenets of an abolitionist social work.[19]

Justice

In the context of abolitionist social work, justice refers to the ways we understand and respond to harm between people and by the state. The PIC and carceral social work have relied on punitive, dominating, and zero-sum justice. Conversely, abolitionist social work can rely on a growing body of ideas and practices that respond to harm in ways that centre healing, accountability, and transformation. These include the theories and practices of restorative, transformative, and reparative justice.

Restorative justice, a western concept heavily influenced by Indigenous approaches to justice, is geared towards responding to interpersonal harm. In responding to harm, restorative justice shifts the focus away from legality and punishment and towards the person who was harmed and their needs and, at the same time, makes the person who caused the harm responsible for making things as right as possible. There is much written about the successes, possibilities, challenges, and tensions in the work of restorative justice. As restorative justice continues to grow and social workers increasingly adopt its ideas and practices, caution and attention is needed with regards to appropriation, co-optation, and restorative justice's relationship to state power.

Transformative justice, a political framework and ever-growing array of practices, has grown out of antiviolence and abolitionist organizing, led primarily by women and femmes of colour. In its approaches to justice, transformative justice thought and practice has come from people at the margins, who are most likely to be harmed by the violence of the state. Transformative justice practitioners believe that interpersonal justice is inextricably tied to structural justice. That is, we cannot seek justice for harm committed between people without attending to the structural violence that has been a primary driver of that harm. Transformative justice is grounded in the reality that the state has failed to provide safety and justice for people at the margins and thus responses to justice cannot rely on the state for help.[20]

Reparative justice teaches us that justice, broadly speaking, is not only about accountability and transformation but is also about making repair, to the degree possible, for the harm caused. Reparative justice and efforts for reparations have focused primarily on institutions and ideologies of racialized harm. Social work, and carceral social work in particular, have a long history of racialized harm. Reparative justice, as developed and written about by Kassandra Frederique and the Drug Policy Alliance, includes the acknowledgement of harm, atoning for the harm, and action, which involves concrete reparations and policy changes.[21]

Reform

Understanding abolition both as a horizon and a theory of change makes room for the necessary reforms and incremental changes that respond to the material needs of today without losing sight of fundamental transformation. While discerning which reforms lead us closer to an abolitionist horizon is not always easy, abolitionists have offered the terms "nonreformist" and "liberatory reforms" to help identify the incremental changes that mitigate the power of the state to cause harm and thus bring us closer to abolition. Distinguishing between liberatory and reformist reforms is particularly important to social work given its regular proximity and partnership with the state.[22]

Dean Spade differentiates reformist reforms from those reforms that retain the liberatory essence of abolition.[23] In a previously written piece, James and I adapted Spade's questions slightly (with permission) to help us consider and discern liberatory social work efforts.[24]

› Is the work accountable to the people it proposes to be working for and with? (Does it include their leadership? Is it shifting power? Is it working to reduce and eliminate coercion?)
› Does it provide material relief? If yes, at what cost to one's agency and at what risk?
› Does it perpetuate dichotomies and ideologies of good vs. bad, deserving vs. undeserving, violent vs. nonviolent, criminal vs. innocent?
› Does it legitimate or expand carceral systems? (Does it use, affirm, or expand criminalization, incarceration, surveillance, or punishment?)
› Does it mobilize those most affected for ongoing struggle? (Is this building power?)

BUILDING ABOLITIONIST SOCIAL WORK PRAXIS

As I write this, fascism is growing in the United States and Canada, and overtly authoritarian regimes and movements are gaining strength in many other places across the world. It is thus appropriate that we should study the thinking and organizing of antifascist efforts. Writings about progressive movements in Italy in the 1930s offer a conceptualization of three categories of work necessary to combat fascism: (a) the work against the state, (b) the work outside the state, and (c) the work inside the state.[25] This framework has also been taken up more recently by abolitionists and racial and economic justice organizers and scholars in assessing and strategizing around the limitations and possibilities of the state.[26] Given the relationship between social work and the state, this categorization can be helpful in localizing abolitionist social work and inviting discussions on the possibilities and challenges of each of the three venues. Of particular utility is identifying, amplifying, and analyzing the unique approach and relationship to power within each category while simultaneously holding onto the broader breadth of work as well as the possibilities—and perhaps the necessity of complementary interventions.

Work against the State

The ability of the state to wield violence, what abolitionist Mariame Kaba describes as the "monopoly on violence," is central to the PIC and carceral social work.[27] Abolitionist social work against the state is primarily focused on ending the harms and violence of the state. Specifically, these efforts work to reduce the size, power, and resources of the carceral state and can include closing jails, prisons, and detention centres; freeing people from these institutions (bail funds, sentencing reform, parole reform, clemency campaigns); reducing the harm of conditions inside these facilities (ending solitary confinement); organizing to get reparations for the harms of white supremacy and the carceral state; and organizing against family regulation policies and practices. In naming these efforts there are at least two important caveats. The first is that while none of these efforts are exclusive to social work, they should be central to abolitionist social work. The second is that the efforts are not necessarily, in and of themselves, aligned with abolition, and without a fundamental adherence to values of abolition and to key political values such as self-determination, equity, reflexivity, and intersectionality, we can at times risk bolstering the state with these interventions.

Working Outside the State

Many of the failures of settler colonial, white supremacist, capitalist, and cisheteropatriarchal states (in this case the US but applicable to many states around the world) are inherent to foundational social, political, and economic infrastructure and *by design* limit its ability to provide justice, safety, and fundamental human rights. The consequences of these failures are felt most deeply by people at the margins, from death by state violence and the criminalization of survival to woefully inadequate access to the things that allow people to lead healthy and fulfilling lives. The work outside the state is aimed at meeting these needs without relying on the state and without having to fit those needs into the confines of existing state power. Mutual aid and transformative justice are among the most instructive approaches and practices to work outside the state. They offer political philosophies for care work and justice work, respectively, as well as a growing array of practices. The practice and promise of mutual aid have become much more visible during the time of the COVID-19 pandemic. These practices can include funds that offer direct financial support, child-care cooperatives, transportation support, education support, food distribution, efforts to support people's physical and mental health needs (such as support groups and nonhospitalized health care), and legal support (such as participatory defense campaigns), to name a few. The practice of transformative justice—politicized efforts for achieving safety and justice outside the state—are also growing in consciousness and practice.

Transformative justice practices span a wide range in terms of their degree of formality and from prevention to intervention. Two of the more recognizable transformative justice practices are community accountability and pod-mapping processes. Community accountability processes are more formalized responses to a spectrum of harmful behaviour, the most visible of which are incidents of sexual harm. Pod-mapping, developed by the Bay Area Transformative Justice Collective, is the practice of building intentional relationships where people can "turn to each other for support around violent, harmful, and abusive experiences, whether as survivors, bystanders or people who have harmed."[28] The politics and practices of mutual aid and transformative justice also offer a range of possible responses to harm in lieu of mandated reporting. Mandated reporting in the US is both law and practice, requiring certain professionals, including social workers, to report specific harms to police or child protective services.[29] Mandated reporting then requires social workers to act as the eyes of the carceral state, meaning their own livelihood is dependent on reporting others to carceral institutions. Navigating the legality and liability of mandated reporting is complex for many in social work. Fortunately, there is a growing push to challenge the existence of this law and to explore how to not report and what to do instead.

Working Inside (and around) the State
The practice of abolitionist social work against and outside the state is more easily and visibly aligned with the politics and praxis of abolition. It is debatable whether any social work in and around the state can be considered abolitionist. Still, a comprehensive response to the carcerality of social work requires that we interrogate how we might disrupt the webs of state power and state violence that

are directly and indirectly tied to the profession. Working towards abolitionist social work in and around the state is fraught, given the many pitfalls of co-optation and the possibilities for the explicit and implicit reproduction of carceral social work. Nonetheless, we can imagine work in and around the state that can reduce the harm of state violence, which like the work against the state, is the primary aim of this category of work.

While it can be difficult to discern which efforts can reduce harm, there are some that have no place in our abolitionist social work practice today. Social workers and social work institutions should not work directly for any arm of the carceral state, including police departments, prisons, or jails. Working directly for the carceral state gives legitimacy to its power and at best maintains and at worst increases its capacity to harm. Still, many social workers and social work institutions work indirectly in and around other arms of the carceral state. From providing mental health care inside jails and prisons to working in public defense, these forms of social work practices have varying mandates in resisting the PIC. Some of this work may be considered abolitionist and some not. Most importantly, we must consider where and how these efforts can work towards abolitionist horizons.

Beyond work in carceral settings, social work has an outsized presence in communities and community-based organizations. Many community-based organizations and the social workers working for them have some tie or obligation to the state, including through policies and regulations that mandate state involvement (such as mandated reporting or the power and requirement to send someone back to jail or prison for not meeting requirements) or through funding that includes stipulations connected to the state (such as limits to who can access resources). Resisting state power in community work can include organizing to directly challenge the existence of policies and regulations, refusing to adhere to them, or pursuing work outside the state.

FINDING A POLITICAL HOME

For me, having a political home has meant having a community to learn with; a community with whom to grapple with the many difficult questions, decisions, and experiences that come with liberatory work and people to be accountable to; it is a foundation for building power with others. Having a political home has been essential to building solidarity and power and practicing the emancipatory relations we seek to realize more broadly. Finding a political home may mean joining an organizing formation, building one where you work, creating your own, or any number of other possibilities—whatever it looks like, building abolitionist social work praxis cannot be done alone.

CHAPTER 2
MENTAL HEALTH WORKERS HAVE NEVER BEEN THE SOLUTION TO RACIAL VIOLENCE BY POLICE

Edward Hon-Sing Wong

On June 23, 2020, the Centre for Addiction and Mental Health (CAMH) joined the chorus of condemnations after the murder of Ejaz Choudry by Peel Regional Police during a wellness check. In a statement, CAMH argued, "Police should not be the first responders ... people in crisis [should be] first met by mental health responders."[1] But this suggestion—to replace the figure of the police with that of the mental health worker—requires closer scrutiny.

Missing in this analysis is recognition of the mental health field's culpability in racial and colonial violence. The mental health field shares discursive roots with scientific racism, emerging out of eugenic desires to control racialized people. These discursive roots led to the advocacy for and engagement in violent and racist practices like coerced sterilization, anti-miscegenation, and immigration restrictions, practices that, shockingly, remain in place today and represent an ongoing entanglement between the mental health field and carceral institutions.[2] Mental health professionals are also already implicated in racist police violence in ways that are difficult to disentangle considering the number of collaborations that mutually reinforce the work of both institutions. Despite apparent calls by mental health organizations for the disengagement of the police from mental health work, there has been little movement or demands made to end carceral practices like involuntary hospitalization, treatment orders, and close collaboration between some social workers and police.

THE INTERTWINING ROOTS OF MENTAL HEALTH AND RACISM

Despite the seemingly eternal nature of psychiatric and race-based conceptualizations of human life, these frameworks emerged out of specific social conditions and practices. Scientific racism, the notion that empirical evidence justifies racial hierarchy, and psychiatry have shared roots in the theory of degeneration. Developed in the late-eighteenth century, degeneration theory posits that all races have a common origin in the "Caucasian race," and those racial differences developed through deterioration and devolution caused by environmental factors like climate, nutrition, and cultural upbringing.[3] This degeneration was thought to cause both differences in physical appearance and the deterioration of mental and intellectual capacities, exhibiting itself as mental disorders. German psychiatrist Emil Kraepelin, who published one of the first compendiums of mental diagnoses in 1883, argued that degeneration "certainly play[ed] a part in the development of dementia praecox," the forerunner to schizophrenia, and could be used to explain many psychological disorders.[4]

The concept of degeneration influenced Francis Galton's theory of eugenics, the science of "improving" the genetic quality of a population by encouraging the procreation of white nondisabled people while preventing the procreation of others deemed as defective and inferior. Two approaches to eugenics were developed and complemented one another: *positive eugenics* for "normals" and "supernormals" and *negative eugenics* for "abnormals."[5] Positive eugenics refers to policies that encourage reproduction for those deemed desirable, while negative eugenics refers to policies that discourage reproduction or eliminate those deemed undesirable.

This deep entanglement between disability and race serves a specific function, and it was no accident that eugenics first gained prominence in the context of colonialism. Eugenics was simultaneously influenced by and helped to justify colonialism by presenting the colonized people as less abled, child-like, and subhuman; consequently, the subjugation of colonized peoples was not considered a moral transgression but simply a natural phase within human evolution.[6] The conceptualization of mental disorder as rooted in race provided the ideological justification for white supremacy and was employed as a means of control. A particularly stark example of this is drapetomania, the "mental disease" assigned to Black enslaved people who ran away. The use of physical violence was prescribed as the cure to return Black enslaved people to their "normal" state of subservience.[7] Psychiatrists also diagnosed thousands of Black civil rights activists with schizophrenia to justify their detention in asylums in the 1960s and 1970s. These activists' resistance against racism was understood as pathological. Eugenicist perspectives on race underpinned the emergence of the mental hygiene movement, which later evolved into the modern mental health field. One of the most prominent mental hygiene organizations in Canada was the Canadian National Committee of Mental Hygiene (CNCMH).[8] Now known as the Canadian Mental Health Association, CNCMH was founded in 1918 and employed some of Canada's first mental health social workers. In "The Scope and Aims of the Mental Hygiene Movement," Dr. Clarence M. Hincks, the cofounder of CNCMH, stated, "The brains of a nation constitute its most important asset. No country can be truly great, and remain so, with a population possessed of mediocre mentality."[9] A nationalist desire for Canada to be "truly great" was a major component of CNCMH's raison d'être, with a particular focus on improving mental aspects of the Canadian people.

These nationalist objectives coincided with the articulation of several foundation myths that form an integral part of Canadian identity. A major myth that has justified the formation of the country and colonialism is the representation of Canada as barren, a tabula rasa.[10] In the early twentieth century, J. D. Page, chief medical officer for the Port of Quebec, cited Sir James Barr, president of the British Medical Association, in an article in *Canadian Journal of Mental Hygiene (CJMH)*, saying, "You have, here, a virgin soil and you should see that it is peopled with a vigorous and an intellectual race. You should shut out all degenerate foreigners as you would exclude a mad dog."[11] Canada's soil is considered untouched and the white race, vigorous and intellectual, is considered its rightful inheritors. Virgin soil alludes to the idea of manifest destiny and the frontier discourse of civilized white men conquering uninhabited lands.[12] The CNCMH rendered colonial violence invisible through the framing of colonialism as the labour of white people bringing about progress. In the same year, W. G. Smith, professor of psychology at the University of Toronto, stated, for example:

> From the day when to the astonishment of the red men the pale faces began to arrive from the East and press their way forward

toward the West, to the present day, when the results of the labour and endurance of the hardy pioneer are manifested in "the star of Empire."[13]

Not only is the violence of colonialism not mentioned, but colonizers are also celebrated for their "labour and endurance." The nationalist objectives held by CNCMH were also tied to an idea of the Canadian nation as "white,"[14] with its literature revealing clear racial delineations that governed access to Canadian identity. Dr. Jasper Halpenny, the one-time medical superintendent of the Winnipeg General Hospital, classified Canadians with other ethnic groups including the "English, French, Irish, Scotch, Icelandic and American," explaining that these groups "spring largely from common stock."[15] In other words, people of Western European descent were considered to possess a shared identity as differentiated from inherently "foreign" people belonging to the rest of the world.

Consistent with the eugenic framing of mental disorder as rooted in race, there were numerous references in mental hygiene literature to the foreign Other as disproportionately affected by mental disorders. In the 1920 Mental Hygiene Survey of the Province of British Columbia, it was reported that despite 43.14% of the population being born in the country, "the foreign born constitute 72.72% of the admissions [to Hospitals for the Insane], a showing that is quite out of proportion to that expected."[16] These statements have as their common argument the idea that a significant number of people understood as "mentally defective" are racialized immigrants. And reading these statements in the context of a history of labelling immigrants and racialized peoples, and their practices, as mentally abnormal, we can understand these statements as reinforcing the pathologization of certain groups.

Connections were then made between immigrants and all people labelled as "mentally defective" with criminality. Hincks stated, "It is probable that about 60 percent of our criminals belong to the mentally abnormal group."[17] Seeing as racialized people and immigrants were considered, disproportionate to the general population, to carry mental defects, it is not surprising that many authors made the leap from "the mentally defective are criminals" to "immigrants are criminals." In a CJMH article, anecdotes from police officers were used as evidence of apparent crime, especially with regards to drugs, associated with the Chinese and Greek communities.[18] Afterwards, the writer cited statistics from the Vancouver gaol, making special mention of the 598 Chinese people detained—a disproportionate 17 percent of the total. These claims were used to justify calls for urgent action to restrict immigration and control racialized communities.

THE ONGOING HISTORY OF COLONIAL AND RACIST VIOLENCE COMMITTED BY THE MENTAL HEALTH FIELD

Driven by its discursive roots in scientific racism, the mental health field has engaged in practices that demonstrate an ongoing pattern of racist violence in collaboration with carceral institutions. The most prominent examples involve the CNCMH's pursuit of eugenic policies by successfully advocating for and implementing violent practices like coerced sterilization, anti-miscegenation, and immigration restrictions, all of which explicitly targeted racialized communities. Much of these practices remain to this day, sometimes with alterations to its form but with very similar practical results.

Coerced Sterilization

To limit reproduction, the CNCMH demanded sterilization. Jessie Taft, the social service director for the Committee on Mental Hygiene of the New York State Charities Aid Association, argued, "Sterilization of the feebleminded is logically the solution for the problem of prevention of propagation of the mentally unfit where feeblemindedness is due to heredity."[19] This advocacy contributed in part to the implementation of coerced sterilization in North America, including in several Canadian provinces. These policies disproportionately targeted Indigenous peoples. In Alberta, Indigenous peoples were disproportionately diagnosed as mentally defective, which allowed the state to waive the consent requirement for sterilization under the 1928 Sexual Sterilization Act of Alberta. Consequently, a quarter of all sterilizations were conducted on First Nations and Métis people despite this group making up less than 3 percent of the entire population.[20] The social worker's primary role in this regard was to identify potential cases for sterilization and to collect case histories.[21] In particular, social workers "were able to infiltrate the home environment and recommend individuals for sterilization."[22]

To facilitate sterilization, guidance clinics were established throughout the province with mental health social workers often placed at their helm. At these clinics, individuals were given physical, psychiatric, and psychometric or IQ examinations. Should these examinations conclude that the individual was "mentally deficient," recommendations were made for "'sterilization and supervision,' 'medical and surgical treatment,' 'modified school work,' 'special class at school,' 'placement in a good home,' 'deportation,' and 'institutional training and care.'"[23] The significant role played by social workers in facilitating sterilization is apparent with Mary Frost, the chief psychiatric social worker, advocating for the employment of greater numbers of mental health social workers to increase the rates of sterilization.[24] By the 1950s, public health nurses involved in sterilization were largely replaced by social workers.[25]

Coerced sterilization continued throughout Canada even after the repealing of sterilization legislation in 1972 and 1973. The most recent documented case occurred in 2017, when an Indigenous woman was asked, while under anaesthetics and in a state of panic, to undergo sterilization.[26] In 2012, another Indigenous woman explicitly refused sterilization but the procedure was done anyway.[27] Health care workers and social service providers would often participate in this coercion, with practices ranging from the gentler coaxing of a patient to undergo sterilization to informing a patient that they were not to leave the hospital without sterilization. Past and current involvement with child protection services is also often used as reasoning for coercion into sterilization.[28] In one example from the late 1970s, Liz, a seventeen-year-old, was coerced into having an abortion and sterilization by a Children's Aid worker at a northwestern Ontario hospital. Liz explains, "It was a matter of me almost [being] cornered, if you will, by my worker at the time saying, 'You better have an abortion because if you don't, either way, we are going to take that child from you.'"[29]

Class action lawsuits regarding coerced sterilization were filed against various levels of government in Saskatchewan and Alberta, turning up hundreds of cases.[30] A 2021 Senate committee on human rights interviewed sixteen women who experienced sterilization, revealing that coerced sterilization affects "other marginalized and vulnerable groups in the country, including Black women and other people of colour," in addition to Indigenous women. The committee concluded that "coerced sterilization of Indigenous women is not a matter of the past and still happens in Canada today."[31]

Anti-Miscegenation and Immigration Control

The CNCMH also opposed miscegenation based on the fear that interracial "breeding" would lead to racial degradation and the desire to maintain Canada as a white nation. While formal anti-miscegenation laws never existed in Canada, advocacy from the mental hygiene movement reinforced attitudes, laws, and practices that mirror anti-miscegenation laws in logic and outcome.[32] For example, the 1876 revisions to the Indian Act included Section 12.1.b, which stipulated that "Indian women" who married "non-Indians" lose their Indian status and children of this marriage were not entitled to obtain status.[33] Interracial relations were also prevented through the Female Refuges Act and the 1946 Canadian Citizenship Act. In 1939, Velma Demerson, a white woman, was arrested and incarcerated for nine months under the Female Refuges Act, which permitted parents to bring about legal intervention for women under the age of twenty-one deemed "unmanageable or incorrigible."[34] Demerson's father reported his daughter to authorities because he was unhappy that she had chosen to reside and have a child with Harry Yip, a Chinese man. Demerson was also stripped of her Canadian citizenship because she had married a non-Canadian.[35] The eugenic fear of the procreation of those deemed mentally ill and the proliferation of mental disorder persist and continue to influence the daily lives of people with mental health issues, especially in the context of contemporary health care and social work practices. Psychiatric survivors report that mental health professionals have discouraged them from having children.[36]

Anti-miscegenation perspectives also influenced demands by the mental hygiene movement for more stringent immigration controls. It was feared that immigrants would ruin Canada's gene pool through miscegenation, overtaking white people in numbers through higher reproductive rates. The work of Prescott F. Hall, an American lawyer who championed eugenics, was highlighted in one issue of the *CJMH*: "Immigration tends to sterilize the people on the higher social and economic levels who are already in the country."[37] Low birth-rates among the white upper-class was understood to be the result of nonwhite working-class immigrants bringing chaos to the nation through criminality and mental defect. This speaks to a discourse of the "unfit" out multiplying the "fit," or as Taft expressed in more overtly racial terms, a commitment of "race suicide" and a "detract[ion] from our racial integrity."[38]

Though earlier pieces of immigration legislation did prohibit some migrants identified as "lunatic, idiotic, deaf and dumb, blind or infirm,"[39] or required the payment of a bond to allow for entry, the implementation of these restrictions were largely limited or uneven.[40] Advocacy by the mental hygiene movement led to the broadening of categories of disability prohibited by immigration policy by the turn of the century.[41] These more restrictive policies meant that from 1902 to 1911, 40 percent of immigrants rejected were for reasons of medical inadmissibility.

The list of prohibited disabilities continued to expand until an overhaul of immigration policy in 1976 marked a shift towards exclusion justified on the more "politically acceptable" basis of "excessive demand" on social services.[42] In 2018, Immigration Minister Ahmed Hussen suggested that changes to the "excessive demand" clause meant that disabled immigrants would no longer be considered a burden.[43] The changes involved the tripling of the cost threshold for determining inadmissibility and shortening the list of services considered in calculating cost, but this was not a repeal of the clause.[44] Alongside the Points System, which determines eligibility for immigration based on the likelihood of integration into the Canadian workforce and society, placing racialized applicants with disabilities at a disadvantage,[45] the latest reforms do not mark a substantive shift away from the discourses and practices of racist violence promoted by the mental hygiene movement. The mental health field remains entangled with border control, another major element of the state's carceral system.

MENTAL HEALTH SERVICES AND POLICE COLLABORATION

Mental health workers also have a strong collaborationist relationship with carceral institutions like policing that perpetuate racial violence. This collaboration occurs right as racialized people enter the mental health system through diagnoses.[46] Racialized people are disproportionately diagnosed with schizophrenia, depression, posttraumatic stress disorder, and other labels.[47] Receiving a psychiatric diagnosis can pave the way for chemical restraints, community surveillance, and involuntary hospitalization.[48]

A major component of these coercive responses is police interventions. In Canada, police killings of racialized individuals like Andrew Loku, Sammy Yatim, Abdirahman Abdi, and Regis Korchinski-Paquet have propelled the issue of police violence against individuals with mental health issues to national prominence. In fact, from 2004–2014, 40 percent of all fatal police shootings involved people in mental health crises.[49] Police violence may also involve the use of force with "hands on, arm lock, handcuffs, pepper spray, Taser, or low-lethality gunshot with beanbags."[50] These forms of police violence can have serious implications, leading to psychological trauma in addition to physical injuries or death.[51] While statistics on the use of force are unavailable, contact statistics can illustrate the scale of policing in relation to mental health crises. In 2012, 18.7% of Canadians coming into contact with the police did so in relation to mental health crises, and this number is growing in Canadian cities.[52]

Mental health workers contribute to these growing police contact numbers. Given the widespread collaboration between the criminal justice system and the mental health field, involvement in one system increases exposure to the other. In Ontario, where I live, collaboration between mental health workers and the police occur through three main processes and procedures: Forms 1 and 2, community treatment orders (CTO), and situations.

Form 1 and 2

In Ontario, forms are legal tools used to order the police to bring a person involuntarily to a psychiatric facility and can be issued by a physician (Form 1) or a justice of the peace (JP; Form 2).[53] Two sets of criteria are used to determine eligibility for involuntary hospitalization. The first set, falling under "Box A," considers serious harm. If a physician has observed or received reports of threats or acts of violence, believes the patient is unable to take care of themselves, and believes that the patient's mental diagnosis will result in serious bodily harm or impairment to themselves or another person, they may use Form 1 to begin involuntary hospitalization. Box B, the second set of criteria, which was added in

2000, allows for the involuntary hospitalization of patients likely to experience bodily harm, substantial mental or physical deterioration, or serious physical impairment should they stop receiving medical treatment.

Social workers often take on the role of providing third party reports and observations for these purposes. A social worker, or indeed anyone including family members and passersby, can appear before a JP to apply for a Form 2 by providing sworn information, in written or oral form, that the patient fits the criteria set out by Box A and B from Form 1. Should the JP determine that the information does indeed meet the criteria, the Form 2 order is then provided to the police to apprehend the patient and bring them to a psychiatric facility, usually a hospital emergency room.

Community Treatment Orders

CTOs came into practice across Canada in the 1990s, with Saskatchewan being the first to enact CTO legislation in 1995, followed by Ontario in 2000.[54] The goal of CTOs is to enforce treatments, not through forced medication but through the threat of hospitalization. Should a patient be deemed not to have followed the treatment plan in the community, they would be brought back to the hospital by the police for a psychiatric assessment and involuntary hospitalization.

While a patient must be offered an opportunity to consult with a rights advisor and consent to a CTO, consent may also be provided by the secondary decision maker (SDM), which is usually a family member, if the patient is deemed incapable.[55] The physician is also expected to seek input from other health practitioners, family members, or social workers involved in the treatment. There is recognition among the legal community that these practices infringe on the rights of psychiatric survivors, but University of Guelph scholar John Dawson argues that courts are likely to consider these restrictions justified if the laws governing CTOs meet judicial definitions of fairness, allow for independent review, and do not impose excessive powers disproportionate to the need.[56] In addition, CTOs are sometimes justified on the claim that they are less repressive relative to involuntary hospitalization. Ironically though, its power lies in the threat to enact the same repressive mechanisms it claims to mitigate against.

Situation Tables

A newer invention is the situation table, "a venue for service providers from various sectors (police, education, addictions, social work, mental health, etc.) to regularly convene and discuss clients who meet a defined threshold of risk."[57] This venue serves as a space to evaluate people deemed at risk of "harm," with cases brought to the situation table by social workers, police officers, and other service providers to determine appropriate interventions to address the issue "before harm occurs" and to lower their risk levels.[58] Interventions are often police-led, including informal check-ins, forced hospitalizations, or even arrests. More than a hundred of these programs exist across Canada, with thirty-seven in Ontario as of April 2018.[59]

The evaluation process involves the use of a provincial Risk-Drive Tracking Database of sensitive personal information of vulnerable persons that were targets of intervention, amassed by social workers and other front-line workers.[60] This information includes age, sex, location, and risk factors like criminal involvement, drugs, antisocial behaviour, housing, suicide, unemployment, and physical violence. The most prevalent risk factor ascribed for all age groups is mental health. These vague risk factors are all that is necessary to justify interventions.

Situation tables are a form of "predictive policing," part of a broader trend by police to use algorithmic technologies (i.e., big data) in their surveillance and enforcement practices. Interventions initiated by situation tables also do not require prior consent from the person intervened on. A social worker interviewed by *Vice* estimated that around 50 percent of all situation table interventions were nonconsensual, many involving people with addictions.[61] Situation tables are also used for police surveillance and investigative purposes.[62] A mental health social worker I interviewed explained that detectives would often use situation tables to conduct environmental scans, to learn the lay of the land in a specific neighbourhood, and to seek out information or observations relevant to ongoing investigations.[63]

FINDING ANSWERS ELSEWHERE

Forming, CTOs, and situation tables make up the constellation of coercive apparatuses that involve direct collaboration between mental health workers and the police. These tools all rely on violent interventions, whether it is the threat of police or psychiatric violence, in the case of CTOs, or direct violence as police officers physically escort the person to a psychiatric facility for assessment and detention in the case of the practice of "forming" or show up unannounced on "welfare" checks in the case of situation tables. These examples demonstrate that professional mental health practices are inextricable from policing because the mental health field both relies on the use of police and also supports policing. The continued uncritical engagement in collaborationist projects with the police is perhaps unsurprising given the shared discursive origins of the mental health field and scientific racism find resonance in current mental health and policing practices. The intertwining of mental health and scientific racism also finds resonance in the mental health field's own long-standing participation in racial violence and the policing of racialized people.

All this to say that people should be critical of calls to replace one institute of state violence through a strengthening of another. Instead, people should consider responses to crises informed by perspectives from mad people themselves. Mad movement activists have long called for mad literacy, a willingness to understand those whose behaviours do not conform to social norms, and skill sharing, to allow for community-driven approaches to crisis intervention not predicated on violent coercion. For example, Bonnie Burstow, the late mad movement activist and professor, suggested community befriending, a return to an emphasis on basic human relationship building by community members to creatively support a person before, during, and after a crisis.[64] Elements of this proposal can be seen in Toronto, where activist-led neighbourhood response groups, organized in the midst of the COVID-19 pandemic, have served as first responders, supporting people targeted by police and white supremacists and engaging in conflict de-escalation.[65] Their objectives are to serve as an alternative to calling the police and to mitigate violence. People should also consider the reminder from Onyota'a:Ka activist-scholar Roland Chrisjohn that emotional distress is a social problem rooted in racism, sexism, capitalism, and colonialism. Substantively addressing this distress requires directly confronting racial and colonial violence in the past and present, including the violence perpetrated by the mental health field.

CHAPTER 3
FOR BLACK WOMEN, HEALTH CARE IS AN ABOLITION ISSUE

Renée Nichole Ferguson

So much of what we know about Black women's health experiences in Canada comes from either self-reported ethnicity survey data with limited sample sizes or the data-rich narratives of qualitative strategies.[1] Much of this work of collecting, interpreting, and analysing the health experiences of Black women is due to the perseverance and leadership of Black women community members and researchers who know that the lives of Black people not only matter, but are also crucial for the overall health of the population in Canada. Standing on the shoulders of this vital research, I argue that a robust understanding of Black women's health and wellness must consider that our experiences with the dominant health care system are deeply affected by the ubiquity of the state's commitment to carceral philosophies. This chapter seeks to offer lessons for thinking about abolition for social workers and health care professionals.

BLACK WOMEN'S EXPERIENCES OF THE SHADOW CARCERAL STATE

Abolitionists like Ruth Wilson Gilmore and James Kilgore have been writing about and resisting the expansion of the carceral state for some time.[2] Their work is important to social service providers because it has made visible the overreliance of suspicion, criminalization, and punishment in our society, including in health care settings. Black people are overrepresented in the prison system in Canada. In the ten years between 2003 and 2013, the incarceration rate among Black people in Canada increased by nearly 90 percent, and the data shows that while Black people made up 3 percent of the total population of the country at the time, they made up 8.6

percent of the federal prison population.³ In Canada's largest city, Toronto, where Black people make up 8.8 percent of the population, they are overrepresented in police use of force, violent encounters, and fatal shootings.⁴

We are living in a time when the disproportionate impact of the carceral state is being made clear through data, and yet, when we talk about prisons and policing in the lives of Black people, the discussion is masculinized; the data collection and ensuing discussions almost exclusively focus on the overt physical harm of Black cisgender and heterosexual men at the hands of police and within the confines of prisons. This experience is unquestionably a crucial part of the conversation, however, the exclusivity renders invisible the ways that gendered experiences of racism permeate punitive state practices and affect the lives of Black women, femme, queer, and trans people in ways that are independent of our relationship to Black cisgender and heterosexual men. When Angela Davis questioned what we miss when we think about prisons without addressing larger socioeconomic questions, she offered us an opportunity to stretch this conversation by expanding our data collection and discussions about carcerality and the Black community to include analyses of criminalization and punishment *within and beyond* the prison walls.⁵ If we do this, we can see a more complete picture of the state's carceral functions, in particular, it's reach into the lives of Black women.

Scholars Katherine Beckett and Naomi Murakawa use the term "shadow carceral state" to describe this shifting and blending of civil, administrative, and criminal legal authority to mimic carceral philosophies outside of prisons.⁶ The concept is applied here to identify how the carceral state inserts itself in the culture and policy of physical health, mental health, social work, reproductive rights, and health care institutions. This includes historical and present-day practices that imitate and rely on traditional forms of punishment within a marketized culture: suspensions, firings, fees, fines, detentions, unwanted medical treatment, and coercion. For Black women, the merger of punishment and health is part of an old pattern; a consequence of the marriage between neoliberalism and carceralism in a country with a rich history of racial punishment.⁷

BREAKING SPIRIT: NEOLIBERAL BUDGET CUTS AND PUNISHMENT IN ONTARIO'S HEALTH CARE SYSTEM

In Ontario, the philosophies of scarcity embedded in neoliberalism have blended with public health policy in an incessant search for waste, finding ways to produce cost-effective budgets and market-style sensibilities in care delivery. The Ontario Government's *Action Plan for Health Care* defines health care for its citizens as an investment of limited resources and an exercise of cost-benefit analysis where the government must choose between different health needs, making "tough trade-offs and shifting spending to where we get the best value for the dollar."[8] This economic language is a cornerstone of neoliberal culture; a justification for spending cuts, downsizing, closures, budget reduction, and, of course, the culpability of individual citizens for the detrimental health impacts they experience due to governmental policy choices and sacrifices.

Deep cuts to health care in Ontario, where I live, began in 1995 with Mike Harris' Progressive Conservative Party under the slogan "the Common Sense Revolution" and were carried forward through successive Liberal governments. Labour studies scholars Bryan M. Evans and Carlo Fanelli recall that by 1999 the Ontario government had privatized health care laboratories, removed twenty-nine hospitals, and cut over ten thousand hospital beds and six thousand nurses' jobs.[9] Mental health and social work infrastructure were equally affected. In Ontario in the 1980s, the divestment, reconfiguration, or closure of six psychiatric hospitals, the amalgamation of four facilities, the closure of fifty percent of psychiatric beds, and the transfer of a portion of the remaining beds to general hospitals significantly transformed mental health care.[10] At the same time, the capacity of community care services was not increased to take over the responsibilities of closing hospitals.[11]

The systematic cutting and divesting from health care are not simply economic and political choices, but mark cultural shifts as well, all of which carry heavy material consequences for communities at the margins. In thinking of this cultural shift, academic Noah De Lessovoy uses the term "carceral turn," within which

> networks of solidarity and obligations to the vulnerable are replaced by a culture of blame and externalization—as those who are unable or unwilling to market themselves, or who are

selected as targets for the collective fears and dissatisfactions that accompany the atomization of public life, are subject to intimidation, violence, and incarceration.[12]

The stress of budget cuts and resulting job losses lay bare the possibility of punishment for what is defined as waste, excess, redundancy, and poor return on investment in health care. And as health care is narrated into a commodity, so too is the citizen transformed into the consumer. In a commodity-based health care culture that emphasizes efficacy, there is an increase in complaints from the public and subsequent punishment of staff and administrators who fail to comply or who are unable to perform along marketized expectations.[13] Finally, where structural inequalities are interpreted as individual failures and resistance to injustice, a moral threat leads to punishing strategies for managing failed citizens.

CONSEQUENCES OF HEALTH CARE RESTRUCTURING FOR BLACK WOMEN

As with other carceral experiences, this culture of punishment within the neoliberalism of Ontario's health care system carried weight for Black people. Literature documents the immense difficulties that Black women have experienced within the nursing profession.[14] For Black women working within the health care system, the mark of suspicion and outsider status is wrapped up with concerns of competency, professionalism, and patient care based on myths about Black womanhood. Characterizations of Black women as aggressive without provocation, sassy, and ignorant of the profession have traditionally presumed that Black women are out of place, out of line, and on the verge of sullying order. Resistance to the unkindness offered to Black women in the workplace has often been recast as unjustified anger. Das Gupta's (1996) study of Black nurses experiences with racism is a testimony to the impact and longevity of social and economic neoliberal reform on Black women's work in health care.[15] For example, Black nurses who stood up against racial bullying on the job were punished through dismissal as a hospital management strategy used to reduce staff costs in hard financial times. Das Gupta's work is consistent with other research from this period that documents the disproportionate impact of punishment on Black nurses in the context of economic and health care restructuring and their resistance.[16] These studies were confirmed over two decades later in a scoping review of Black nurses in Canada by Jefferies and colleagues who report stories of Black nurses experiencing unjustified termination and enhanced surveillance in the workplace today.[17] While this may not be a direct experience of imprisonment, the experiences of excessive monitoring, discipline for minor or nonexistent problems, and oversurveillance speaks to a culture of punishment of Black women in health care.

With neoliberalism as a driver, there are a number of ways that Black women's experiences with the mental health system have been embedded in the carceral heritage of social policy. Written into Ontario's Mental Health Act are several points of interconnectedness between mental health, policing, and punishment. For example, community treatment orders (CTOs), as discussed in Wong's chapter in this book, are a form of mandated treatment developed within the more neoliberal policy landscape of deinstitutionalization.[18] The act allows a psychiatrist the authority to treat patients living with persistent and serious mental illness by mandating psychiatric treatment in the community and to use the police to bring patients in for an assessment if an individual does not follow through with the mandated plan.

Carcerality, social work, and psychiatry have a long interrelationship, tied up in rituals of exile and exclusion.[19] Black women are affected by these carceral mergers in uniquely gendered and raced ways; almost every aspect of our lives are already under scrutiny and surveillance and our existence is often treated as out of place and interpreted as difficult. These experiences often fall outside traditional analyses of mandated psychological treatment, sustaining intersecting racial and gendered surveillance and punishment that Black women navigate and negotiate daily within the health care system.

The growing role of law enforcement in mental health support, embedded in Ontario's Mental Health Act, makes the experience of mental distress appear criminal and has proven to be deadly for some Black women. Recent stories of Black women requiring emergency mental health support and being met by police officers operating through a "public safety" lens are concerning. In May 2020, Regis Korchinski-Paquet, a twenty-nine-year-old Afro-Indigenous woman, fatally fell from the balcony of her twenty-fourth floor

Toronto apartment after police entered her home. A family member who was trying to support her in distress called 911 for help. Instead, just twenty-six minutes after that call and her interactions with police, she fell to her death. Six months after her death, an unnamed thirty-year-old Black transgender woman in Toronto was found dead after being taken into custody by police for what was deemed as mental health care under the Mental Health Act. Death was the response to their calls for help rather than care, kindness, and support.[20]

The punishment allotted to Black women extends, of course, beyond the Mental Health Act. Annette Bailey, Manoj Sharma, and Michelle Jubin, researching the relationship between traumatic stress and resilience among Black women who have lost children to gun violence, found that compensation and grief counselling are provided for most families of victims of crime in Canada except in cases where the victim is deemed responsible for their own death.[21] In 90 percent of the cases the study looked at, Black women were excluded from these supports because their children were known to the police. The Bailey, Sharma and Jubin study is important because it is an example of how Black women's experiences have been suppressed and dismissed in developing health policy in this country.[22] Specifically in this case, by limiting access to mental health care based on police involvement in the context of a long-patterned history of mass incarceration, oversurveillance, and overrepresentation of Black people within prisons across Canada, social work and health care practices grounded in abolition strategies need to be seen as legitimate supports for Black women. As a strategy, abolition offers possibilities for addressing the material and emotional harm of marginalization and injustice; when we question and unsettle the inevitability of punishment and prison, we have no choice but to return to creativity and imagination in our practice and dream up new ways to organize our world and shape our relationship to each other.

In 2019, abolitionists Ruth Wilson Gilmore and James Kilgore wrote a piece for the Marshall Project making a case for abolition. They write that, "ultimately, abolition is a practical program of change rooted in how people sustain and improve their lives, cobbling together insights and strategies from disparate, connected struggle . . . to imagine a world without prisons and jail is to imagine a world in which social welfare is a right and not a luxury."[23] Below, I outline several clear strategies that social workers can take up in this regard.

THINK DEEPLY AND CRITICALLY ABOUT THE SOCIAL DETERMINANTS OF HEALTH

Through its interest in social and economic justice, social work is committed to addressing the social determinants of health. This is enshrined in the *Canadian Association of Social Workers Code of Ethics and Scope or Practice*, a practice document that highlights the profession's commitment to "health and social well-being using the social determinants of health framework when delivering services, navigating systems, and advocating for equitable access to and improvement of the multiple dimensions that impact health and well-being."[24] Yet, despite over a decade of social determinant public policy implementation and a recent—albeit slower—shift to collecting race-based health data, the connections between health, well-being, and social determinants are still imagined as distinct, individualized, and static identities that influence health outcomes and thus require policy redress at the microlevel.

For example, in a summary of lessons learned about the connections between the social determinants of health and COVID-19, Public Health Ontario notes that "Social determinants of health (SDOH), such as gender, socioeconomic position, race/ethnicity, occupation, Indigeneity, homelessness and incarceration, play an important role in risk of COVID-19 infection, particularly when *they* limit ability to maintain physical distancing" (emphasis mine).[25] This framing of identity as a causation of adverse health outcomes is popular in Canadian narratives of health, and it insists that individuals embody particular identities that make them vulnerable to detrimental health outcomes. This thesis has been useful in galvanizing conversations about the relationship between race and health, but it maintains naturalistic and medicalizing understandings of race that promote individual interventions at the expense of inciting moves for transforming structural inequalities.

Racial identity does not affect our ability to maintain physical distance, but structural consequences do. The research is clear: unfair labour policies prevent people from taking time off if they or a family member is sick; lack of affordable housing and city designs keep people in close quarters, preventing them from isolating if they are sick; and transit decisions that cut routes result in streetcars and buses that are more crowded. These are all things that prevent people from being able to maintain physical distance, and these are decisions that disproportionately affect Black, Indigenous, and other racialized people, who, because of racial capitalism, are most likely to work in industries and live in neighbourhoods that are affected by these policies. This is how race gets made: it is a dynamic process. Thinking deeply about SDOH would mean a recognition that our health experiences and outcomes are a result of processes of racialization.

Writing on dominant meanings of Blackness, Rinaldo Walcott reminds us, "Black people are constantly understood to be out of place. This out-of-place-ness, especially of poor Black people, is one which has profound life and death consequences; it has become highlighted in the extreme by the carceral state"[26] The regulation of this out-of-placeness with surveillance and carceral consequence has become synonymous with Blackness and is a social determinant of our health. It is braided into our health care experience. Race is not a determinant of our health experiences, rather it is the meaning that we attach to Blackness and the material consequences that ensue; this means cultures of carcerality and surveillance are also determinants of health.

RECOGNITION OF SOCIAL WORK AS ABOLITION WORK

Ostensibly, social work prides itself on being a profession committed to social justice, and yet it is a profession with deep and historical roots in settler colonial punishment and carcerality. Historians have documented the development of social welfare policy in Canada, growing out of the colonial charitable sector and organizing into a wide range of government-led social services.[27] Early social work, handmaidens to the developing welfare state, professionalized alongside the growth of moral surveillance, invested in separating the deserving from the undeserving beneficiaries of the welfare state. Participating in the genocide of Indigenous people across Canada, social workers accompanied Indian agents on to reserves, supporting the removal and institutionalization of Indigenous children, whose entitlement to citizenship and state support depended on their Europeanization.[28]

As Chanelle Gallant points out in her chapter in this book, individual social workers do not design the institution of social work and have little control over the policy codes and budgets that govern their work and their professional responsibilities. This becomes challenging when social work, as an institution, continues to find itself deputized and called upon to participate in punishment. Recently, with growing calls to defund the police, social workers are increasingly presented as a viable option for replacing the work of police in wellness checks. We should see the history of social work and its relationship to punishment as cause for concern for improving the "wellness check" process. We need to see our work as pushing back against the call to punish and instead use our energies and creativity to address injustices and support people getting the resources they need when in crisis.

BLACK SOCIAL WORK, INTERCONNECTEDNESS, AND ABOLITION

Black people birth cultures of resistance. These are the cultural, political, economic, emotional, and spiritual sites of being in this world that affirm our dignity and humanity, recapitulating futures where freedom is possible. Black social workers and health care workers have both conceptualized and put into action ways of supporting communities that offer lessons in resisting policing, refusing participation in surveillance, and rejecting the enactment of punishment in favour of the politicizing of love, mutual aid, and care.[29] These practices are based on African and diasporic understandings of interconnectedness; an insistence that we exist today because we are in constant relationship to our ancestral and earthly communities. Part of this symbiosis is an accounting of these relationships with each other, within ourselves, and with broader structural systems.

Black social workers have documented this work. For example, writing from long-standing practice experience, Black social work scholars, MJ Rwigema, Onyinyechukwu Udegbe, and David Lewis-Peart call upon social workers to take up social work interventions such as community witnessing, making room for Afrocentric spirituality, and case management strategies that ask workers to treat clients as if they are part of one's own family and community.[30] For Black social work scholar Akua Benjamin, front-line social workers cannot provide health, employment, education, and counselling supports in Black communities without overcoming the fear of addressing racial profiling.[31] These experiences are intimately connected. Early writing from Wanda Thomas-Bernard, Lydia Lucas-White, and Dorothy E. Moore in *Canadian Social Work Review* shows a call for social work education that gives students the capacity to redress *systemic* discrimination.[32] This is an example of the type of abolitionist approaches to social work that are being advocated by Black women in the field. Instead of looking for ways to regulate or monitor our work, we look to find ways to solve problems or prevent the behaviour that brings about the problem in the first place. Our work involves rethinking what is punishable in the first place. Engaging as Black social workers with Black people should not be left simply at the one-on-one level, we need to practice with the systemic context in mind. Providing health care with dignity is practicing with this interconnectedness between Black people's experiences and the racialized context in which they access services. We must engage in microsupports while actively working to address issues of policing, racial profiling, and stigmatizing Black people with individualized mental health issues when they reject the racist context in which they exist. It is also a recognition that we keep each other safe and that our relationships with each other become a key part of working towards and calling for fully funded, quality health care that is not based on punishment and surveillance.

CONCLUSION

One of this chapter's broader concerns is to look at how Black women have experienced carcerality in health care and social work settings to add to a more fulsome understanding of how carcerality operates in Canada. This expanded definition is important because it focuses on what we know about state violence and punishment at the intersection of race and gender identity. I recognize that there are limits to using this framework in the way I have. Tracing the carceral logic in some of the health care experiences for Black women runs the risk of becoming a damage centred analysis and leaves room for misinterpreting this analysis as evidence of Black brokenness.[33]

Still, I would like to speak back to this. Black people have and continue to respond to carcerality in ways that reaffirm our dignity and humanity by asserting ways that we see each other and care for each other through mutual aid formation. Even from a social work perspective, a review of Black women's scholarship in social work demonstrates this. Thus, while some argue that Black life remains stuck in the afterlife of slavery, for me these affirmations remind us that the afterlife has moments of comfort delight and merges with an unbroken critical hope for the possibility of future freedom. I use critical hope in the way Carl James and Akua Benjamin have described it, as

> action that is based on the critical analysis of a situation and the recognition that wishing alone is not sufficient to make change. It involves an understanding of the forces that produce injustice and an imagining of what the world without these forces, and without the injustice, might look like.[34]

This is abolition. It continues the work of ancestors who fought to end the transatlantic slave trade. Taking up an abolitionist lens in social work recognizes and identifies prison and punishment as experiences that go beyond the actual physical walls of an institution and allows us to see how health care institutions and social work philosophies can be sites of abolitionist resistance.

CHAPTER 4

"KEEP THIS UP AND THEY'LL BE PULLING YOU FROM THE RED"

Young People Are Dying to Survive Winnipeg's Child Welfare System

Juvie[1]

> I'd like to dedicate this piece to all current and former street kids who experienced violence from caregivers, and institutions that framed it as "care." To those who survived in whole. To those who survived in part. To those who didn't survive at all.

The Red River is an important piece of Winnipeg's geography, winding through the city and joining together with the Assiniboine River at a central meeting place called "The Forks," a historical trading post that played a key role in the development of the Prairies earliest railroad system. The Red River is also an important piece of what it means to live on the street in Winnipeg. Not only because of the parks, trees, and greenspaces that line its riverbanks—providing places to hide, rest, or seek recluse from judgmental eyes—but also because of the evocative imagery social workers, police, and media routinely invoke of poor people, homeless people, and street kids being pulled out of the Red River as a consequence of our poor choices: poverty, crime, promiscuity, drug use, etc. It's just as much a promise as it is a threat that the poor, the homeless, the undesirable, and the forgotten will one day find themselves helpless, lifeless, washed up on the banks of the Red River covered in the red-brown silt that famously tints the entire stream a light auburn. It's something that was repeated to me and others regularly throughout our time in and around Winnipeg's child welfare system—from cops, social workers, therapists, teachers, and politicians.

If you're not careful it could be you.
If you don't make better choices this could happen to you.
This is where you're headed.
This is what you're destined for.

I can't use terms like "care," "welfare," or "protection" to describe my experience with social workers, therapists, police, teachers, and the whole host of adult figures who participate in the web of surveillance that Child and Family Services (CFS) Manitoba creates. A web that is just as thin, fragile, and ineffective as it is expansive. It wouldn't be accurate to say I "fell through the cracks"; rather, I and too many other street kids were actively failed by a system operating just as it was intended to. A system that labeled me *high risk*, minimized the violence I experienced, dismissed my suffering, my pleas for help, and my pain precisely because I was seen as high risk and disposable. I was young. I was Black. I was poor. I was angry. I was defiant. I was also a child fighting to survive some of the nation's coldest winters outdoors, dodging physical and sexual violence in foster homes, circling in and out of the orbit of CFS social workers, police, counsellors, and others as I was kicked out or ran away from home after home after home. The only reason I escaped and ultimately survived after twelve years in the orbit of CFS is because of the love and the care of other street kids who saw me, helped me, clothed me, fed me, and recognized my humanity in moments where I struggled to see it in myself. I survived *in spite of* the violence I experienced at the hands of CFS Manitoba, Winnipeg Police, and the far-reaching networks of social workers, health care providers, teachers, and others tapped to surveil, profile, and write me off as a street kid through an adversarial system framed as "care."

CFS Manitoba is often referred to as "child protective services" or "child welfare"—programming that works directly with young people and families—in theory intervening in "unstable home environments" with supportive programming and services, placing us in foster homes, removing us from communities of caregivers, and providing ongoing case management until we age or die out of their system. In my experience, the language of "care," "protection," and "child welfare" was largely used to mask a deeply racist, antagonizing system that works to further marginalize Black and Indigenous youth. The language and framing of "care" was used to strip us of our community ties and trap so many young people in a web of policing, surveillance, and punishment that follows us across generations. This language was deliberately invoked to take punitive action against us. Police and social workers used it to justify ticketing, arresting, and detaining young people looking for food, shelter, community, and other basic necessities on the streets of Winnipeg. Therapists and case managers used it to coax young people into divulging their deepest, most intimate personal traumas—experiences of physical and sexual assault, struggles with addictions and mental health, suicidal thoughts and ideations—and weaponized this information by sharing it widely, using it to institutionalize us or justify further surveillance. Judges and politicians used the language of "care" to justify criminalizing and incarcerating us—framing it as much-needed *tough love*—while implementing rigid social policies that failed to keep us safe, marked us as social problems, and effectively left us to die. The framing of child protective services as "care" gives social workers, police, and the state unrestricted access and control over our lives. To be seized, surveilled, and institutionalized under the guise of "care" strips us of our agency and with that, any ability to say "no," assert boundaries, or exercise any meaningful form of control over our lives. For those of us who experience violence, abuse, or harm at the hands of a system so adamantly framed as "care" and "protection," the consequences are life-altering.

The rates at which youth in the "care" of CFS Manitoba are reported missing and murdered in Winnipeg and struggle with intergenerational trauma and the life-long impacts of being so heavily policed, surveilled, and scrutinized through critical phases of development are devastating. Young people should not need to *fight to survive* Canada's child welfare system. They are the perpetrators, the accomplices, and the enforcers of a violent system. We are the casualties. And while we are hustled through a system framed as "care" and "protection," many of us struggle to find any real semblance of love, care, or protection from the violence we endure at its hands.

CANADA'S "CHILD WELFARE" SYSTEM AND CFS MANITOBA

Canada has one of the highest rates of child apprehensions in the world.[2] The 2011 Census was the first time a national survey attempted to track the total number of foster kids in Canada, identifying a total of 47,885 youth. In 2011, 29,590 or 62 percent of youth in care were aged fourteen and under, another 11,455 youth in care were fifteen–nineteen, 1,730 were aged twenty–twenty-four and 5,115 were over twenty-five.[3] What this survey and most data around foster care cannot capture are all of the informal arrangements and alternative settings youth living away from biological parents or primary caregivers find themselves in: informal agreements with friends, family, and peers; living out of shelters or group homes; couch surfing or living on the streets. The logistics and structure of foster care systems in Canada have fallen largely under provincial and territorial jurisdiction, meaning the eligibility criteria for entering and exiting care, readily available supports, and data reporting tools for rates of apprehension, mistreatment, even death rates, vary across each province and territory. Within each province and territory, child protective services tend to be run across multiple agencies with varying systems for tracking, reporting, and publicly communicating information related to their work.[4]

In the 2011 Census, Manitoba reported the highest rates of youth in care in Canada—1.9 percent of the total youth population ages fourteen and under.[5] When accounting for all youth under the age of eighteen at the time, this rises to just over 3 percent of the total youth population.[6] In 2011, 7.5 percent of *all youth* in Manitoba had been in the orbit of CFS, receiving "supportive" or "protective" services by the age of seven.[7] While many with limited experience in or around Canada's child welfare system think of apprehension as a last resort following particularly extreme cases of child endangerment, the reality is that CFS agencies in Manitoba often preemptively determine who is unfit to parent. In 2015, on average, CFS agencies across Manitoba seized one newborn a day, directly after delivery. In that same year, CFS Manitoba seized forty Indigenous children from a single Winnipeg hospital through a formal "Birth Alert System" where social workers would warn health care workers about potentially "high risk" patients about to give birth and apprehend the babies just after they were born.[8] CFS agencies have a history of marking Black, Indigenous, and racialized people as "high risk" by profiling parents and targeting the children of current and former CFS youth.

Canada's child welfare system has been widely recognized as

an extension of the residential school system—an act of genocide that seized Indigenous youth from their homes, families, and communities, stripped them of their language, culture, traditions, kinship, and identity, and forced on them the cultural practices and standards of the Canadian state. Residential schools operated under the guise of "civilizing" Indigenous youth and used the language of assimilation to justify horrific forms of physical, sexual, and psychological abuse that many survivors have had to carry with them across generations. As communities across Canada continue to discover mass graves at former residential school sites, the direct connections between state-sanctioned child apprehension and family separation framed as "care," "protection," and "assimilation" to white, Anglo-Canadian values cannot be separated from the current practices CFS agencies use to identify "high risk" families. CFS agencies overwhelmingly target Black and Indigenous youth from Manitoba's poorest communities and justify the violence of family separation, isolation, youth detention, and criminalization with the language of "care" and "protection." In 2011, 85 percent of youth in Manitoba's foster care system were seized from Indigenous communities.[9] As a result, 22 percent of First Nations children in Manitoba end up in child protective services compared to just 1.5 percent of non-Indigenous youth in the general population.[10] Several First Nations across Northern Manitoba report their entire youth population having at least one interaction with CFS agencies before the age of eighteen. While many provinces, including Manitoba, openly acknowledge the profound harms of residential schools and the Sixties Scoop, there are currently three times more Indigenous youth in child welfare than there were at the height of the residential schooling system.[11]

The lack of transparent reporting around CFS Manitoba's apprehension rates, demographic information, activities, and complaints helps agencies evade accountability and minimizes the struggles and experiences of youth in care by quite literally erasing them from the official record altogether. Consider that CFS agencies in Manitoba mobilize an expansive network of social workers, case managers, police, health care workers, even teachers, caregivers, and foster parents for the purposes of tracking, pathologizing, criminalizing, and institutionalizing young people. While CFS agencies and political leaders across Manitoba, even nationally, remark on the inefficient bureaucratic processes within and between CFS agencies and how these lead to youth "slipping through the cracks," it speaks to the reality that *violence* and *erasure* within state-run "care" and "protective" services is not limited to our immediate experiences of physical, emotional, and psychological abuse in care—it also extends into the bureaucratic tools and processes CFS agencies engage in to serve and protect themselves. Provincial leaders are also implicated in how rates of youth in care are manipulated and, since 2016, have played a key role in attempting to shift language and definitions around what it means to be "in care" to reduce Manitoba's publicly reported rates of youth in foster care. From 2000 to 2016 the percentage of Manitoba youth in care rose from 1.9 percent to 3.5 percent—totalling around 10,500 youth in care.[12] In 2016, the provincial government moved to exclude seven hundred youth who were *voluntarily placed* in care and youth who *preemptively moved* into the care of others to bring the annual figure below ten thousand.[13] Comparatively, Saskatchewan, a neighbouring province with a comparable population, reported around four thousand youth in care in the same year.[14] In 2017, Manitoba again revised their definition of what it meant to be "in care" to remove youth in "non-paid care" settings (arrangements where caregivers are not compensated) and "out-of-home care" arrangements (young people living with a family member, friend, or caregiver). Through working to redefine what kind of "care" settings are included in publicly reported rates of youth in care, Manitoba reported its first decrease in 2018 and continues to report steadily declining rates of youth in care to date.[15] In 2020, CFS Manitoba reported 9,849 youth in care and an additional 527 youth in "out-of-home care" arrangements.[16]

THE IMPACTS OF BEING IN AND SURVIVING CFS MANITOBA'S "CARE"

The negative outcomes associated with navigating foster care are far-reaching and long lasting, ranging from negative impacts on a survivor's physical and mental health and interpersonal relationships, social and economic outcomes, and long-term, intergenerational trauma. Youth in care are more likely to be hospitalized, report suicide attempts at twice the rate of youth who are not in care, and commit suicide at three and a half times the rate of youth who have never been in contact with child protective services.[17]

Youth in care are more likely to struggle in school and be suspended or expelled.[18] Of youth in the permanent care of CFS Manitoba, 33.4 percent are expected to graduate high school compared to 66.8 percent of youth who have received *any services* from CFS Manitoba and 89 percent of youth who had never been in care.[19] The long-term impacts of family separation and isolation affect every aspect of a survivor's interpersonal, romantic, and familial relationships to come. The mental health outcomes—grief, depression, PTSD, anxiety, and more—can be carried through an entire lifetime, even passed down through generations of a survivor's lineage.

There is also a strong relationship between youth in the "care" of CFS agencies and their exposure to the criminal justice system. Social workers, police officers, media, and local politicians use the term "crossover kids" to refer to youth who are both in care and in the orbit of the criminal justice system. In 2015, 83 percent of all missing persons cases in Manitoba were youth meant to be in the care of CFS agencies at the time of their disappearance.[20] Kerri Irvin-Ross, a local politician (NDP) and social worker who served as Manitoba's minister of family services during this time, said these numbers were the result of a few "frequent flyers"—young people who continued to run away from foster homes or end up in police custody.[21] Local politicians, social workers, and CFS agencies often reduce the struggles of young people in care to individual cases of "frequent flyers," "street kids," and "troubled youth" who are "acting out," refusing to see *running away from foster homes; stealing food, clothing, basic necessities; and connecting with local gangs for community, safety, and protection* as an implication of the *lack* of meaningful supports their "care" offers.

THE PIPELINE: FROM FOSTER HOME TO GROUP HOME TO SHELTER TO HOTEL/MOTEL TO JUVIE

Manitoba has always had more youth in care than readily available foster homes. In 2012, CFS reported a shortage of foster homes with about 4,800 placements available across the province for the ten thousand youth in care.[22] In an effort to increase the number of available foster homes, provinces generally offer compensation to families who take youth in. Compensation models for foster parents were designed to cover basic expenses: room and board, food and clothing, and other basic necessities—but because CFS has so many youth in care, their ability to follow up with families, ensure funds were used accordingly, or even ensure the safety and security of youth in care can be largely nonexistent. Because of the chronic shortage of foster homes, there has historically been an intolerance for foster kids reporting issues with their existing placements. The sentiment communicated to many of us was that we should be grateful for any placements—our reports of physical, sexual, and psychological abuse often went unattended to or were used to antagonize us directly as "troubled," "attention-seeking," or "disturbed" youth in need of "care."

In Winnipeg, when CFS couldn't place you in a foster home, their next step would be to send you to a group home or youth shelter, and then to a hotel or motel as a last resort. I, and others, often *chose* to live outdoors, to sleep in bus shelters, in secluded alleyways, abandoned buildings, and park spaces because they were safer than many of these placement options. Shelters and drop-ins were often overcrowded and underfunded and hotel/motel options were unsupervised in areas with no real support from CFS staff. Between 2011 and 2014, the Province of Manitoba spent $18 million on hotel accommodations and staff support roles related to housing youth in care.[23] It was through this time that hotel and motel placements increased, hitting an all-time high in March of 2014 when eighty-one youth were sheltered in hotel settings in a single night.[24]

In August 2014, fifteen-year-old Tina Fontaine's body was recovered from the Red River in Winnipeg, wrapped in a duvet cover and weighted down by rocks. She weighed seventy-two pounds. Left in an unsupervised hotel setting in downtown Winnipeg, she'd interacted with police, social workers, and medical staff at Winnipeg Children's Hospital. Tina Fontaine had asked social workers and health care workers for resources, bed-space, and addictions and mental health support that never came. She ran away from an unsupervised hotel placement shortly before her body was pulled out of the river. It was only in April of 2015, following a series of high-profile cases, including the discovery of Tina Fontaine's body and widely publicized CCTV footage of a youth in care being violently physically and sexually assaulted at an unsupervised hotel site, ultimately leading to her death, that CFS Manitoba committed to ending the use of unsupervised hotel and motel spaces.[25] CFS set an end date of June 1, 2015, but that was gradually extended to November despite young people in care reporting violence and abuse while staying in these unsupervised spaces.[26] In 2016, CFS Manitoba continued to house young people in hotels unsupervised, citing a lack of alternative placement options, and by 2017, CFS had stopped collecting data on youth in unsupervised hotel and motel settings altogether despite advocates flagging these continued arrangements.[27]

The less publicized reality of what it meant to be a young person in care in the midst of a foster home shortage, overcrowded shelters and group homes, and unsafe hotel and motel sites was how the criminal justice system and jails were then used to house young people "in care" with nowhere else to go. In 2015, the lack of available foster homes and alternative placements for youth "in care" led to judges keeping youth in detention facilities for extended periods of time.[28] It was routine for judges who could not secure placements for young people to leave them at the Manitoba Youth Centre. When child advocates flagged this as a human rights violation, CFS Manitoba and the provincial government could not produce any data identifying exactly how many youth had been held under these conditions and admitted that no one was keeping track.[29] No agency was keeping track of how many young people "in care" were warehoused in detention facilities, just as no agency was keeping track of how many young people "in care" were left to die in unsupervised hotel/motel settings, just as no agency was keeping track of how many young people "in care" died across the country.

What's overlooked in the decision to keep youth in custody for extended periods of time are the violent conditions many face while detained. In 2013, sixteen-year-old Roberta "Gracie" Daniels hung herself from a ceiling vent at the Brandon Correctional Centre while in the care of CFS Manitoba. Her family's subsequent lawsuit notes, "At the time Gracie committed suicide, a fellow inmate, who was supposedly on suicide watch and from a different cell, observed her attempted suicide and repeatedly yelled for the guards to intervene but no one came to prevent the suicide."[30] Detention facilities are not an alternative to stable housing options, counselling, or mental health support for youth "in care." Many youth in the orbit of CFS Manitoba are brought to detention facilities, ticketed, and arrested for minor acts: missing curfew, talking back to an officer or social worker, running away, basic probation violations, and simply being *perceived* by others as suspicious or threatening. While police in

Winnipeg often profile and harass Black and Indigenous people on the streets, prisons (adult facilities and juvenile detention facilities alike) work as an extension of this to disappear street kids, troubled youth, and communities marked as social problems. Youth "in care" die in jails and at the hands of police. Youth "in care" kill themselves in jails because *death* feels like the only way out. For those who make it out of the physical cell, the charges, the record, and the impact of having been incarcerated lives with them over decades—through school, work, family planning, and other areas of life.

Two years after Gracie's suicide, Kerri Irvin-Ross, in her capacity as Manitoba family services minister, was approached by children's advocates receiving calls from judges who did not want to release incarcerated youth nearing the end of their sentences back into unsupervised hotel/motel settings. Irvin-Ross refused to acknowledge that this amounted to any form of human rights violation and instead stressed the need for a clear reintegration strategy:

> When we're talking about moving a child from the youth centre back into the community, we need to take a lot of care and attention. When a child is ready to be released, there needs to be a plan in place. If that plan is not in place the time needs to be made to ensure that plan is developed and implemented. That's our responsibility.[31]

This response is characteristic of CFS Manitoba's approach: invoking the language of care, safety planning, and protection to justify violating the human rights of young people in their custody.

DEATH IS EXPECTED: THE UNDER-REPORTING OF YOUTH DEATHS "IN CARE"

In 2017, 13 youth died in the custody of CFS Manitoba.[32] Between 2008 and 2016, the Assembly of Manitoba Chiefs (AMC) reported 546 youth died while in the care of child protective services across Canada, around 68 each year.[33] The reported rates of death in care from AMC and child advocates has always differed from the death rates CFS agencies in Manitoba and child protective services across Canada report. In *A Life Discarded,* investigative reporters from the television program *16x9* identified 320 youth who died between 2010 and 2015 with active files in child welfare agencies across Canada or within their first twelve months of aging out—69 from Manitoba in this period.[34] When they expand this figure to include youth who died at home with active case files at child welfare agencies, the total number of deaths in care increases to 500 between 2009 and 2015.[35] Reporters and child advocates have struggled to access clear and consistent records of youth deaths in care from child welfare agencies. When Kenneth Jackson attempted to investigate the 102 reported deaths of Indigenous youth in Ontario's child welfare system between 2013 and 2017, the investigation identified issues in child welfare agencies' data collection and reporting process that led to a number of deaths not being accurately reflected in state-reported figures.[36] Child welfare agencies across Canada have not been able to accurately account for how many youth die in their care for decades, leaving child advocates, youth in care, and investigative journalists to piece together the true rates of death, suicide, and mistreatment on their own.

From the limited data available on the rate of youth deaths in care, some of the most important details can't be captured, including the personal histories and struggles of youth, how "child protective" services failed them, and how many fought to survive and were ultimately left to suffer, struggle, and die at the hands of this violent system. Youth dying in care are publicly vilified and made responsible for the violence they've endured. In life we are made out to be "troubled," "disturbed," "violent," and "hopeless"—and when we die in the clutches of a violent system that has failed and discarded us at each turn, we bear the brunt of the responsibility in the eyes of police, press, politicians, and social workers. Black and Indigenous women and girls are slut shamed. Our faces, bodies, clothing, public profiles, and sexual histories openly remarked on in the public eye. Our deepest struggles, histories of physical and sexual abuse, addictions, mental health struggles, and crimes are picked apart. We are given no grace or sympathy, forever branded "troubled youth" and "street kids" deserving of the violence we endure. The most disturbing function of this system is how it thrives on beating into so many of us the idea that we *are* responsible for the violence we face, that we *are* troubled and disposable, that we *are* no better than the trash bags we'd carried our entire lives from placement to placement, and that ultimately, we would be better off dead.

DYING TO SURVIVE: THE LASTING IMPACT OF "SURVIVING" CFS MANITOBA

I was in "care" for twelve years. I ran away as a teenager and made it out before many of the young people mentioned in this piece entered the system. I didn't have access to any language or data surrounding rates of apprehension, experiences of violence or abuse, or youth deaths. I didn't need it to understand that the violence I endured "in care" would be life-altering. I didn't plan to live more than a few months to a year at any given moment. I was a child sleeping in bus shelters through the bitter cold of Winnipeg winters; curled up in a tarp behind Portage Place, in alleyways, in malls and vacant buildings, in parkades and bike paths at The Forks, in schools and late-night campus hangouts, in empty cars and abandoned buildings. All of this was safer than returning to some of the homes I'd been placed in. I remember digging through trash bins for food, being so hungry that I'd pass out and ride the bus for hours on end in loops just to get out of the cold. I would sleep under bridges, seek refuge in crack houses, compromise my boundaries for a shot at safety, and stare into the Red River wondering when someone would be fishing my dead body out of it.

I watched other street kids die out in the cold, commit suicide in jails, and face violence at the hands of police, social workers, and other adult caregivers who saw no future for us. Often, I was so exhausted and so scared that I would wish for death. I found many foster placements to be so degrading, so physically painful and sexually exploitative that I would wish for death. I never planned to live more than a few months at a time because I didn't want to. There was no control or say over where I went, how long I stayed, or what living with dignity looked like. It was its own kind of slow and painful death. I found living, surviving, and seeing so much loss around me to be so draining and so painful that I would wish for death, or at least the strength to kill myself. I believed in my heart that it had to be better than life.

I found it easier to deal with Winnipeg Police than social workers because they were at least open about their disgust towards me and others. CFS social workers, therapists, and case managers would often couch their disgust in a humiliating and adversarial process that was built to blame me and other street kids for our circumstances in the name of "care" or "protection." Winnipeg Police didn't care to *protect* me, and they were clear about our relationship, their intentions, and what kind of pain to brace myself for. By casting us as "troubled," "disturbed," "calculated" youth and blaming us for our own poverty, mental health and addictions, broken relationships and past traumas, social workers never had to interrogate the violent systems they upheld at our expense. The systems that *facilitated* this abuse. We were the broken ones. We were the criminals, the liars, and the troubled youth. When foster placements physically and sexually assaulted us, misused funds, or violated our boundaries, *we* were the problem—the ungrateful ones and the troublemakers. *"What's wrong with you?," "What did you do?," "Why are you lying?," "Why are you causing trouble?," "Are you drinking?," "Are you using drugs?," "Are you having sex?," "Are you with a gang?," "If you keep this up, they'll be pulling you out of the Red."*

I struggle to cope with the regular use of the Red River imagery so many social workers, therapists, and political leaders would invoke. This terrifying culture of surveillance and punishment taught me very early on to censor myself for my own protection. I could never find meaningful forms of support or intervention through my time "in care" and this has impacted how I understand care in my life after aging out of the system. Instead of food, clothes, health care, confidential counselling, safe shelter, and resource, I was tracked and documented for the purposes of pathologizing, institutionalizing, and criminalizing me. Communicating my experiences honestly felt like risky and with every new foster home came a balance of probabilities: *It's bad here, but could it be worse somewhere else? Can I risk being re-homed? Is a bus shelter safer?*

By seizing Black and Indigenous youth from Manitoba's poorest communities at greater rates and driving us into underfunded shelters, group homes, motels, and detention facilities, Canada's child welfare system ultimately functions to disappear those of us marked as social problems, undesirable to our surrounding communities. Too many youth die, commit suicide, run away, sleep on the streets, or just fall apart and lose themselves in Manitoba's foster care system. When I think of what it means to "survive" a system as violent and dehumanizing as CFS Manitoba, I often think about the deep physical and psychological wounds many of us carry through our lives as a result of facing off against this system. For Manitoba's political leadership to back discriminatory Birth Alert programs and hospital seizures, use detention facilities as stand ins for meaningful placement options, and refer to us as "frequent flyers" while youth in care go missing and experience profound forms of violence, abuse, and harm through their time "in care" is dehumanizing. I remember what it felt like to sleep under a tarp in the snow, to sit across from social workers, police, and abusive foster placements and see a system designed to make us either run away or die. For some, it's a violent death, and for others, it's a series of slow deaths that kill us from the inside out and leave a person marked in the orbit of CFS Manitoba and the criminal justice system for life. A system meant to "care" for and "protect" some of Manitoba's most marginalized youth leaves such deep scars and robs us of the ability to recognize and accept care from others, to trust people and form meaningful, loving relationships.

I don't identify with the language of "survivor." I feel that some small part of me survived but many other pieces of me died painful deaths. A piece of me died with each friend that I lost. With every home I was hustled through, never quite belonging. With each trash bag I was made to pack my life into in ten minutes or less. Each time I was made to choose a bus shelter or an underpass or an alleyway to sleep in because it was safer than "home." Each time a social worker or cop wrote me off as troubled, distraught, or broken while I begged for help, parts of me died. For every second of every beating, every rape, every moment I was made to feel disgusted, ashamed, and dirty in my own skin by adults pushed on me as "caregivers," I lost parts of myself that I will never get back. Any part of me that survived did so at the expense of others who showed me how to live and survive on the street and "in care."

My survival comes at the expense of people who taught me how to find food, shelter, and warmth through the winter months. Young people who were marked and discarded in the same way I was. My survival comes at the expense of people who taught me how to avoid and minimize scrutiny from cops, social workers, and other immediate threats. People who'd wrap their arms around me to stay warm through the cold, break into cars and abandoned buildings to find shelter, and steal food, medicine, and anything else to keep me and others alive. Selfless people who gained nothing from showing me love, kindness, and basic decency. Often, they made a choice to *sacrifice* and *share* to keep me alive while I'd just hoped to die. My survival comes at the expense of good people denied humanity and care from a system that deliberately labelled us "troubled," "hopeless," "street kids," and "frequent flyers." The people I lost taught me love, trust, compassion, and safety and they are the ones who deserve life, family, love, and safety in return. The guilt of surviving is overwhelming and often feels insurmountable. I wish I'd done more to keep them safe and if I could, I'd give my life for theirs.

CHAPTER 5
NOT CRIMINALLY RESPONSIBLE
The Fatal Intersection of the Mental Health and Justice Systems

Carly Seltzer, Lue Palmer, and Golta Shahidi

The forensic mental health system is where the mental health system and the criminal justice systems intersect. In Ontario, where we live, it is governed by the Ontario Review Board (ORB), a tribunal established under the Criminal Code of Canada to annually review the status of every person under its jurisdiction.[1] In thinking about abolitionist social work, we felt it was important to address the misconceived notion that mental health and psychiatric institutions are inherently different than prisons and the carceral system.

We write from different positions within the system: Carly is a social worker, Lue is a family caregiver for someone in the system, and Golta is a criminal defence lawyer. In each of our unique experiences, we have seen the mental health system use the same disciplinary principles and tactics as the carceral system, including punishment, detainment, surveillance, degradation, control, restriction of movement, restraints, coercion, risk assessments, and an emphasis on the idea of public safety over personal liberty. The forensic mental health system claims to be rehabilitative versus punitive, but that is far from true. Social workers and other health care workers continue to play key roles in upholding carceral regulations and policies that target, constrain, and often make life harder for people with neurodiversity and mental health issues, particularly if they are racialized. Meanwhile, it is unclear whether the forensic mental health system actually contributes to making our society a safer place for all. We, like the other contributors in this book, dream of a world where care is not carceral, madness is not criminalized, and support is accessible. We hope this chapter will inspire you to continue dreaming, resisting, and embodying new ways of working within this system in hopes of abolishing it and building something new.

CARCERAL CARE

Social workers play significant roles in the forensic mental health system, with the power to influence and direct families in responding to their loved ones, call the police, obtain forms for involuntary admission to mental health facilities, and encourage ongoing detainment. Social workers' documentation can be used as evidence in a hearing or in court. Every word, phone call, letter, and note has the power to detain and incarcerate. Carly points out that "we don't actively consider the immense power we have over people's lives." Social workers are often the outward face of the mental health system and have a direct impact on how families engage with and support their loved ones.

Carceral responses to crises are entrenched in the code of ethics governing social workers. We begin our relationships with service users by stating our duty to report (i.e., call 911) should we suspect (not necessarily know) that someone may harm themselves or others. In this sense, our desire to help is informed by the need to control or manage, a presumed intention of violence, and a fear of being liable. Operating from a risk or liability standpoint drives social workers to support psychiatric incarceration. The sentiment often being, "well at least they are in a safe place," to justify the outcome. Ultimately, the ways we are tied to the state mean that our care cannot be divorced from state violence. Though we have the capacity to be helpful, and social workers do have a choice in how we care for and support the people we work with, the move to call for the abolition of social work in its current form is important and necessary.

Often, a person's first point of contact with the mental health system occurs when they experience a serious episode of psychosis, depression, or other mental health struggle that requires them or their family members to seek medical attention—including at the emergency department of their local hospital. Despite seeking medical assistance, they may be unwittingly opening themselves up to a years-long involuntary relationship with the mental health system through carceral mechanisms that are racialized, institutionalized, contradictory, and based on patient observation that is decontextualized from a person's social conditions.

In Ontario, the Mental Health Act—the set of laws governing how and when a person can be involuntarily apprehended and detained in a psychiatric facility or forced to take medication[2]—is a primary example of how the mental system can be punitive and carceral rather than rehabilitative. If medical professionals deem a person in crisis to be a risk to themselves and/or others, the patient is placed on a Form 1 and can be involuntarily detained in a mental health inpatient unit at the hospital for up to seventy-two hours so a psychiatrist can reassess them.[3] Once one becomes an involuntary inpatient, you can lose access to your cellphone and may be told to change out of your clothes and given a gown, making it easier for the hospital to identify inpatients if they escape or to discourage them from attempting to do so. Your stay is often in a small, fluorescent-lit room without much privacy. An inpatient can also be involuntarily placed on medication, including antipsychotic medication. There are restrictions on your personal freedoms: your access to fresh air is limited, your visits with family and friends could be monitored, and you are unable to attend to your life commitments. If a psychiatrist finds that a patient continues to meet the conditions for involuntary admission, they can extend their stay using additional Forms.[4] The similarities between being apprehended to a mental health facility and being sent to jail are striking.

One of the most severe forms of restriction on one's liberty is being locked in a seclusion room and put into four-point mechanical restraints; strapped to a bed and unable to move your arms or legs. You may also be given an injection of sedating medication.[5] These harsh forms of restraint are justified when a patient is deemed a threat, but this response can also be understood as another form of violent punishment that can have severe psychological and physical consequences for the patient involved.

Reflecting on our independent experiences supporting people who are involuntarily detained in psychiatric facilities, we know that those first few days are extremely challenging. You are often under constant observation and scrutiny and your response to this highly disorienting and frightening process can be interpreted in negative ways by social workers and clinicians causing them to add notes to your file that have serious consequences for your future.[6]

In Carly's reflection of how social workers are trained to do their job, she notes that by virtue of displaying mental health distress or psychosis, you are considered a threat. Symptoms of mental health distress are therefore thought of as a "pretext to violence," though expressions of distress are normal responses to trauma and other precarious living conditions.[7] Hearing voices or experiencing paranoia are not in and of themselves signs of crisis or impending violence.

Carly further reflects that under the ORB, ordinary conflicts over personal autonomy are often labelled as delusions or as oppositional defiance. The forensic mental health system does not acknowledge the ways detainment, restriction of liberty, restraint, and seclusion create and contribute to distress, which can cause and perpetuate symptoms of illness. In addition to the distress this can cause to someone's mental health, the apprehension itself can destabilize someone's life and upend it into chaos.

Forced treatment can also dramatically affect one's liberty and autonomy. In some cases, patients are prescribed, or overprescribed, medication against their consent. Medication can have severe side effects, including an impact on memory, increased agitation and dysregulation, and lethargy and low motivation to participate in programs on the unit. Unwillingness to participate in unit programming or with staff can cause a patient to be labelled "antisocial." On the other hand, if a patient challenges the medication, they could be labelled difficult, generally noncompliant, and as lacking insight. Lacking insight is an oft-used phrase in the mental health field and can be defined as someone's inability to accept their condition. It implies that people do not know what they need, that a professional understands their experience better than they do, and that patients are unreliable in defining their experiences and advocating for their own treatment.[8] This designation can be used as a punitive threat of rehospitalization should the person not follow the treatment plan. As a racialized person in this situation, you are often more likely to experience these types of coding.[9]

In their experiences supporting a racialized loved one in psychiatric detention, Lue observes that daily criminalization on the ward is far-reaching and insidious, especially when combined with daily racism and microaggressions. Actions that might be punished by staff include asking questions, making suggestions on how to improve one's care, regular expressions of joy or individuality, touching or making contact with family members, wearing clothing in a way the staff considers not presentable, or expressing concern about the side effects of medication. Punishments include seclusion, restricted access to food or products from outside, and limited privileges to leave the hospital. These punishments can isolate you from your support network and further exacerbate your mental health. This can also affect someone's support network, reducing their ability to properly advocate for their loved one.

Lue recounts how a friend witnessed the death of another Black inpatient on the ward. This inpatient had been detained for months in isolation and there was an observed history before his death of harassment by the staff for activities such as letting his pants hang below his buttocks. This was considered an act of noncompliance. The level of secrecy within the ward places them under the violent guise of being helpless and divorced from their own decision-making, basic civil liberties, and humanity.

EARLY PSYCHOSIS INTERVENTION AND NCRS

Once discharged from a psychiatric hospital, the hospital social worker may refer someone to an Early Psychosis Intervention (EPI) team, but from our experiences, people can wait three to six months for a referral. EPI teams are interprofessional teams consisting of nurses, social workers, psychiatrists, and occupational therapists that provide intensive case management to people experiencing a first episode of psychosis.[10] Should a person who is discharged and being monitored by an EPI team experience another bout of psychosis or extreme mental health crisis, options for support are limited to assist them in this distressed state, often leaving the individual or their family and friends with no choice but to call 911. Once 911 is called, police involvement is almost guaranteed, even in cases where police are asked not to attend. Toronto has a Mobile Crisis Intervention Team (MCIT), which pairs a trained mental health nurse with a police officer, but the accompanying police officer still has the right to cuff or use force at their discretion. Police interventions often escalate situations that would be more appropriately dealt with by other professionals using nonviolent crisis de-escalation.[11] The data has shown that the use of force by police or police interactions resulting in fatalities are far higher when the individual is Black or racialized.[12] Even if people supporting the individual in psychosis call 911 and request the assistance of the MCIT instead of the police, there is a very strong chance that the police will respond to the call first because the MCIT is not widely accessible and is often not immediately available.[13] Police intervention can often result in a physical altercation and lead to arrest.

If the police lay charges, the person arrested may be assessed under the "Not Criminally Responsible" (NCR) regime to avoid criminal conviction. If approved, the person would be placed under the control of the ORB.[14] Long before a person with a history of psychosis is declared NCR, they have often experienced preventable stress, an inability to access support, and psychiatric trauma. Trauma from psychiatric incarceration could exacerbate symptoms such as paranoia, anxiety, depression, and auditory hallucinations.

From the perspective of a lawyer, Golta reflects that there are numerous considerations that inform the decision to pursue an NCR defence. For example, absent other options, a client might view a successful NCR defence as the safest means to avoid conviction. This is a strong motivating factor for those with precarious immigration status—including permanent residents and visa holders—because an NCR defence could protect against deportation. Even among those who may be found not guilty after trial, the threat of deportation may persuade the defendant into an NCR defence. While these calculations are understandable, the consequences of opting into an NCR defence can be severe. An NCR finding can result in a longer period of detention than would have resulted from a formal conviction. Still, for those with precarious immigration status, prolonged detention, a strict treatment regime, or other conditions may be more favourable than deportation.

The Centre for Addiction and Mental Health (CAMH) in Toronto has the largest forensic program in the province and admits approximately 150 new NCR[15] patients per year.[16] There are approximately 4,600 people in Canada under ten provincial Review Boards.[17] In Ontario, there were 1,684 people under the ORB's jurisdiction according to its 2019/2020 Annual Report; however, demographic data and other information on the conditions and outcomes for inpatients at forensic hospitals is not readily available.[18] Recognizing this lack of data, we submitted Freedom of Information Act (FOI) requests to CAMH and

Waypoint Hospital, the only maximum-security forensic facility within Ontario.[19]

In an email response to our FOI, CAMH stated that they did not begin collecting race-based data until 2016.[20] Similarly, Waypoint Hospital stated they did not begin collecting race-based data until 2017.[21] Reportedly, the ORB has no plans to collect race-based data "anytime soon."[22] Given our limited resources, we were only able to afford data from Waypoint and have not completed our quantitative analysis at the time of writing.[23] However, from our anecdotal experience working in the system and investigative news reports, we observe that Black people in Ontario are overrepresented in the mental health system but experience "disproportionately negative outcomes" and are more likely to access mental health care as a result of an emergency or by force of the police.[24] At CAMH, "recent data reveals that Black patients are restrained at a rate that is 44% higher than white patients, and 22% more than patients overall."[25] Black, Indigenous, and people of colour are disproportionately affected by the complexities and contradictions within the forensic system.[26]

Those caught in the ORB system face an impossibly high threshold to demonstrate rehabilitation, leaving people stuck in a system far into their life. There is an important case in Ontario called *Re: Sim*, which involves a man who was under the ORB's jurisdiction for twenty years.[27] The case eventually went to the Court of Appeal. Sim's first index offence occurred in 1997 when he stole a car from an acquaintance and abandoned it when he ran out of gas. While Sim returned the car key to the owner, he was charged with theft under $5,000 and found NCR. Sim's second index offence involved assaulting two staff members at CAMH in 2007. Sim was found NCR for both offences. Since then, Sim made a significant effort to finish school and find employment. The Court of Appeal described his state as stable with no significant behavioural problems. Despite this progress throughout the last two decades, the ORB decided that Sim continued to pose a significant threat to the public. Two factors that the board seemed to focus on were that he appeared to "get angry" when his doctor wanted to discuss his cannabis use and that his high quality of work at the car wash had deteriorated. In 2020, after twenty years, the Court of Appeal decided that the decision to keep Sim under the ORB was unreasonable and issued an absolute discharge.

As we see in the Sim case, it is possible to face an indefinite amount of time in the forensic system. The litany of noncompliances reported to the ORB during a patient's hearing continues to affect their detainment. Social workers can play a pivotal role in a patient's trajectory and in the outcome of their hearing because their observations are heavily relied upon. For example, one time during a hearing it was reported that a patient posed a significant threat to the public because they were uncooperative with their care plan and treatment team. After questioning by the patient's lawyer, it was revealed that this assessment of uncooperativeness was the result of the patient being late for one appointment and refusing to take part in a program they had already completed. Considering how even minor transgressions can be represented as serious noncompliances, a patient can begin to feel hopeless at ever getting out of the hospital or the ORB.

THE FORENSIC MENTAL HEALTH SYSTEM

At CAMH, the highest level of security is the medium-secure unit where those detained face metal detectors, searches, the removal of their belongings, and restrictions from going outdoors. Those held in the facility cannot leave until they receive passes and privileges. Units are often old and cramped and there is a high staff-patient ratio. As Carly recalls, many inpatients refer to the secure unit as "the range"—a common term for a prison section. Inpatients have access to large teams of specialists including psychiatrists, nurses, social workers, behavioural therapists, spiritual counsellors, and peer workers. Some workers are friendly and helpful, while others are cold and demeaning.

Patients are told they are detained, restrained, and secluded for their own good. Within the mental health system, restraint and seclusion are synonymous with treatment, but we do not believe you can use coercive interventions therapeutically. There are few to no publicly available reports in Ontario on the use of seclusion and restraints[28] in hospitals, inpatient suicides, inpatient fatalities, and inpatients with precarious immigration status, let alone a breakdown of the racial demographics related to these issues. Chemical restraints, in the form of antipsychotic medication, for example, are often forced upon individuals when they first become inpatients and can be legally mandated through community treatment orders

(CTO). A CTO means an individual must take medication for a defined period of time—usually six months with a reassessment of capacity.[29] If you stop taking medication, family members or treatment teams can notify the police, who can apprehend you to a hospital, perpetuating a traumatizing cycle. From Carly's experience supporting individuals with psychosis, medication works well for some people and not so well for others. Everyone should have the right to choose if medication is right for them, with informed consent, yet this is rarely the case. We need to ask ourselves why our response to distress is to violently restrain and control versus de-escalate when models of nonviolent intervention exist and are used successfully.[30]

Patients are granted an annual review once per year to determine whether they can be released from the jurisdiction of the ORB. For these hearings, the hospital will prepare a report based on the patient's mental health history, prior convictions, and interviews completed by a psychiatrist. The board assesses the risk they pose to the safety of the public based on their index offence and other factors, like the ones described above.[31] The victim can submit a victim impact statement to the board for consideration. The board and the treatment team can then consider preferences expressed by victims of index offences, like where a patient may live in the future.[32] The patient could either be absolutely discharged, conditionally discharged, or given a detention order with conditions. An absolute discharge means you are no longer considered a significant threat to the public and are free from the ORB. A conditional discharge means that you do not have to live in the hospital but must adhere to conditions outlined by the ORB (e.g., not consuming drugs/alcohol, taking your medication, and regular urine/drug screening). If you break these conditions, you could be brought back to the hospital. A detention order means you will be held in a secure unit until your next ORB hearing or until you can find approved housing in the community.

The threshold for meeting the criteria of being considered a "significant threat" to the safety of the public is technically onerous. It requires that there be a "foreseeable and substantial risk of physical or psychological harm to members of the public" with evidence to prove this.[33] Yet, even with ongoing treatment, abstinence, and no additional offences, many people are deemed significant threats for years. Legally speaking, individuals are supposed to be placed under the least restrictive conditions possible; in reality, this is not the case.[34] The ORB's mandate is to "balance individual rights with public safety," but the board often agrees with the hospital's recommendations, which are largely informed by social workers' observations. Many patients have been consistently detained or detained on and off for many years—with some staff referring to CAMH forensics as a "revolving door" and to patients as "institutionalized"—implying that the hospital had become more familiar to them than the outside world.

According to a 2020 report looking at data from 1987–2012, "the average length of time spent in the forensic was over 7 years" before receiving an absolute discharge.[35] Mental health lawyer Anita Szigeti has stated, based on her twenty-five-plus years of experience, that many people are under the ORB for upwards of ten years, often for decades, sometimes forever.[36] Carly discussed how she has seen people be discharged from the hospital into supportive housing, breach their detention order by consuming drugs/alcohol or being late for curfew, be brought back to the hospital, and then lose their housing. These people essentially start back at zero and end up detained for another year. Moving through the system is very slow and forensic housing is very limited. Hospitals also make it difficult for people inside to maintain outside support, whether from family or other workers. They may claim workers from an outside agency constitute a "duplication of services," leaving people to advocate for themselves, which is scary, difficult, and isolating.

We believe that abolitionist social work, in this context, is a framework and way of practicing that identifies these mechanisms of carcerality and seeks to intervene at the front-line and institutional level to support people struggling in the system to find better stability and support—care rather than control. In her chapter in this volume, Chanelle Gallant provides an extensive though not exhaustive list of recommendations for how to practice what she terms "abolitionist social work," which lends itself well to our discussion of what it means to work within a carceral system of "care."

When Lue reflected on the use of NCR as a defence, they suggested that someone who is declared NCR should receive therapeutic rather than carceral treatment. However, there is a lack of recognition that these offences are the result of mental health distress rather than malice. The notion of therapeutic care is a misnomer. You instead enter a marathon of incarceration, with punitive actions so commonplace that they may even result in death. As a family advocate, one thing that is persistently clear to Lue is that racism, poverty, and mental health stigma funnel communities of colour into the prison system across North America. They note, "When we are in crisis, we are treated as a threat." For social workers to play an active role in transforming such a system, we need to affirm the importance of practicing from a place of care that sees people in mental health crises as needing support and not solely as a threat to themselves and other peoples' safety.

DREAMING OF AN ABOLITIONIST SOCIAL WORK APPROACH TO MENTAL HEALTH

We dream of a model of mental health support that is therapeutic rather than punitive, where people with disabilities and particularly people of colour are not punished, criminalized, or dehumanized for having a disability. We must make possible early access to interventions that do not remove a person from their community or isolate them from their support networks. If resources are funnelled into supporting family and friends to support people in mental health distress, we would be able to create networks of caregiving, peer support, mentorship, and skill building that allows people to stay in the community. This approach emphasizes sustainable long-term support and nonpunitive de-escalation tactics that do not necessitate police involvement. Like the disability rights movement of the 1980s that sought the abolition of institutions housing people with physical disabilities and created supports and funding models to facilitate that, we must work towards the abolition of psychiatric institutionalization and build alternatives that have at their centre autonomy, choice, and the ability to access a multitude of therapeutic supports within one's community.

We imagine a system of care that does not have control as its undercurrent—where individuals experiencing mental distress can receive support unconditionally without the looming threat of police, state, and institutional violence. The 2022 pilot project to provide nonpolice crisis intervention teams in Toronto is hopeful.[37] Yet, at the same time this is happening, police budgets are being expanded exponentially.[38] In his chapter in this volume, Edward

Hon-Sing Wong speaks about the dangers of replacing cops with mental health workers. Social workers as agents of state violence with "good intentions" are no less harmful. In our work, we try our best to always consider the power dynamic at play and the risks we can take to break the rules. Though at times this has meant discomfort and anxiety, the extensive power we have and the minor consequences we face for violations are outweighed by the importance of providing the people we work with the care they need and deserve. Though there are legal limits to registering with the Ontario College of Social Workers and Social Service Workers, we can actively consider and use our position of power and privilege to advocate for and support our clients in their own agency and choice. This might look like careful consideration in case notes, persistent advocacy within institutions, not reporting your clients to ODSP or other welfare services, advocating for your clients within your own agency, and constantly collaborating with them to take their lead on how they want to be supported.

We need increased capacity for networks of care and peer-led support that are robust and adequately compensated. We need care environments that do not use violence and restraint. We need safe places for people to go to for help and support that they don't fear. We need to meet people where they are and not try to control, fix, or manage them but provide them with care, autonomy, choice, and leadership. People who experience mental health crises are regularly framed as solely responsible for their challenges and behaviours; instead, we must recognize how society perpetuates trauma and creates the conditions for violence and harm to occur.

CHAPTER 6
SHIFTING PRAXIS
Social Work and Community-Based Approaches to Abolition

Krystle Skeete and Heather Bergen

This is such an exciting time to be talking about abolition. It is a rethinking of what it means to be in society together. Since conversations about abolishing the police came into the wider public consciousness during the spring of 2020, it feels like there has been a big shift in openness to these ideas. All the years of hard work and consciousness raising done at the grassroots level by primarily Black and racialized folks have started to gain credence within our society. It feels like a generative time where new things are possible. There is a long lineage of people thinking about how to address violence and harm in interpersonal relationships, such as gender-based violence, that is not based in state-sanctioned systems of surveillance and punishment.[1] Sometimes people think abolition is just about getting rid of the carceral system, but it is also about creating alternatives to these structures. Abolitionists create new ways of addressing harm so that we can no longer pretend there is a need for police and prisons. It is about resisting current state practices of violence and creating alternative approaches that address the root causes of that violence.

This chapter came out of a desire to reflect intentionally on our experiences of community organizing as social workers and social work students and to explore concrete, imperfect, and hopeful work being done in the spaces between social work and abolition. Our conversation revolves around three key questions: (a) the history and philosophy of our two community-based groups, (b) the tensions and gifts of doing this work outside of traditional social work settings, and (c) the relationships between abolition and our vision for the future.

We have both been involved in distinct community organizing projects that are rooted in community and seek to create structures of mutual aid and solidarity among members. Krystle is involved in a youth arts program called Freedom Fridayz (FF) that is located in the Black Creek / University Heights area of Toronto, commonly referred to as Jane and Finch. Heather is part of an organization called Community Action for Families (CAF), a mutual support group for families who are impacted by the family policing system (FPS).[2]

For both of us, our involvement in these projects is about shifting social work away from its preexisting assumptions, a move away from relying on "outputs" and focusing on the "human" service element. Although social workers want to demonstrate the impact of their work, it's necessary to understand that's not the sole reason why people should be doing the work. We need to challenge capitalist ideas of production within social work because it removes the human/personal elements of this relationship. While FF and CAF are smaller-scale initiatives, we still have a demonstrable impact at a local level. We address immediate needs through mutual aid and try to mobilize and bring change about at a systemic level.

FREEDOM FRIDAYZ

The FF program was established over a decade ago to create spaces that empower residents to build stronger and healthier communities. In addition to Kofi Frempong, the founder, FF includes five core members: Byron "B Grizzy" Gray, Felix "Flex of all Trades" Cabrera, Prince "Classiko" Attah, myself, Krystle "ohsookrissi" Skeete, and Andrew "Uncle Drew" Newsom (RIP).[3] Each member of FF is or has been a resident of Jane and Finch, and each of us brings a unique lens and expertise to the group.

Kofi had a vision for FF as a community arts-based initiative. He identified a need to create a platform for Jane and Finch residents to play a meaningful role in celebrating and building community. To provide context, Jane and Finch is in the northwest area of the City of Toronto. It is one of Canada's most diverse communities, with a high concentration of youth, immigrant, and racialized residents from over eighty ethnocultural groups, speaking over 112 languages and dialects.[4] FF started with around ten participants and slowly grew to bring in about one hundred to five hundred people per event. FF was much more than just a celebration of our community, it became a space for advocacy and awareness raising, a space to express yourself and share through the arts, and a space of healing for individuals as a community.

Many residents of Jane and Finch, especially youth, are exposed to violence, racism, and discrimination, especially in their interactions with government and social service institutions. For too long residents yearned to reclaim their voice and have ownership over their narrative and experience. Freedom Fridayz provides a space to counter hegemonic and systemic narratives of the community and its residents through poetry, song, rap music, visual arts, and graphics that encourages storytelling, counternarratives, and owning one's reality. Residents share their feelings and emotions and use that space to heal and talk through and about trauma. It is all about positive vibes and having a space to escape and enjoy culture and community and feel safe to be yourself.

The space creates a nontraditional approach to healing and sharing. One of the biggest challenges that we find with youth, children, and to some extent families is that it is difficult to be honest and own your truth out of fear of stigma, reprisals, ostracization, or to some extent, the unconscious harm or impact that sharing may cause. For many folks in our community, sharing or expressing feelings tends to be taboo, especially in spaces where you are supposed to be "hard" or protective. Sharing is no longer a natural way of being because you're always fearful of what that sharing is going to do, whether it's going to have a negative impact, whether your child is going to be taken away, whether you're going to be looked upon as unfit, or whether you're going to be looked upon as not keeping it real or being hard enough.

FF became a space to discuss, advocate, and share how systemic issues like racism, poverty, and violence affect residents and how the power of community can drive change. FF is one of the few collectives that comes together in our neighbourhood regularly, based on word of mouth, and with minimum promotion. Because of the values, relationships, and hyper-focus on the residents of the community, we have been able to build a strong and sustained collective. FF has also had a domino effect. A lot of young people, through the relationships they made at FF, have been able to start their own grassroots organizations or create their own entities that focus on advocacy and systemic change and to become a voice for the injustices within their community.

The culture we create at FF is based on a deep understanding of freedom and care and we are very intentional with which non-profit agencies we partner with because many social work organizations are focused on surveillance and control. As FF, we ensure the groups and organizations we work with align with our principles and values in relation to community and the arts. When we consider whether collaboration makes sense for us, we always start with one key question: Will this collaboration, initiative, or agency (un)intentionally harm or exploit the community? We want to be the driver in negotiations and make this question the key consideration throughout the process. We also consider how a partnership affects how FF is seen in the broader community.

One of our last events was in partnership with the Community Healing Project.[5] The goal was to engage youth remotely and address the mental health impact of the increasing exposure online and in social media to police brutality and homicides against Black and Indigenous peoples across the US and Canada. The event fostered an opportunity to heal as a community and mourn the deaths of individuals who have lost their lives because of a system that's supposed to be helping people but instead authorizes violence, without real rationale, against us. Instead of working to de-escalate situations, many government and social work institutions seek to manage, control, and subdue racialized bodies. They have an unwillingness to change, allowing for biases, discrimination, violence, and harm to be reproduced within these systems. This collaboration, where members of our community were able to come together and talk about their experiences collectively and with trust and care is a contribution that FF makes that is often minimized in social work practice. The focus on clinical work as the primary site where we address trauma fails to see the importance of community mobilization and informal but collective forms of grieving. In this way, FF seeks to address mental health issues both at an individual and community level—to work with members of our community to have a larger impact on both the healing process and the struggle to end systemic racism.

COMMUNITY ACTION FOR FAMILIES

CAF was started by Sheryl Jarvis in 2012 following her personal experience having their kids taken by the FPS, which had a devastating impact on her life. While taking the Assaulted Women and Children's Advocate program at George Brown College, she was politicized around her understanding of her family's experiences with the FPS and motivated to start organizing. She started reaching out and having conversations with people who were either involved with the FPS themselves as parents or allies, including some radical community workers.

CAF is an explicitly abolitionist organization. While some of our work overlaps with the work social work agencies do, our principles and frameworks differ drastically from how these organizations intervene in people's lives. Witnessing and experiencing the struggles of mothers who were amazing parents and fierce advocates but could not get the FPS out of their lives exposed the deep-rooted colonialism, anti-Blackness, antimother, and antipoor ideologies at every level of the FPS; from policies that blame mothers for experiencing gender-based violence to individual workers who equated a crowded apartment with inadequate parenting. Through this analysis, CAF seeks to provide supports for women who are impacted by the FPS with the explicit goal of abolishing this system. We are also inspired by the peer-support work being done by RISE in NYC and Fearless R2W in Winnipeg.[6]

CAF also fulfills needs that social service agencies cannot because, unlike social service agencies, we do not contend with "liability" and all these rules about what you can and cannot do. For example, we can do things like chat with people outside of "office" hours, hang out and be friends, help with cleaning someone's place before an FPS worker comes, or pitch in with babysitting so parents can prepare for court. This is not to say we don't work hard at having boundaries when supporting each other. For mothers with their own experiences with the FPS, this type of support can be really draining—but we aren't constrained by arbitrary rules made to protect organizations from liability.

A key part of our work is running regular support meetings. Depending on people's capacities, we sometimes do them once a week or once a month, and we've been doing them on and off during the COVID-19 pandemic, though video conferencing is not ideal for sharing and building trust. Often, a meeting can just involve a two-hour check-in. These support meetings can be really powerful because people often feel this deep shame about the circumstances that led to FPS involvement in their lives and that can be very isolating. Even if you recognize that FPS being involved with your family is partly shaped by racism, classism, and other factors that are outside of your control, parents may feel like they've failed at parenting or failed to protect their children. During the meetings, people can share their stories and, through sharing, become aware of how similar other people's experiences are. We've had meetings where there's literally been eight mothers who all had FPS enter their families' lives because of gender-based violence. The FPS forced them to separate from their partners before they were ready. So, they didn't have plans in place, didn't have money saved, and weren't emotionally ready. Then after complying with the demands of the FPS and leaving their partner, the scrutiny and surveillance abruptly switched from the partner to the mother. Their struggles with mixed emotions over separating from their partner, their mental health, PTSD, poverty, and substance use as a coping method were used against them. In a shocking number of cases, FPS forced them to leave their partner because their partners were abusive, and within a year or two, the kids end up in the abusive partner's care because the mother had been so demonized for coping less than perfectly. While every experience with the FPS is unique, sharing stories can facilitate the recognition that this is a systemic issue.

Unlike FF, which in many ways started as a celebration of community, CAF has come to realize over time the importance of celebrating small victories and spending time together outside of meetings. We've experimented with different forms of support over the years, depending on interest and energy. We've had social events in our homes, especially around holidays, which can be very difficult for folks separated from their children. We intentionally make time to hang out, have potlucks, and just socialize. It's important to avoid focusing exclusively on traumatic issues because that quickly becomes emotionally intense and can create unbalanced group dynamics. While spending time eating and chatting is not valued in traditional social work, we find this practice acknowledges the fullness and complexity of people's lives, helps to build trust and community, and supports the rest of the work we do.

Finally, CAF engages in public education, speaking in social work and legal classrooms, as well as conducting creative interventions. One year we ran a Jane's Walk, which is an annual festival of community-led walking tours inspired by the work of Jane Jacobs. We gave a tour around the downtown FPS office and went to a couple different places. The demographic who participated in that event was mostly rich white people who had little knowledge of how the FPS actually operates. Tour participants were taken aback by the stories shared by our members because, for many people, their privilege protects them from interactions with the FPS. The tour served as a great educational opportunity. Recently our public education work has resulted in political action and organizing activities like attending protests and sit-ins and participating in the MotherRisk Commission.[7]

AN ABOLITIONIST RETHINKING OF SOCIAL WORK

Both these projects reflect, in their own way, the possibilities of what an abolitionist social work can look like. Initiatives like FF and CAF were formed to debunk myths and initiate change that shifts people's thinking and mentality around the impact and role of government and social service institutions in reinforcing community violence, racism, and poverty. We think one of the benefits of organized groups like this is that they allow individuals to have control over their own narratives rather than cede it to "professionals." bell hooks writes, "One of the most vital ways we sustain ourselves is by building communities of resistance, places where we know we are not alone."[8] Through the community work of FF and CAF, participants are better able to navigate and understand systems and mobilize and support each other. It's this idea of forming a community of care instead of relying on the system to support you that makes our work powerful. In adopting this abolitionist lens, we are actively trying to end interpersonal and structural forms of violence while creating alternative spaces for healing.

Sometimes when people talk about abolitionist social work it can be very abstract, and we believe it's important to talk about concrete examples of abolition in practice. The examples we share here are complicated and real. They are not perfect examples of abolitionist social work, but they carry that spirit and, as Mariame Kaba says, "There must be a thousand different, parallel experiments in our communities."⁹ One overlapping practice between FF and CAF is an emphasis on flexibility to provide support and healing outside of traditional social work settings. Both groups leverage resources from the social work field to engage in more radical practices outside of it. This is the work of building alternatives, of building the world we need.

And there is a need for more initiatives like FF and CAF. Groups such as these protect individuals from revictimization through collective learning from experiences; they build communities of care. Through FF's public education work, for instance, people are better able to navigate and understand systems and come together to support each other. While social justice is avowed as a core principle of work by most social workers, institutionalization and continued reliance on practices of coercion and control have diminished this social justice piece.¹⁰ Collectives like FF and CAF are catalysts of social justice change; we push the social work organizations we work with to acknowledge that there is more relational work that needs to be done, there are better alternatives to their professional approaches, and there is a need to address social injustices at local, institutional, and systemic levels—not just among individuals and families. We are showing these institutions how to align theory and practice—how to shift their praxis.

DEALING WITH CHALLENGES

In more traditional social work settings, we imagine healing and community organizing as disconnected. There's this split between counselling in one space and activism in another space. Counselling, activism, and structural change work must be deeply intertwined. Emotional, practical, and systemic support work is the strength of both FF and CAF, but they are also big challenges. These things take energy, and long-term structural advocacy work can easily fall by the wayside when dealing with immediate crises. We want to do political and systemic change work simultaneously, but we are dealing with folks experiencing a lot of trauma—moms whose kids are caught up in the system right now or youth dealing with police harassment and violence; finding a balance where support is intertwined with activism is a delicate dance.

Trying to stave off burnout from the immensity of the trauma that comes into our spaces, with limited resources, is also a real struggle. Our numbers were especially low during the pandemic because as we weren't able to do outreach. Yet, as soon as we put up posters or sent out an email for an event, people came. People are thirsty for understanding, for a listening ear, and for concrete support. Providing that support can also come with such a heaviness; there is so much trauma, and supporting even one person can take so much time and emotional energy.

It's hard for us to find that balance between working with people where they are at and meeting their very immediate needs while also figuring out how we can work on larger structural issues—while also holding down our own personal, work, family and school commitments. Making that longer-term structural change is what ultimately needs to happen, but we also need to sit with the tension between individual support and activism because it is such an important space for ongoing dialogue and knowledge production. We continually grapple with whether to go after more funding or stay at a basically unfunded grassroots level. While having more funding would allow us to dedicate more time and resources to this work, we would also need to become more formal, and then what stops us from becoming a regular social service organization whose accountability is to funders rather than our members?

Nonprofit structures limit the amount of political advocacy work we can do, and political advocacy is at the heart of the work we are currently trying to do. This struggle is addressed so clearly in the edited volume by INCITE! called *The Revolution Will Not Be Funded*, and we continue to struggle with these contradictions.[11] At times our funds are accessed through the "trusteeship" of social work organizations, which has meant that we haven't had to go through all the paperwork to become a nonprofit organization ourselves. These types of partnerships can be difficult to maintain, especially if/when our work directly challenges policies that affect our nonprofit partner. Our lack of meaningful funding has, however, challenged us to be creative in our organizing. Sometimes we leverage our paid jobs in traditional nonprofits to do things like free photocopying or work for our projects on agency time. Other times we work to build relationships with organizations that may be able to offer a free meeting space or resources for our communities.

We want to stay grassroots, responsive, and accountable to our members and able to publicly advocate for abolitionist policies, and we don't want to be constrained by funders or disconnected boards of directors. However, we know that this limits the amount of time we can put into our groups and the material supports we can offer, in a context where there is so much need for these types of resources and for this type of organizing. This precarious balancing act forces us to be adaptable and inventive; but it can feel like we are often scrambling for basic things.

Our groups were founded by community members, not professional social workers, and being peer-led fundamentally shapes our work. There are many fruitful options for relationships when the starting point is not "I am the expert" and you are not "the person who needs my expertise." Being peer-led forces us to acknowledge that we are all people who will be able to give and receive support in different ways at different times. When we break down dichotomies of service provider and user, so many other possibilities and potentials emerge.

Being peer-led also gives members the freedom to determine how they participate in our organizations and creates a space to celebrate people's strengths and victories. The communities that we work in often have a lot of court-mandated activities. There are all these areas of life where you have very little control. Because of that, creating peer-led spaces where people can choose how much to engage, and who to engage with, is so important. We don't dictate how people introduce themselves at meetings. We don't have an intake form where you must tell your traumatizing story. Being peer-led means we try to see people in their entirety, not just as service users. We really try to celebrate successes and value the variety of contributions each member makes. Our commitment to abolition has been profoundly shaped by our experiences working with FF and CAF. Through our individual experiences we recognize and see the long histories of colonialism and anti-Black racism that structure social work institutions. We urgently need to start over, both to develop systems and structures that better address violence in the lives of individuals, children, families, and communities and to end a system that disproportionately creates violence against Indigenous, Black, racialized, queer, trans, and poor people.

CHAPTER 7
THE ANTITRAFFICKING MOVEMENT IS NOT ABOLITIONIST
How Carceral Feminists and Social Workers Harm Migrant Sex Workers

Elene Lam

I have worked with the migrant sex worker community as an organizer and activist for over twenty years. After moving to Canada from Hong Kong, I founded Butterfly, an Asian and migrant sex workers organization focused on sex worker rights.[1] Though we provide various social supports for our members, Butterfly is not a social service organization. Instead, we are oriented towards building power and solidarity among sex workers themselves—creating networks of mutual aid and mobilizing to fight anti–sex worker legislation and policies.

This chapter focuses on the proliferation of antitrafficking activism among feminist and social work organizations, arguing that despite the good intentions of many involved in these campaigns, their actions disproportionately harm migrant sex workers. This chapter draws partly from interviews I conducted in my dissertation, "An Institutional Ethnography Inquiry into the Policing and Investigation of Migrant Sex Workers in Canada," which sought to better understand how the everyday lives of Asian and migrant sex workers (including massage workers) are shaped by institutional actions and to uncover the day-to-day implications for sex workers of legal and policy frameworks adopted and enabled at multiple levels.[2] In that research, one of my informants, Yu, recounted her traumatic experiences with police and social workers:

> A few police officers broke my door in an early morning, I was naked. They handcuffed me and did not allow me to wear my clothes until I answered their question. They asked me if I was

safe. I told them that "I was safe before you came." Then they took all my money and phones. A social worker told me that she was not police and tried to help me. She gave me a very shitty phone and little money. I told her I am an adult and no one controls me. I don't need your help. I don't want your phone and money. I want my phone and money back.[3]

In my interviews with Yu and twenty-four other migrant sex and massage workers, as well as fifteen service providers and sex work activists (extra-local informants), I show how antitrafficking campaigns increase the policing and criminalization of sex work and are a major source of violence for sex workers in Canada. In this chapter, I focus more specifically on how social workers operating through a nominal "feminist" lens contribute to the carceral conditions for sex workers in Canada, making their lives more rather than less dangerous.

The participation of social workers in the current wave of abolitionist movements, such as the defunding the police movements, inspired hope among migrant sex workers and their supporters that social work professionals might join the fight for the abolition of the carceral system. However, many social workers and feminists who claim to be concerned about sex worker rights have aligned themselves with the antitrafficking movement in the belief that ending human trafficking into the sex industry is an abolitionist goal. In my advocacy work, I have found that these antitrafficking feminists and social workers are often the greatest opposition to sex worker justice because they seek more rather than less criminalization and policing of the sex industry. Though these carceral social workers and feminists use the term "abolitionist" to describe their work, in actuality they are fighting against the values and principles of abolitionism.[4]

DISJUNCTURE: TO PROTECT VS TO HARM

"Help! Police have come to arrest me!" I received this message while at an antitrafficking meeting with policymakers, law enforcement officers, and antitrafficking organizations who were arguing that antitrafficking investigations would save and protect women exploited by the sex industry. But the person who sent this text, and the other migrant sex workers I've spoken with, tell a very different story: instead of offering them protection, these antitrafficking investigations actually target and harm them. Despite government claims that these investigations aim "to protect trafficked victims," Asian migrant women are surveilled, abused, arrested, detained, and deported.[5] The disjuncture between the actual experiences of migrant sex workers and the stories told by these organizations warrants closer examination.

Carceral logics focus on punishment and the expansion of the criminal justice system to deal with real and perceived harm in society, like domestic violence and human trafficking.[6] The harm becomes merely a technical problem that can be fixed by improving laws and law enforcement, involving social workers, and adopting a "do no harm approach."[7] However, as critical trafficking scholars have argued, the problem of human trafficking itself has been constructed as a means to control sex work and migration.[8] The negative consequences faced by migrant sex workers are neither technical problems nor unintentional effects of otherwise good policies; they are foundational to the antitrafficking industry.

Elizabeth Bernstein uses the term "carceral feminist" to describe how some currents of feminism have become vehicles for punitive state policies.[9] She suggests that "neoliberalism and the politics of sex and gender have intertwined to produce a carceral turn in feminist advocacy movements previously organized around struggles for economic justice and liberation."[10] Others have noted how carceral logics among social workers result in punishment for those who are perceived as disobedient, marking certain bodies, behaviours, and actions as unrespectable, undesirable, dangerous, threatening, and criminal (e.g., BIPOC; migrants; the unhoused; drug users; sex workers; people with disabilities; gender non-binary, transgender, and queer people; youth; undocumented people, and so on).[11]

For many sex workers, social workers are as dangerous as the police because, through the welfare and legal systems, they impose institutional violence on and exercise power over them, including surveillance, policing, and the removal of their children. A growing number of social work organizations operate through carceral feminist logics, seeing sex work as a form of sexual violence and commodification and refusing to believe that any women can actively consent to sell sex. They provoke concerns about sex trafficking and conflate all forms of sex work with human trafficking, regardless of how sex workers see themselves.[12] These anti–sex work organizations often promote themselves as feminist and abolitionist and use antiracist and antiprison language. In this respect, they are not abolitionists but prohibitionists.[13] Feminist scholar, Mechthild Nagel also questions whether they are feminist, arguing that "these pro-women neo-abolitionists share their passion with the conservative anti-sex, pro-abstinence right-wing Christian 'soldiers' for prohibitionism."[14] Nagel notes that there are fundamental differences between the anti-sex industry movement and the abolitionist movement. For example, the anti-sex industry movement relies on "inciting moral panic through media, juridical, and political mechanisms, which enforce a carceral surveillance system," and they often "ignore the racist effects of their ideology,"[15] whereas contemporary abolitionists who engage in anticarceral and defunding police movements "neither rely on a moral panic rhetoric nor on bolstering the criminal injustice complex."[16]

SOCIAL WORK AND NONGOVERNMENT ORGANIZATIONS IN ANTITRAFFICKING INITIATIVES

Many social workers, nongovernmental organizations (NGOs), and social service and violence organizations involved with antitrafficking initiatives have received significant funding to carry out the political agenda of governments in pursuit of so-called abolition through awareness campaigns, intervention initiatives, social policies, and exiting programs. The Canadian Association of Social Workers, for example, has emphasized the funding and expansion of the exiting program, despite hearing from sex workers' rights groups that the program is harmful and violates their agency and self-determination.[17]

Stephanie Wahab argues that social work has historically identified sex workers as "fallen women," "victims of sexual slavery," or "pathological deviants" who need to be helped and protected for "their own good."[18] Ann De Shalit, Emily van der Meulen, and Adrian Guta similarly show that social service organizations that receive government funding for anti–human trafficking programming often "pathologize sex work and sex workers, rendering purported victims both agency-less and responsible. Those who access services must demonstrate a desire to remedy their exploitation and abuse by distancing themselves from sex work and/or drug use."[19]

They also found that social workers often interpreted sex work activities as flags, self-evident indicators, or symptoms of human trafficking and believed that sex workers must surrender to state-guided rescue.

Law enforcement often collaborates with NGOs, children's services, or victim's services units to carry out an antitrafficking investigation. For example, the Children's Aid Societies of Toronto and Durham have formed a special unit with police to investigate trafficking and identify victims. This collaboration, often couched in a carceral feminist politics, fosters what Jennifer Musto calls "carceral protectionism," which consolidates state power and control.[20] Human trafficking "rescues" often end in the criminalization, arrest, and deportation of sex workers as they get caught in the protection-to-prison pipeline.

Abolitionist scholars and activists have expressed concern about the power and authority of law enforcement and social workers to criminalize rather than protect sex workers.[21] They argue that using social workers as "soft cops" does nothing to change the fact that sex workers' lives are being made more dangerous and precarious through these types of antitrafficking collaborations.[22]

As Patricia O'Brien and colleagues explain, "Carceral feminisms have further fueled the dual subjectivities of women and girls engaged in sex work as both victims and criminals."[23] This logic of risk management is being applied to surveillance through the language of "helping."[24] The state, through social workers, can then use the language of "protection" to surveil, control, arrest, and impose other kinds of punishment on sex workers. The use of protection as a framework is a powerful tool to justify violence, oppression, and other harms against marginalized communities. It is also difficult to push back against because "rescuing" people from human trafficking is a good news story. The antitrafficking movement has successfully dictated the terms of the conversation.

MORAL PANIC ABOUT HUMAN TRAFFICKING

In Canada, a broad coalition has formed to create moral panic about human trafficking and sex work. Some of these antitrafficking NGOs are led by the Christian right. For example, the Evangelical Fellowship of Canada and Defend Dignity not only lobby Parliament, but they also develop action kits, sample letters, and campaigns to mobilize others to push for punitive laws, limit access to pornography, criminalize the sex trade, and impose municipal bylaws to shut down body rub parlours. However, feminist organizations such as the Canadian Women's Foundation, the Canadian Association of Elizabeth Fry Societies, and the Canadian Centre to End Human Trafficking have also actively lobbied and advocated for this punitive approach to human trafficking, including the criminalization and policing of the sex industry. This coalition of rightwing Christian groups and supposedly progressive feminist social service organizations have had a material impact on federal policy regarding sex workers.

Different levels of government in Canada have employed various measures to investigate, identify, and rescue victims and target and prosecute traffickers. Robyn Maynard argues, however, that "while Canada's Conservative government appeared to be combating trafficking, it was, in fact, largely responsible for creating so-called trafficking victims by advancing a political agenda that was hostile to migrants, sex workers, and Indigenous peoples."[25] Many of these initiatives claim to rescue innocent victims by helping them exit the sex industry, end demand, and abolish sex work altogether. But rather than offering protection, antitrafficking initiatives force sex workers further underground or into involuntary contact with police.[26] These operations often intensify racial profiling, surveillance, and the targeting of Asian migrant sex workers who work in hotels, massage parlours, and other indoor venues, including those who are permanent residents or Canadian citizens. That antitrafficking raids often violate the human rights of the victims and sex workers has been extensively documented, with sex workers reporting that they are physically and sexually assaulted by law enforcement and experience inhuman and degrading treatment.[27] When I interviewed Yu, she shared her troubling experiences of an antitrafficking investigation: "I was handcuffed and arrested. Why do they arrest me when they said they came to protect me? If they care about my safety, why don't they arrest the robber, instead of arresting me?" Another migrant sex worker, Mi, who I spoke with in June 2020, reported that she was locked up for almost two months, and her wrists, waist, and legs were chained. Mi felt humiliated and traumatized. Her phones and other communication devices, as well as over $10,000 of her money, were seized by the police. Yet, the police and the court said she was detained for her own safety.

Sex workers, particularly women of colour and migrants from countries of the global South, are constructed as trafficked victims to justify repressive policies against migrants and the sex industry.[28] Researchers such as Lyndsey Beutin describe how the covert goal of antitrafficking initiatives is to end sex work, not exploitation. Antitrafficking laws and policies are also used to illegalize migrants and tighten border control measures.[29] These investigations are fraught with anti-Asian racism and quickly become new avenues for criminalizing marginalized migrants who do, in fact, possess agency and who are making decisions based on their circumstances and experiences. Migrant sex worker organizations emphasize that sex workers are not unilaterally victims of trafficking and have expressed concerns about their victimization through these new initiatives. They strongly oppose the raid and rescue approach taken by law enforcement, arguing that instead of protecting trafficked victims, the antitrafficking policies and initiatives create harm.

RESISTING THE SAVIOUR COMPLEX OF ANTITRAFFICKING

The "white saviour complex," which relies on colonial concepts of rescue, is foundational to social work as a profession. All too often, social workers are complicit with state violence against marginalized people. Social workers have a long and troubling history of being the agents that conspire with the state to produce and reproduce its power structures such as racism, white supremacy, sexism, and colonialism.[30] Historically, Christian faith-based organizations have been influential in the education of social workers and the provision of social work services. Seeing themselves as the guardians of moral order, Christian organizations often use social services to shape public opinion, promote and maintain colonialism, and advance particular religious-based moralist values.[31] Between 1888 and 1942, for example, the Christian-run Chinese Rescue Home was used to implement the imperialist agenda to "rescue, convert and 'civilize' Victoria's Chinese prostitutes."[32] Today, these organizations continue to use their moral authority and significant institutional power to influence state policies and moral regulations, control abortion, and increase policing and the criminalization of sexual minorities and sex workers.

Carceral logics such as these remain deeply infused within social work today. As a result of the lobbying of social service, carceral feminist, Christian, and anti-sex work organizations, the Immigration and Refugee Protection Act (2001, s. 118) and sections of the Criminal Code (1985, ss. 279.01 to 279.011) were amended to criminalize human trafficking. The government also passed immigration regulation that banned suspected trafficked victims from entering Canada and prohibited all temporary residents (including those with open work permits) from working in sex or sex-related industries.

The targeting of Asian massage parlours is the direct result of this moralistic discourse becoming public policy and social work practice. Many antitrafficking organizations (including women's and social service organizations) are highly involved in policy-making processes to eradicate sexual services, calling for the criminalization of sex work (including clients and third parties) and expanding punitive laws and law enforcement against sex workers and related industries like massage parlours and strip clubs. The government acknowledges that "marginalized groups are at a higher risk of being trafficked; yet, it does not address current and historical colonialism or the criminal and immigration laws that place people in a rights-vacuum, leaving them vulnerable to labour abuses."[33] The antitrafficking industry has often claimed that women engaged in sex work are too victimized to be able to speak out, necessitating speaking for them—further silencing and dismissing self-organized workers.

When sex workers in Canada argued that the criminal laws regarding sex work are unconstitutional because they violate the rights and security of sex workers, a group of women and social services organizations formed a coalition to advocate for the criminalization of the clients and pimps of the sex industry. While the Canadian Association of Elizabeth Fry Societies has positioned itself against the criminalization of women and subscribes to the abolition of prisons, until very recently they contradictorily advocated in favour of criminalizing sex work, and they were central to the Women's Coalition of intervener groups fighting decriminalization in the *Bedford v Canada* Supreme Court case in 2013.[34] According to them:

> Criminalizing johns, brothel owners, pimps and profiteers is consistent with principles of fundamental justice. The criminalization of men who buy, sell, and profit off women in prostitution is neither overbroad nor grossly disproportionate. It is consistent with Canada's domestic and international commitments to protect prostituted women and to interfere with their exploitation.[35]

With the support of these organizations and in response to their lobbying efforts, in 2014 the Canadian government passed the Protection of Communities and Exploited Persons Act to recriminalize sex work. They also developed other antitrafficking initiatives. The conflation of sex work with human trafficking has led to sex workers being arrested and charged—and this extends even to those who merely play a supporting role, such as answering the phone, screening clients, advertising, or providing a place to work. Criminal and immigration laws empower police and law enforcement to enter the lives of sex workers, but they also provide powerful tools for social workers to surveil, racially profile, and report sex workers to police, particularly those who are migrants and racialized.

In the past few years, Butterfly has lobbied many social services and women's organizations to end these campaigns. Despite the recognition by some of the harms caused by the criminalization of sex work through their advocacy work, few have changed their position to publicly support the full decriminalization of sex work. At the municipal level, anti–sex work organizations have promoted their agenda and called for an increase in policing, expansion of punitive policies, and an end to sex work–related industries, such as body rub parlours, massage parlours, and strip clubs. In 2020, the Ontario government allocated over $300 million to combat human trafficking and, in 2021, introduced the Combating Human Trafficking Act (Bill 251). Sex worker organizations, with support from racial justice and migrant rights groups, health professionals, academics, and other groups, spoke in one strong, united voice against the proposed antitrafficking legislation in the consultation meetings of the provincial Standing Committee on Justice Policy, raising their concerns about the increases in police power, racial profiling, and harm to sex workers, especially those who are BIPOC. Nevertheless, when the bill came to vote in the provincial legislature, not a single MPP voted against it.

SEX WORKER–LED ABOLITIONISM

Sex work is not inconsistent with feminism; many women's rights advocates and feminists have expressed support for the self-determination of sex workers. These feminists recognize sex workers as the experts of their own lives, and they support sex worker-led movements and fight alongside them for full decriminalization. Echoing O'Brien and colleagues, I call for social workers who claim to be committed to social justice principles to "remain vigilant in [their] opposition to the 'punishment industry' in all of its forms."[36] Instead of taking the punitive approach, adopt grassroots and redistributive approaches as solutions to social issues.

Maynard suggests that sex workers should be given "support for the choice either to enter, remain, or leave the sex industry. Ethical support requires letting sex workers themselves determine their own needs and recognizing that each individual has different experiences and is the most capable of determining the course of her life."[37] Rather than being mere victims, sex workers are increasingly empowered to organize themselves. Sex worker–led organizations such as Stella's, Butterfly, and Maggie's have long spoken out, supported their own communities, and advocated for their rights. These sex worker groups have also collaborated with organizations in other cities to form the Canadian Alliance of Sex Work Network and to advocate for the full decriminalization of sex work.

Sex worker–led organizations such as Butterfly have built solidarity with various social justice entities, including racial and migrant groups, violence against women organizations, progressive social worker groups, abolitionist movements, and Indigenous women's organizations to push back against the antitrafficking movement and to advocate for the full decriminalization of sex work. Instead of relying on policing, social workers, and state power, sex workers, particularly BIPOC and migrant sex workers, are building their own community to develop new abolitionist tools and approaches based on transformative justice.[38] At an anti-Asian racism rally in Toronto, Asian migrant and massage workers spoke out, saying:

> Calling the police doesn't work for us. The police and law enforcement officers treat us with disrespect, conflate our profession with human trafficking, and disrupt our work. We can only rely on ourselves to keep ourselves and our sisters safe.[39]

Migrant sex workers have also called for social workers and social services organizations to participate in abolitionist movements led by directly affected people and to come together to understand the role social workers play in creating a context of social control, victimization, policing, and institutional violence in the name of protection.

Growing recognition of intersectionality and problems with the carceral approach has led some feminist organizations to acknowledge the harm caused by their advocacy work and position. For example, the WAVAW, a rape crisis centre in British Columbia, has formally apologized to the sex worker community for framing sex work as inherently exploitative. The Canadian Women's Foundation also acknowledged their problematic position on sex work and have built stronger relationships with the sex worker community and shown their solidarity for the decriminalization of sex work as well as developing program supports for sex workers. The Canadian Association of Elizabeth Fry Societies recently publicly announced that they intend to "grapple with the harm" caused by their stance on sex work and review their position on sex work. These significant and long-overdue changes will hopefully push other organizations to similarly recognize the historical and ongoing harms caused to sex workers across the country. Sex workers are key contributors to our collective imagining of a world without police, prisons, immigration detention, child apprehension systems, and state control—a world where all people are free to choose how they live and work and to do so with dignity, safety, and respect. Abolitionist social workers should see self-organized sex workers as leaders in movements to end carceral violence in our society and join their movements for decriminalization.

CHAPTER 8
A MASTERPIECE WE CAN CALL ABOLITION

Reflections from the Pages of *Cell Count*

Sena Hussain, Nolan Turcotte, and Zakaria Amara

Five years ago, I was hired by a prisoner health and harm reduction organization in Toronto to revive a newsletter called *Cell Count*, written by and for people who are incarcerated. *Cell Count* provided me with a space to engage in abolitionist politics through my public health work as a social worker with incarcerated people. *Cell Count* is an abolitionist publication, but we also provide information on HIV and hep C and other health and harm reduction information. These are important issues that affect the prison population and prisons rely on publications like ours to get public health information out to incarcerated people because there is a huge amount of distrust between prisoners and health staff in the prisons. We provide a space for incarcerated folks to talk about their experiences of incarceration and their criticisms of corrections, the trauma they are experiencing, and the myriad injustices and harms they face while inside.

This chapter seeks to highlight the writing and experiences of two of the folks I've worked closely with over the last few years, Nolan Turcotte and Zakaria Amara. I went through the back issues of *Cell Count* and selected two pieces that I felt resonated most closely with the themes of this book. The first piece, "#FreeTheYouth," was first published in *Cell Count*'s Vaccination Issue in 2021 and is written by Nolan Turcotte. "My spirit name is Stands with the Wolves. I am from Flying Dust First Nation, Kopahawakenum Band. I was born in Regina, Saskatchewan," writes Nolan in an article titled "One Drop Is All You Need," in issue #85 of *Cell Count*. Nolan is currently surviving a life sentence at a medium security prison in Ontario.

The second piece, "The Boy and His Sandcastle," was first published in *Cell Count*'s Spring 2018 issue and is written by Zakaria Amara, who is surviving a life sentence for his involvement in the "Toronto 18" terror plot; he was recently released from prison.

I met Nolan and Zak on the same day, back in either 2017 or 2018. At that time, they were both at Millhaven Institution, a maximum-security prison in Bath, Ontario. I was there to participate in a health fair. I met Nolan first as I was working on a project to connect tattoo artists on the outside with tattoo artists on the inside and to educate folks about health issues related to tattooing in prisons. Nolan's whole body is covered in tattoos, it is amazing artwork. I asked if he could tell me a story of one of his favourite tattoos and he agreed. After that conversation, I asked him if he'd be interested in writing for *Cell Count* and he accepted.

Zak was the opposite, he was very shy. I saw this group of Muslim dudes just standing over in a corner looking at me and I was like, "Hey, come over and talk." One guy came to my table and said, "My friend really wants to come over and talk to you, but he's really shy." I decided to just go over and talk to them and he *was* super shy, but I asked if he wanted a copy of *Cell Count* and he did, so I signed him up for a subscription and went back to my table. Later, as I was packing up my things to go, I found a little note tucked underneath a pile of *Cell Counts* that said, "It was really nice to meet you." So, I wrote to him and told him that if he ever wanted to write for *Cell Count* these are the ways he could go about it, and he started writing. I present both Nolan and Zak's pieces below and then connect it to the role of abolitionist social work thereafter.

#FREETHEYOUTH (NOLAN R. TURCOTTE)

I was asked by a friend of mine to write a piece on "Abolition." To be completely honest, I'm not that well-informed on the whole concept of abolition, aside from the obvious; putting an end to incarceration. Since my friend's request, I've spent much of my time considering the possibilities and trying to understand exactly where abolitionists are coming from.

Let my experiences be the brushstrokes that lead to the completion of a masterpiece we can call "abolition." My Indigenous father grew up in a violent household that practiced alcoholism and lacked culture. His intergenerational impacts became mine, which momentarily damaged our relationship and affected my upbringing. I vividly recall the kind of child I was, and my parents hands were more than full. Nothing they did worked, so they sought "professional help" from social workers, psychologists, and psychiatrists when I was four years old. According to the doctors I was hyperactive and defiant. I was prescribed medication such as Ritalin and Risperdal to calm my ass down, but I wouldn't take them because I found the medication crushed up in my peanut butter-jam sandwiches. LOL! My parents continued to struggle with me, but little did they know their first-born son was being molested, which only enhanced my acting out.

A few years passed and things only got worse. In grade three, I began to get bullied and was constantly a victim of racism. My behaviour in school deteriorated and I was in trouble every day of the week. When I was pressed by my parents, my truth was never believed, and my father began to discipline me through physical abuse. I got sick of getting my ass beat, so I chose to run away every chance I could to avoid the physical pain, but the mental and emotional pain followed me everywhere I went. I felt unloved and unwanted, so I distanced myself from my family. In turn, I was introduced to the system. I was in and out of group homes and foster care, meeting like-minded peers I could relate to and bond with through similar interests and misbehaving.

My life of crime really began at the age of thirteen after my first arrest in 2003. A group of classmates surrounded me after school, so I pulled out a Swiss Army knife and fought back. The knife wasn't used in the altercation, but I ended up getting charged with assault causing bodily harm and weapon concealing. I remember being court ordered to participate in a Healing Circle with my "victims," and the charges were subsequently withdrawn. The ceremony was facilitated by an Indigenous organization, and we were to discuss what took place, what we were thinking and feeling, and what we'd learned from the incident. It was an extrajudicial sanction that took a couple hours to complete and wasn't taken seriously by those involved. I learned nothing and continued my immature path of defiance.

As time went on my involvement in criminal activity and drug abuse became a regular pattern. I was absorbed by the streets, disregarded the importance of education, and developed an obsession with establishing a reputation that's both feared and respected. I entered the Paul Dojack Youth Centre (PDYC) for the first time at the age of fourteen. My five-day stay was sad and lonely, but for some reason, I returned eight more times. During every stay, I became more familiar with the staff. Some were kind, while others were assholes, and there wasn't much mentoring between the staff and the youth. There was structure such as designated times for school, meals, chores, physical activity, showers, laundry and leisure time, but there wasn't much effort put into rehabilitation.

While in the PDYC, the youth offenders were expected to write essays on their anger, drug abuse, and family relationships and were to present them to their peers and staff. This didn't necessarily help the youth gain insight; rather, it gave them the opportunity to boast about their violence and gang involvement, what drugs they've used, and the crimes they've committed. On a spiritual aspect, interactions with the Elder were sporadic, and it didn't seem like facilitating ceremonies was a top priority for the PDYC. Furthermore, when it came to programming, the only youth permitted to participate were the ones serving a secure sentence, which excluded the remanded youth from receiving any benefits the programming had the potential of providing.

In addition, as I was going in and out of the PDYC, I had multiple youth workers and continued to meet with doctors for pre-sentence reports and other assessments. The diagnoses kept adding up and before I knew it I was diagnosed with the entire alphabet, had antisocial personality disorder, and was a Level 5 risk of reoffending. As a youth, I was misunderstood more than I am today, and nobody took the time to understand me. All those so-called professionals chose to scold me, blame me, and tell me how wrong I was. Their initial impression of me was blinded by prejudice, which caused our rapport to be built on distrust rather than trust. When questioned, it didn't matter how I replied because when I told the truth they assumed I was being dishonest, and when I decided to exaggerate to sound cool, they took me at face value and labelled me callous and unremorseful. I never stood a chance against such a corrupt system.

In 2006, at the age of sixteen, I was arrested for accidentally stabbing a twenty-eight-year-old man to death. I've always held myself accountable for my mistake, and I've maintained that my intention was never to kill him. Given the unfortunate circumstances, I was remanded to the PDYC for the ninth and final time, tried as an adult, found guilty of second-degree murder, sentenced to Life, and transferred to the Saskatchewan Penitentiary at the age of eighteen. But, while on remand, upon my admission to the PDYC, I was placed in solitary confinement. I sat there for six months, before the director, Al Manning, decided to let me integrate into the population. He claimed my involuntary placement in administrative segregation was due to my security concerns.

Finally, in the summer of 2007, I was released from solitary confinement and housed in a unit designated for sentenced youth. Due to the severity of my index offence, I was considered a long-term remand case, which meant I was able to earn some of the same privileges the sentenced youth could by displaying consistent positive behaviour and leadership. I earned privileges, such as wearing my own clothing, having a radio in my cell, and playing the PlayStation 2. Since I knew my good behaviour equaled better living conditions, I tried my best to refrain from trouble. For the first time in my life, I was focused on changing my lifestyle, and I even approached one of the program facilitators and inquired about participating in her group. She informed me that only sentenced young offenders can be referred to programming. No matter how much interest I showed, nor the fact I explained how I would soon be sentenced, I got rejected. Nobody wanted to help me when I needed it the most, which is such a disgusting thought, but the worst part of it all is that when I went to trial, there were multiple reports stating I have apathy towards programming and refused to participate in it while on remand at the PDYC. The prosecution ate that up and emphasized those reports at trial to prove I am a high risk and an unlikely candidate to receive a youth sentence. My fate was sealed. How can the PDYC rehabilitate youth when they place them in solitary confinement and deny them programming?

Now, when I think about the abolition of the prison system, I can't help but picture the majority of society ripping their hair out, screaming, "Are you fucking nuts!?!," because who really wants murderers, rapists, and drug dealers roaming free after committing such offences? Sounds insane, right? Even I find it to be a little extreme and I'm currently imprisoned, I have suffered from many injustices and endured too much oppression throughout the past fourteen years. You'd think I'd be all for it, but I believe in a way, the prison system does aid in public safety. I don't mean to sound like I'm on CSC's side because I'm not. I just prefer to keep an open mind and consider both sides because I always want our side to be considered by others rather than overlooked.

As I sit here weighing the pros and cons and imagining a country where prisons cease to exist, I can't stop thinking of other solutions. Why aim for adult prisons to be abolished when we can target the youth? It makes more sense to focus our time and energy on freeing up the youth because they will gain more from our investment, which will be beneficial to society and the future well-being of humanity, or at the very least Canada. If we target at-risk youth and create relatable programming to fit their mental, emotional, physical, and spiritual needs, we can ultimately preclude them from becoming hardened career criminals. In a perfect world, wouldn't that mean there would eventually be no use for penitentiaries in Canada, if we can successfully stop the youth from offending before they are declared adults? It would seem that if we went this route, in time, prisons will slowly but surely become irrelevant, unnecessary, and a thing of the past.

THE BOY AND HIS SANDCASTLE (ZAKARIA AMARA)

My beloved twelve-year-old daughter asked me to share my story with you. I am having a difficult time deciding what to write and from which point to start. Perhaps I should begin from the present and work my way back to the past. I've been in prison for twelve years now. I received a life sentence after pleading guilty to being one of the ringleaders in the "Toronto 18" terror plot. Thankfully, no one was physically hurt. I was twenty then, I am almost thirty-three now. In pretrial custody, I was deemed a radical threat to the inmate population, and so I was involuntarily placed in solitary confinement for three years. After receiving my sentence, I was once again considered a radical threat and sent to Canada's only Super Max prison (usually, you have to kill or stab someone inside to be sent there). I spent six difficult years there before finally getting transferred to Millhaven Max.

Based on what you just read, it is easy to imagine me as a tough, violent, angry man with a threatening demeanor. The truth is that I am the exact opposite of that image. Guilty, I am. Radicalized, I was. Yet, I still find my entire situation incredibly surreal. I often go back in time to retrace my steps and figure out how I ended up here. Every time I engage in this exercise, I find a young man who was caught up in a perfect storm of internal and external influences. The inevitability of it all is what I find most remarkable.

After any major terrorist attack, there is usually a fierce debate about what makes individuals susceptible to radical ideologies (unfortunately, this rarely occurs when the perpetrators are non-Muslims—e.g., right-wing extremists). If I had a noose around my neck, and the only thing that could save my life was the answer to this apparently dumbfounding question, then I would have to say that it is the emotional state of feeling utterly worthless. I have always felt worthless. I still struggle with this feeling to this day. Perhaps I feel this way because I carry within me a strong inner critic that has been ripping me apart since childhood. Perhaps I have always felt like an outsider. Even though I am a citizen of this country, I have never felt Canadian because ever since I arrived here as a twelve-year-old-boy, in my mind, to be a real Canadian, you had to be white.

Prior to immigrating here, I lived in my mother's country of birth, Cyprus. There too, I felt like an outsider, since I was keenly aware that my Arab features automatically disqualified me from claiming to be Cypriot. Prior to that, I lived in Saudi Arabia, where native citizens are infamous for looking down upon all non-Saudis. I still remember the words of a Saudi boy who referred to us Palestinians as "Phalas-Teezi" (a hybrid word that combines "Palestinian" with the Arabic word for "ass"). The sad fact that I was sexually molested while living there could have only intensified my feelings of worthlessness and inadequacy. Even in Jordan, my own country of birth, I never considered myself Jordanian since I belonged to a family that came to Jordan as refugees after losing their land to the Israeli occupation.

Many of you probably wonder why the Muslim world has produced so many radicalized individuals in the modern era. Blaming Islam for it is incredibly simplistic, if not absolutely wrong. When I look at what the people of that region have been going through for over a hundred years, I am surprised there aren't more radicals, not less. I can't imagine how utterly worthless many of them are made to feel. The culprits are foreign and local governments who systematically strip the people of their dignity. Bush's 2003 invasion of Iraq and its resulting massacre of hundreds of thousands of innocent Iraqis represented the crossing into radicalism for me. You can pretty much draw a straight line from there to my arrest in 2006.

How does it feel to be radical? You feel worthy, righteous, and heroic. You see yourself as a saviour of your people. Your mind is obsessed with the injustices they are suffering from, and that's all you wish to talk about. You see the world in strictly black and white terms. Deep inside, you suspect there may be other colours, which subconsciously drives you to engage in constant reinforcement of your beliefs. It is said that those who are the most dogmatic are usually the least certain. A vivid depiction of this internal struggle is that of a boy who is perpetually fortifying the walls of a sandcastle he built too closely to the waves.

When I arrived at the Special Handling Unit (SHU, Canada's Super Max), I was willing to give change a chance for the sake of my family, but unfortunately, the administrators were unresponsive. Feeling rejected once again intensified my radical state, and in fact, I became more extreme in the SHU than I ever was on the outside. I adopted a standoffish attitude towards the administrators and refused to meet my parole officer for many years. This state of affairs continued until ISIS declared its Caliphate and news of its atrocities began streaming in. Prior to ISIS, whenever innocent people were killed, I would simply tell myself that it was "collateral damage," if those killed were non-Muslims, or a "mistake," if they were Muslims. Every atrocity committed by ISIS was like a tsunami that would violently demolish my sandcastle and leave no trace of it behind. Yet, I kept frantically rushing back to rebuild it.

Eventually, the hideousness of this group led me to periods of depression that followed every massacre. At the time, I did not see my radical ideology as separate from my religion, and this caused me to fear that abandoning it would lead to abandoning my faith. I also feared confronting the reality that I may have thrown my entire life away and brought so much suffering upon my family for no good cause.

Holding on became harder and harder until it finally became impossible, and I simply had to let go out of sheer disillusionment. What followed was not a free fall into a dark abyss of disbelief but rather a surprising spiritual ascent. I felt liberated to finally be able to see the world in its true colours. This feeling only intensified as I slowly took the shackles off, one by one. This process began a few years ago and continues to this day. How do I view my experience? Despite its hardships and painful losses, I see it as a blessing. Sometimes I tell myself that I am acquiring a PhD in Life Studies from the University of the Incarcerated. I live a very meaningful life despite living behind bars, and I am incredibly optimistic about my future. To God, I am ever grateful for all of this.

I ask the Canadian public to forgive me for betraying their trust. I ask the Muslim community to forgive me for causing them so much apprehension by helping to cast them under a dark cloud of suspicion. I ask my dear parents to forgive me for breaking their hearts. I ask my brother and sister to forgive me for causing them so much stress and sadness. I ask my ex-wife, whose loss I never recovered from, to forgive me for abandoning her and devastating her in such a way. I ask her entire family to forgive me for turning their lives upside down. I ask all the young men who became involved because of me to forgive me for everything. I ask their families for forgiveness as well. Last but not least, I ask my beloved daughter to forgive me for leaving her without a father. Princess, when I see you in my dreams, I sometimes hold you in my arms, and weep, and weep, and weep 'till I awake. Beloved, knowing what I know now, if I could go back in time to be with you, I would be there in a heartbeat. But grieve no more, for I once heard that "the Truth shall set you free" . . .
And now I know . . .
That what I heard is true.

SOCIAL WORK, YOUTH, AND INCARCERATION

I wanted to highlight these two pieces because of the way both authors directly and indirectly raise questions about the social supports available for young people dealing with trauma, racism, and displacement. Although they are from different backgrounds, Zak and Nolan both felt a deep sense of injustice as young people and lacked the types of relational and ongoing supports that might have helped them navigate these feeling. They both think very deeply about what they did and understand their own complicity in the harm they were convicted of causing. But they also both talk deeply about systemic gaps that create conditions where youth who are struggling face carceral responses to issues that require care and support. They both want change. They have both expressed that if and when they get out, they want to be involved in social services themselves. They want to help youth. Both of them.

However, they are both wary of abolitionist politics that don't take into account the real-world experiences of people on the inside. Despite both inferring that incarceration doesn't necessarily help young people, they are both tentative about their support for a politics of abolition without addressing the multiple needs of their respective communities. Youth don't end up incarcerated solely because of individual failures; rather, it's a series of systemic failures—racism, colonialism, imperialism, poverty, not enough understanding around boys and masculinity at a younger age, etc. For example, how do we support young boys, girls, people struggling with mental health or rage issues? Everything we do as social workers should be towards trying to meet people's needs. That's not always easy to do. Nolan's right, the bureaucracy keeps people working in those systems and keeps institutions in place. People are weighing their own job or license against the interests of the people they are working with. Maintaining these structures and systems produces burnout. Burnout leads to working uncritically and starting to have less compassion for the people we work with.

Before his recent release, Zak was denied parole. They agreed that he'd done all the programs and done everything they asked him to do. He's clearly shifted his entire belief system and his mindset—and it's something that he wanted to do himself, but it was also what the courts and government wanted him to do. He did it all on his own because there were no appropriate support systems in the prison to help him. At the parole hearing, they said, "We can't let you go because we didn't have those programs for you." Basically, they had denied him parole because the system failed to meet his needs. They admitted it was a failure on their part—to provide these programs—that they didn't know what to do; they just wanted to put people convicted of terrorism in prison, but they did not provide any rehabilitation services around that.

Through *Cell Count,* my community health organization is able to give voice to the experiences of the folks we work with inside prisons—it pushes us to incorporate the theories and knowledges that comes out of the lived realities of prisoners into our work in meaningful ways. Nolan and Zak are both very well-respected writers in *Cell Count* within the prisons we distribute this publication. It's validating for people to read Nolan's and Zak's work and see themselves in what they are writing. Nolan will tap into people's sense of injustice, their anger, and their grief—and Zak will tap into some of the deeper philosophical thoughts people might have, reflections that people might have while in prison. What they write in *Cell Count* is going behind those walls and showing everybody their vulnerability—but it's also being circulated in our communities and workplaces—among social service workers, prison support workers, and social workers in general. In this way, they are helping to change how we think about our role as social workers and to be clear about our responsibilities to provide care and support for folks on the inside.

PART TWO
SOCIAL WORK ABOLITION

CHAPTER 9
SOCIAL WORK ABOLITION IN UNSETTLING TIMES

Craig Fortier and Edward Hon-Sing Wong

This chapter was written at the conjuncture of two moments of historical reckoning for social workers in North America: the push to defund the police and to promote social work as an alternative, spurred by the 2020 rebellions against police killings of unarmed Black people including George Floyd, Breonna Taylor, Tony McDade, and Regis Korchinski-Paquet; and the current era of "official reconciliation," in Canada, a response to the Truth and Reconciliation Commission of Canada's (TRC) *Calls to Action*.

Abolitionist and decolonial political movements have created the space for substantive critiques and prefigured radical alternatives to violent state practices. While influenced by these movements, Canadian social workers have struggled to come to terms with what abolition and decolonization look like for a profession that is intimately ensnared in both carceral and settler colonial projects.[1] Social work, *as a profession*, is produced through the continuing disruption of long-standing forms of community-based mutual aid practices, replacing these with forms of racial and class control that maintain the status quo. Grassroots initiatives seeking to support members of one's own community are chronically underfunded, disrespected, and labelled as too radical or hard to work with.[2] Drawing on our experiences as activists, educators, and social workers, we join the call for social work abolition—the systematic and total dissolution and restructuring of social work as we know it—as part of a framework for social work decolonization. Rejecting the practices and values encapsulated by professional social work, we argue for a move towards a social work guided by principles of mutual aid and accountability led by Indigenous, Black, queer/trans, racialized, immigrant, disabled, poor, and other communities for whom social work has inserted itself.

We have been engaging in a dialogue with each other and with colleagues and friends in activist, social work, and educational spaces about the risks associated with proposing professional social work as the solution to problems that we face in society (police brutality, the impacts of settler violence, mass incarceration, confinement of mad people, etc.). We write this chapter in relation to wisdom and teaching shared by BIPOC women, trans, and nonbinary folks; incarcerated folks; and fellow social workers who have been on the forefront of exposing the limits of the social work profession and imagining abolitionist and decolonizing possibilities outside its framework.

SOCIAL WORK ABOLITION AND DECOLONIZATION

Professional social work is marked by a top-down, distant, and unidirectional way of relating to marginalized people. In fact, the very basis of professional social work involves working to "lay claim" to knowledges and practices that distinguish practitioners from other helpers in the "everyday world."[3] Social workers have gained their expertise through the extraction of practices, traditions, and processes of mutual aid from marginalized communities.[4] With the fraying of community-based and familial networks of support in the early twentieth century in North America, social workers constructed a professional identity out of filling these gaps while also serving a carceral function of surveillance and control.[5] In this way, social work can be understood as a form of what Anna Lowenhaupt Tsing calls "salvage accumulation," the creation of capitalist value from noncapitalist value regimes.[6] By diminishing and disrupting community-based forms of mutual aid, social workers create jobs and careers out of professionalizing practices that had otherwise been taken on in informal and relational ways, such as conflict resolution, resource and information sharing, and caring for infirm community members. These practices are then reimagined by professional social workers through a hierarchical structure that imposes itself upon Indigenous peoples, Black people, and other marginalized communities as groups to be monitored and forced to behave in specific ways to receive support. This reimagining of community care into professional social work often empties the original practices of their values and politics. Through formal streams of professionalization (including social work education or registration with the professional associations), the relationships formed between social workers and the communities that they seek to "help" are circumscribed by a set of principles that position the social worker as the provider of knowledge/services and the people they serve as the recipient or beneficiary.

It does not have to be this way. Social work(ing) can become a critical part of the "array of institutions" that form the social infrastructure of a decolonizing abolitionist society. We offer four (of many) examples of how social work can be transformed to meet these needs below: reckoning, accountability, mutual aid, and unsettling.

RECKONING

Social workers need to identify and reckon with the parts of our work that are carceral and colonial in nature. Social workers are often quick to defend our profession today without carefully considering how our histories reverberate in the actions we take in the present.[7] Social work was (and continues to be) a disruptive and controlling apparatus in the lives of people. One that sees local forms of mutual aid, rebellion, and solidarity as competition and threat rather than as parallel processes. For instance, social workers in Canada lobbied extensively (and successfully) to replace the Indian agent (the chief colonial agent based in Indigenous communities) as the primary colonial force on reservations.[8] This led to the Sixties Scoop, which stole hundreds of children from their communities to be adopted out to white settler families (often as servants or labourers), and the contemporary Millennial Scoop that has resulted in more Indigenous children in care than were in the residential school system despite public declarations by social workers in support of reconciliation.[9]

Social work also disrupted forms of mutuality among new immigrants (both those arriving from Europe and Black folks escaping the Jim Crow South) who had been mobilizing community associations and labour actions at the turn of the twentieth century. Both settlement houses and charitable organization societies had the underlying effect (if not the express goal) of demobilizing autonomous community support in favour of a top-down white Anglo-Saxon led civilizing practice that promoted containment, assimilation, and control among migrant communities.[10] As we've previously written, "Charitable organization societies and settlement houses [both] preached self-reliance and used social welfare as a mechanism of control... to manage and assimilate new immigrant settler populations... [and] were operationalized in Canada (and the United States) for the purpose of settlement and colonization."[11] The construction of professional social work institutions as mechanisms of social control within poor and marginalized communities expanded in the late 1960s–early 1970s as a response to and pacification of widespread revolutionary movements such as the Black liberation movement, the feminist movement, the gay liberation movement, and many others. This process laid the seeds of what INCITE! describes as the "nonprofit industrial complex" (NPIC), the growing and expanding industry of social service provision funded primarily through private donations and governed by government regulations that limit transformative social change in favour of maintaining order by engaging exclusively in short-term crisis management.[12] A reckoning that the present reality of social workers in North America is circumscribed by the legacy of these histories should provoke serious and ongoing conversations and actions to divest from and work with communities to support alternatives to the carceral and colonial practices of social work in our society.

ACCOUNTABILITY

Social workers have been called upon to be accountable to our histories of violence and to our treaty obligations. Theorists Eve Tuck and K. Wayne Yang argue that settler organizations should stop engaging in the commerce of Indigenous pain and instead focus on issues of power and complicity in colonial violence as an unsettling project.[13] This critique has been levelled at activists as well. The extensively circulated pamphlet "Accomplices not Allies" calls out activists and "solidarity" groups who have developed our self-worth and our own political careers through avowed allyship with Indigenous communities without directly and forcefully confronting the state, capital, and our own complicity in settler violence.[14]

To be accountable requires that we act meaningfully as both individual social workers and as social work organizations and institutions to stop the harm we cause, to listen to community, and to participate meaningfully in abolitionist, anticapitalist, feminist, queer, disability justice, and decolonizing movements (among others.) Social work scholars Bindi Bennett, Joanna Zubrzycki, and Violet Bacon argue that non-Indigenous social workers should participate in decolonization through recognizing and addressing "the powerful influences that the history of colonization and the ongoing nature of colonizing practices have" on their current work.[15] While awareness of our complicity in settler colonial and white supremacist violence is important, how do we mobilize this awareness towards accountability? What does collective accountability look like for a profession that is enmeshed so deeply in carceral and colonial structures like the prison/criminal justice system, child apprehension, psychiatric surveillance, and other forms of social control?

Accountability does not mean that we fix all the problems (especially in our lifetimes). Following Tuck and Yang, we realize that at times the goals, desires, and values held by people within transformative movements can be incommensurable. Indigenous practices of decolonization and resurgence or Black-led movements for abolition will and should seek to move beyond the limits of other social justice movements and institutions—and that also means accepting that they may envision worlds where professional social workers cease to exist. The goal to create an abolitionist social work might, in fact, be incommensurable with the goals and desires of Indigenous and Black movements. As Tuck and Yang note, "There is so much that is incommensurable, so many overlaps that can't be figured, that cannot be resolved."[16] To live in this incommensurability is both vital to our long-term transformative goals and extremely uncomfortable. As philosopher Alexis Shotwell explains in *Against Purity: Living Ethically in Compromised Times*, "Patterns of social relations, as structure not event, then predict the practices of the future."[17] This means that we must understand that transformative processes must be accountable for the harm being caused in the present, and we must resist the tendency to locate harm as occurring in the past. But we also have to be attentive to the possibility that the futures we are trying to collectively create might not include institutions, professions, or jobs that we currently see as oriented towards the goals of justice and liberation. We need to respect the self-determination and autonomy of communities engaged in transformative processes, and that might mean that our greatest value as social workers oriented towards abolition and decolonization in the present is through rule breaking, resource redistribution, and potentially illicit activities, as Gallant suggests in her chapter in this book.[18]

MUTUAL AID

The NPIC and the social work profession do not emerge out of a vacuum. Both are top-down projects that aim to disrupt mutual aid practices among poor and marginalized communities. Through the process of professionalization, social work becomes, as Nilan Yu argues, "invested in the established order."[19] By gaining our legitimacy through state-sanctioned professional associations, social work is securely nestled within the given social order. It also incentivizes social workers to conceptualize organic forms of mutual aid as rudimentary, unsophisticated, disorganized, and at times, *as competition*. Indeed, at the heart of the current NPIC is a desire to co-opt mass political movements that advocate for substantive social change by proliferating the nonprofit organization as a legitimate alternative to extra-legal political forms of helping, resisting, and caring.[20] With the expansion of the nonprofit industry came the diversion of energy and funds to nonprofit agencies for the purpose of "monitor[ing] and control[ing] social justice movements; and ... manag[ing] and control[ing] dissent in order to make the world safe for capitalism."[21] This included the containment and pacification of Black and Indigenous communities resisting white supremacy and colonization.[22]

Western evidence-based practice is a major component of contemporary social work. Positioning social workers as experts applying scientific methods to service users, Alexandra Crampton frames these practices as based on notions of permanence, whereby social work practices are understood as universal, without concern of local contexts.[23] The medical approach in social work practice is especially reflective of this perspective, granting the social worker, and other medical professionals, the power to define certain behaviours or individuals as deviant.[24] When found deviant, the social worker attempts to "fix" the person, but with little consideration for that person's wishes, needs, or perspectives, nor the context in which they live their lives.[25] This monopolization of knowledge is also fundamentally undemocratic.

As an alternative to this undemocratic professionalization, Crampton advocates for approaches rooted in concepts of impermanence.[26] This rejection of professionalism is made in an effort to elevate the work of relationality. This refocus on relationality challenges the identities of the helper and the helped, allowing for the emergence of "mutuality between people, all of whom had gifts to offer."[27] While at no point should social workers presume that power imbalances can be made to disappear without substantive social change, moments of mutuality within the context of our work in various sectors provide an opening into imagining the possibilities of abolitionist and decolonizing forms of practice.

UNSETTLING

In Canada, the era of official reconciliation is touted as a "new relationship" between the Canadian state/settler society and Indigenous peoples, but it fails to actually reconcile ongoing settler colonial violence and land theft. It portends instead to be an expansion of the NPIC that ensures state and settler control of any reconciliation efforts that protects Canada's economic goals of continued resource extraction on Indigenous lands.[28] As Yellowknives Dene scholar Glen Coulthard articulates:

> In settler-colonial contexts where there is no period marking a clear or formal transition from an authoritarian past to a democratic present—state-sanctioned approaches to reconciliation must ideologically manufacture such a transition by allocating the abuses of settler colonization to the dustbins of history, and/ or purposely disentangling processes of reconciliation from questions of settler coloniality as such.[29]

Through this type of sleight of hand, the Canadian state (and in our case Canadian social workers) apologize for the wrongs of residential schools and the Sixties Scoop respectively by advancing a narrative that such incidents are *historical events* and that our present moment requires simple *recognition* of these injustices to undo the harm rather than *substantive action* to dismantle the *ongoing structure* of settler violence. As Coulthard further explains, under such conditions, reconciliation takes on a temporal character, the individual and collective processes of overcoming the legacy of past abuse, while seamlessly ignoring the ongoing harm that is occurring.

Anishinaabe scholar and activist Kimberly M. Blaeser argues that the "'institutionalized words' or 'white words' of social work cannot initiate the kind of healing achieved through tribal rituals."[30] Reconciliation does not move beyond an individualized framework of social work practice guided by the logic that positions social disadvantages and social problems as issues that can be overcome through therapy, hard work, and integration into the Canadian economy. We suggest that as non-Indigenous activists and social workers we must work through the process of unsettling through the dismantling of narratives, institutions, practices, and position that structure the settler colonial project.

Through our engagement with the Grassy Narrows River Run and other actions in support of the community, we have witnessed settlers and non-Indigenous allies following leadership from the community to put significant pressure on the state to act on their demands. This has been done through public education, by confronting politicians at press conferences, in videos and documentaries, and through the co-creation of a biannual event called the River Run—where people from Grassy Narrows come down to Toronto to push the provincial government to follow through on commitments to clean their water and open a treatment centre in their community. However, this work has also included significant relationship building, with consistent travel between supporters living in Winnipeg, Ottawa, Toronto, and other major Canadian cities to visit the territories, spend time on the land, and engage in ceremony with people in Grassy Narrows. Such a process is grassroots, relies on the leadership of the community itself, and attempts to refrain from the white saviour approach to organizing that has permeated the culture of both social work and activism in North America. It is a rejection of top-down professionalism in favour of respectful relationships and humble service towards the work of decolonizing led by the Grassy Narrows people—often willing to be accomplices in resisting current policies and laws—rather than seeking recognition as allies.

CONCLUSION

We offer these critiques not to be contrarian but rather to raise serious questions about the viability of professional social work as we know it to address the most pressing questions of our current era. We hope that this piece provokes further conversations rooted in the emerging paradigm of abolitionist anticarceral social work but also through the realistic need to unsettle and decolonize social work as we know it. As we continue to engage in struggles within, against, and beyond the structures of power that oppress, marginalize, and harm many people globally, we are reminded of and take heart in the multitudes of emerging movements that have reimagined relationality, mutuality, and care to create the societies we wish to bring about.

CHAPTER 10
THE ONLY GOOD SOCIAL WORKER IS A CRIMINAL SOCIAL WORKER

Chanelle Gallant

This is an invitation to social workers and social service workers.[1] It is an encouragement of what you may have already sensed—the systems you work within are set up to keep people down, and ethical and principled social workers must break the rules of those systems and fight to change them. This chapter is about how social workers can be social work *abolitionists*.

Mainstream culture teaches us that social workers can heroically and selflessly save people, and some social workers do amazing work supporting people and helping them navigate crises in their lives and families. But social workers are also paid to uphold the very systems that hurt people. Social workers are not always a welcome presence in the lives of poor families, especially those that are Black and Indigenous. That's because social work is rooted in systems of oppression, and social workers have played a violent role in capitalist settler societies.[2] Even when they are trying to do good, social workers are often expected to serve as the managers, administrators, and enforcers of the moral agendas of the wealthy, white, and powerful. When the elite want to make sure that some groups of people are treated as backward, dangerous, immoral, contagious, antisocial, or criminal, they often hire social workers to do their dirty work for them. Because social workers have access to people's intimate lives, in their homes, hospitals, and schools, they can serve as the eyes and ears of the ruling class in poor and racialized communities (or in foster homes, institutions, shelters, and so on). These dangers are insidious, intimate, and often underestimated. Unlike police officers, social workers can be deeply embedded in the everyday lives of poor and racialized people. Other chapters in this anthology speak to the role social workers have played in colonial policies to steal Indigenous land by disrupting families and culture. From residential/assimilation "schools" and the Sixties Scoop to the crisis of Indigenous children in state "care" today, some social workers have the power to tear a family apart forever by apprehending a child and setting off a chain reaction of trauma and cultural destruction that ripples out for generations.

Social workers also have the power to withhold small amounts of money that can be the difference between life and death—money that could help a young trans person escape the streets, a woman flee an abusive partner, or a disabled person purchase food or medicine that makes them less sick. Some social workers hold the power to report their clients for working without immigration status, or for parole violations, or for their health status (like being HIV positive), or to deny parents access to their children for moral infractions. Their power can send someone to jail or get them deported. Social workers may also decide who will get their basic needs met and who will stay hungry. In short, some social workers are invested with an obscene amount of power to watch over the lives of marginalized people and communities and sometimes make life or death decisions for them. At their worst, social workers are expected to behave as the state's morality squad, terrorizing Indigenous and Black communities by stealing their children; withholding the necessities of life (like food and shelter) from poor people; reporting people to the authorities; and enforcing sexist, racist, and colonial agendas.

To be fair, social workers do not design the system, nor do they make the rules or the laws. They have no say over the criminal code or municipal regulations that govern their work and their professional responsibilities, and they typically have no say in their own budgets.[3] Some social workers are in it to provide the kind of support they themselves (or their families) needed at one point. If they could, some would redesign our social and economic systems to actually meet people's needs, providing them with enough money to live on (universal basic incomes) or universal services and ensuring they are treated with dignity and have what they need to thrive. But the system of social work is so implicated in every form of social and economic oppression that one person's good intentions can't change that injustice is baked into the DNA of professional social work. In a just world, we wouldn't need a professional class of social workers. The system we have now would be abolished and we would have systems of support by and for the communities they serve that work to meet people's needs.

I have been an activist in sex worker communities for nearly two decades, working with sex workers who are facing many forms of criminalization due to their sex work, race, Indigeneity, poverty, drug use, immigration status, or their gender as trans women. I have witnessed social workers attempt to intervene, sometimes support, and sometimes interfere with sex workers safety, dignity, and autonomy. And I have on occasion trained social workers on providing competent and respectful services to sex workers. I was also raised in a family that came into contact with social workers, including the child welfare system, income supports like welfare and disability, and so on. My family is largely poor and working class and a mix of white and Indigenous adults and children. What I have witnessed through my own family's encounters with the social service sector and those of sex workers is how scary, disrespectful, and exploitative social workers can be. But social workers and social service workers also taught me that it is possible to "act like an abolitionist" and serve our communities. And that might include ignoring, breaking, and directly challenging harmful, racist, sexist, and antipoor rules and laws.

From Black women abolitionists, such as Rachel Herzing, Ruth Wilson Gilmore, Mariame Kaba, and Robyn Maynard, and organizations, such as Critical Resistance and INCITE! Women of Color Against Violence, I have learned that abolition is not a one-time event—not for police and prisons and not for social work. It is a process of building a just, caring, and fair society where people have what they need. Experienced social justice activists teach us that meaningful and lasting changes that shift how we live and who holds power never come from any one individual or group of individuals. Big institutional change happens when people come together in social justice organizations and movements that are fighting to transform the root causes of our social, economic, and ecological problems. Social workers can support these movements, not as charity or saviourism, but in solidarity with the people most affected by systems of power like racism, poverty, colonization, and patriarchy. Social movements reduce our reliance on social workers when they are able to win changes to policies that harm people. By winning immigration status for all or a national affordable housing program, for example, we reduce social problems and crises that are created by harmful policies. When social movements win policy changes that reduce sexual and intimate partner violence, there is less need for crisis counsellors and emergency women's shelters. This relationship goes both ways: these movements can often benefit from social workers who follow their political lead and are willing to speak out to the media or government representatives about the harms bad policies cause for the people they serve. People in power will listen to social workers, who can leverage their role and the legitimacy they are granted.

Some will say that even if we abolish social work, we will still need people who provide support to those experiencing grief or trauma, health crises, ageing, parenting, immigration, and so on. But consider that for poor and racialized people, social workers often do not provide support; instead, they provide state surveillance and control over essential resources. Without oppression and injustice there would be far *less* grief, trauma, loss, and illness to deal with. A world with no poverty or homelessness, without domestic violence, where Indigenous people are not being poisoned by corporations and have the right to make the rules that govern their land, is a world where communities have the power and the resources to take care of themselves, where they no longer have to rely on a professional class of people with state power. This is a world where communities have the resources they need to support people with violence prevention programs, good housing, mental health care—in short, a just society with a social safety net.

Abolition is a process and it is a culture, a way of being in our everyday lives. How do we live out social work abolitionism today? But even trickier, how do *social workers* live an abolitionist life today? Many social workers are already attempting to practice this ethos, deciding how to use their role to support people in navigating the systems to get their needs met. In the next section, I describe a couple of small moments that illustrate what abolitionist social work practice can look like.

"WORK-FREE DRUG SPACE"

For a few years, I worked at a social service agency run by and for sex workers. Early on, a friend suggested I meet with a social services worker who ran a drop-in for sex workers at a nearby church.

I was hesitant—she had no experience in the sex industry and, uh, a church? Those aren't usually the most sex worker friendly environments. But my friend reassured me, she wasn't as bad as some of the truly awful Christians running "white saviour" missions in the city. I called her up and we met in the back room of the church, which like most church social spaces, felt like a small school gym, and I asked her about the program. At first, I was grateful when she told me about how they opened their doors in the predawn hours of the morning at a time when many street workers were finishing work for the night. That's so helpful, and god knows I didn't want to be up at that hour. Then she mentioned having to call the cops and throw some workers out for using drugs in the bathroom. I cocked my head and looked at her sideways. I'd never worked in social services before and I didn't understand the culture, so naively I asked her why. Why call the cops? She hesitated and said, "I mean," she shrugged, "it's policy." "But isn't that harmful? Couldn't you just . . . not follow it?," I replied. Now she looked as confused as I did and quickly changed the subject.

Later, I was shocked to find out that the vast majority of social service agencies in Toronto ban service users for drug use, even when this increases the risk of using drugs alone—and *during a crisis of toxic drug supply and overdose*. It is not enough for social workers to hide behind policy and say that they are just "following the rules." Abolitionist social workers must work to avoid enforcing racist and fatal rules that are devastating to communities, like anti-drug laws. Social workers can face risks in not reporting suspected criminalized activity, but in many cases, the risks of reporting—such as the possibility of an arrest, an overdose, or being barred from essential services—far outweigh the risks to the social worker.

Back at my workplace, our policies were designed to protect people and their right to make decisions over their own lives and bodies. Because we know that police encounters are extremely dangerous to criminalized people, we avoided working with police. We made it clear to our community members that we were not there to watch them and "catch" them but rather as peers in solidarity. The walls of the drop-in were lined with safer drug use and sex work supplies and harm reduction information pamphlets, and we used respectful language that was not rooted in criminalization or stigma ("drug user" not "addict," "sex worker" not "prostitute") and asked that others did too. We actively supported drug users and sex workers rights movements and organizations. A sign hung on our bathroom door read "work-free drug space," a pun on the "drug-free workspace" signs often found at worksites. It was just one part of how we communicated our appreciation for drug-using sex workers and made the space safe for them. By having policies and protocols that support the safe use of illegal drugs, many peer-led, harm reduction-based organizations would be considered at the very least "inappropriate" or bad social workers and at worst "criminal," but breaking the law can be evidence-based and ethical care.

COMMUNITY MEMBERS CAN BE THEIR OWN SOCIAL WORKERS

I want to share another example of how marginalized community members develop alternative systems of social work to care for each other in ways that build their power and skill. Years ago, I was invited to be part of a Restorative Justice Conflict Resolution/Harm Reduction (RJHR) project through Rittenhouse, a prison abolitionist and transformative justice organization in Toronto. This project gave me insight into another way of doing abolitionist social work—empowering community members to do their own social work.[4] The RJHR project began at St. Stephen's Community House, a Toronto-based drop-in centre catering to the needs of drug users and street-based folks in the downtown area. It used a peer-based model that included twelve weeks of training, an ongoing support team, stipends, and social justice organizing activities. Joan Rusza, one of the project founders, described it this way:

> We recruited and hired service users of agencies—who were current or former drug users and who had been criminalized by the legal system—and trained them to be transformative justice facilitators. The idea was to build the capacity of participants to resolve conflicts in their own communities, and to reduce the use of barring in community agencies.[5] We see this as an abolitionist strategy with the broader goals of strengthening community capacity to address social harm and reducing contact with the legal system and incarceration.[6]

When criminalized community members provide social work services to each other, they focus on support, and their solutions are often the exact opposite of how the cops and courts might respond. Karen Daniel, one of the group members, said in an interview before she passed away in 2015:

> When the law gets involved, they take this person and put him in the corner, take that person, put him in the corner, [they say] "never speak to each other again, and be on your way." And that's how society is. We're just out there by ourselves. And you meet somebody who you can identify with, and you get in trouble for hanging out with that person because of the stigma, like, "Oh, they're a crackhead." "Oh, don't hang around with them, they're no good for you." And you can have more community with that one person than with somebody that's supposed to be there to serve and protect. They're not really protecting me.[7]

Daniel is pointing towards how most authorities default to state control and severing relationships as the only solution to harm. But when people who have been criminalized are given the power, training, and resources to work through their issues on their own terms, they often want to bring more understanding and reconnection and avoid further criminalization and harm to others. It's a practice of social care rather than social control.

SOCIAL WORK ABOLITIONISTS ARE POLICE ABOLITIONISTS

Abolitionists and criminalized people showed me how social work can be a form of care, support, and community power—not charity. They showed me the responsibility that social workers have to keep police out of the spaces where people who are racialized, poor, disabled, and drug users congregate, to act as a buffer, and to refuse to enforce bad laws. They might refuse to cite people on parole violations, get them access to welfare by ignoring technical disqualifications, keep their mouths shut to police officers about service users who are selling sex or drugs, let trans people use their real, chosen names instead of government names on their paperwork, creatively use funds to get cash into the hands of a mother fleeing violence, and fudge grant applications to get the money for critical work that never gets funded by granting agencies. *A special shout out to social workers who have stuck their necks out to protect their clients from police and gotten money into the hands of domestic violence survivors by whatever means available, you are the real MVPs!*

Social work abolitionists are police abolitionists. They become very skilled at de-escalation and avoid calling the police on poor and racialized people. Police encounters can be very violent but, even when they're not, being "known to police" increases the chance of further police harassment. Police often escalate situations, especially with Black and Indigenous people. The threat or possibility that the police are called brings fear, anxiety, and in some cases terror for people who have PTSD from their encounters with police and prisons. Social workers can build trusting relationships with the community by avoiding contact with police where possible and showing their service users over time that they can trust them on this. I have seen it go very badly for poor people of colour and migrants when well-meaning social service workers who are less criminalized (white, middle class) downplay the dangers of interactions with law enforcement and trust "this one good cop I know." Abolitionist social workers refuse collaboration with the cops—and that might require concealing information from police, authorities, funders, and management for the well-being and self-determination of program users.

ON RISK

Abolitionist social workers side with the people—those who are targeted by criminalization—not those in power, not the corporate state. The provocative title to this chapter was meant to challenge social workers' internalized superiority, their sense that they are better than those who break the law. I am not calling for social workers to sacrifice themselves or to rush headlong into trouble. I understand the duty to report and the risks that social workers face in failing to do so. What I am proposing is that social workers must take some risks and oppose the harmful aspects of their profession. Social workers who break the rules do face real consequences, but I want us to put those risks into context. The risks to social workers are usually far less severe than the risks that poor and racialized people must take to survive. To get the absolute bare minimum of services and support, poor people must mislead, lie, or withhold information, like not reporting drug use, or that they have some under the table income or a live-in partner, or don't meet the eligibility criteria. And they can expect to be harshly punished for breaking, or simply not knowing, the rules and cut off from essential services like housing. The risks of being badly "social worked" are usually far more dangerous than the risks to social workers if they break the rules.

The social workers who are more likely to be punished for rule breaking are the low paid precarious workers on the front lines. They are sometimes drawn from the same marginalized communities they serve—Black, Brown, Indigenous, drug-using, poor, working class, migrant, or trans—and less likely to be in senior administration roles. They are often the ones taking bigger risks and fighting to make things more just. Their advocacy means they have a higher risk of being punished, demoted, fired, or charged with criminal code violations. They could use some help. Social workers who are less directly affected and more protected by privilege can share the risks of breaking the rules as they fight for their community members and fight to change rules that hurt everyone.

ABOLITIONIST SOCIAL WORK, A STARTING POINT

Here is my incomplete, totally not exhaustive reflection on what I'd consider to be pieces of a social work abolitionism:

- Do not steal babies. If your job requires apprehending children from Black, Indigenous, and poor families because the parents are poor and lack support, then quit your job.
- Understand the personal, professional, and criminal risks that social workers face and learn how to manage them so you can maximize your client's autonomy and dignity.
- Learn the difference between something that is *actually harmful* and something that's just against the rules or that violates the morality norms of social workers. For example, selling sex or getting high might be someone's best life choice, whether or not social workers can relate and understand.
- Resist working with state authorities who could endanger your clients such as police, immigration enforcement, parole officers, etc.
- Reduce the harms of the state when you have no choice but to involve state authorities. For example, avoid providing information about clients such as whereabouts, immigration

status, health status (like HIV and mental health diagnoses), "criminal" activity, who they associate with, etc.
- Actively work to protect and insulate clients from interactions with law enforcement. For example, helping to create a paper trail that would protect a woman if she were to have to deal with courts or CAS interference in her family life.
- Do not report clients for violations of rules or laws unless it is unavoidable.
- Help people get around the rules to protect your clients' access to essential services such as welfare, food, harm reduction materials, medical treatment, and community support).
- Work to change the rules by following the leadership of those who are directly affected.
- Do not make people beg, perform humility and gratitude or assimilate to bougie white people's norms and goals for their lives to get access to care, money, or services.
- Recognize and respect clients' greater knowledge, experience, and insights about how to navigate and survive the systems and oppressions that the social worker does not experience.
- Encourage clients' participation and leadership in peer-led social groups and social movements that campaign to change the root causes of their problems.
- Actively and respectfully integrate and amplify the voices of directly affected clients in places that privilege social worker's voices.
- Join, support, and donate to social movements that are led by those who are directly affected, working to build their power and end the problems they face.

Finally, abolitionist social workers fight the power as principled objectors, as rebels, and as comrades in struggle with those they serve.

CHAPTER 11
CONVERSATIONS ON DECOLONIZING JUSTICE
With Members of It Starts With Us and No More Silence

Audrey Huntley and Carol Lynne D'Arcangelis

Audrey and Carol Lynne have been working together in No More Silence since the early days of its founding, circa 2004.[1] An important component of the network's activities has been creating opportunities for MMIWGT2SQ (missing and murdered Indigenous women, girls, trans, Two-Spirit, and queer people) organizers who share a commitment to radical decolonization to meet and strategize. Bringing together women from around the country, mostly in Toronto, these Violence No More events are video documented and can be accessed on the It Starts With Us website.[2] The following is a conversation between Audrey and Carol Lynne about a series of interviews Audrey did with members of this initiative. They are excited to be anchoring this form of oral knowledge transmission in book format and hope their contribution will be the catalyst for much reflection and exchange.

CAROL LYNNE: Can you talk about the genesis of this chapter?

AUDREY: For several years, No More Silence had been gathering with individual organizers, family members, folks from Families of Sisters in Spirit, and the Native Youth Sexual Health Network in Toronto (and once in St. John's) to talk strategy and connect our struggles. By 2020, it had been awhile since we met in person and we hoped to bring everyone back together to grapple with a fundamental tension in our work; namely, how do we confront the injustice of the impunity experienced by killers of Indigenous women, girls, trans, Two-Spirit, and queer people (and men for that matter), especially when those killers are settlers, when the response by many of our community members is to equate justice with carceral punishment? After all, No More Silence works outside the state and seeks fundamental decolonization as the solution to ending femicide and genocide.

The pandemic meant it would be a while longer before we could gather in person, so I decided to initiate Zoom conversations. I am honoured and privileged to be working for about a decade now with some amazing organizers in It Starts With Us. They are wonderful, committed, dedicated, and powerful. The conversation included Wanda Whitebird (Mi'kmaq), Sheryl Lindsay (Mixed Indigenous and Settler), Beverley Jacobs (Haudenosaunee), Terri Monture (Haudenosaunee), Alex Wilson (Cree), Christa Big Canoe (Anishinaabe), Sarah Hunt/ Tłaliłiláogwa (Kwagu'ł), and Krysta Williams (Lenape).[3]

CAROL LYNNE: How does this tension—wanting to decolonize and reject settler institutions like the prison industrial complex when many equate justice with carceral punishment—play out in the personal or professional lives of the women you interviewed?

AUDREY: That question resonated with every one of the women with whom I spoke. For example, Aboriginal Legal Executive Director Christa Big Canoe described the conundrum as a daily internal struggle:

> It's like your brain and heart struggle with each other all the time on some of these issues . . . I particularly felt it when I was working with the National Inquiry [into Missing and Murdered Indigenous Women and Girls]. My job [as Commission Counsel] was to put evidence before them. What that meant is I'd be sitting beside families who were calling for the death penalty or stricter punishments and I had to maintain my unbiased approach. I had to ask them the questions so they could give the evidence. And even if, you know, in my core being, I was thinking we can't have capital punishments . . . I had no choice, but to ask the questions and allow them to speak their truth.

Christa explains how this tension is made worse by Eurocentric forms of justice in Canada:

> Most of the processes we work in are very ... colonial or very Eurocentric or Euro-Canadian. And so, it's really hard sometimes to even reconcile what we know of Indigenous knowledge and practice to what's happening with us. So, the approach I've taken at least in the last fifteen or twenty years has been to try to take some of that knowledge for the greater good and to convince others that there's other opportunities or ways. But when you're working within a system, you're often stuck in that conundrum.

Others, including Krysta Williams, describe how incredibly disconcerting, let alone disempowering, it can be to engage with the settler colonial justice system for those involved in trials or hearings. She paints a vivid picture:

> [The tension] shows up as very practical stuff, you know, for anybody that's done in-court support, it's right there and you walk into the courtroom and it's so weird and so colonial and they're swearing oaths to the Queen and family members are there. It is so far removed from those experiences and from people's wants and needs and yet they go into extreme amounts of detail about ... whatever acts were committed. It's surreal and it doesn't connect to this very human experience ... You see the limitations of what [the colonizer's legal system] can do and what it can't do and you see how easy it is to set people up to fail, because they're expecting a certain level of control or communication. But that's not how, you know, the settler colonial justice system is set up, right? You're lucky when [the judge] tells you when the next parole hearing date is, let alone involves you in any sort of meaningful way. So, it really just kind of reinforces this idea that, you know, the person who's experienced this harm has no control over what happens and doesn't have much of a say other than doing impact statements.

Krysta's experiences are typical of how the system retraumatizes Indigenous people. Several of the women interviewed agree that the Canadian legal system simply does not work for Indigenous individuals and communities, especially if we redefine the goal of that system as one of redressing harm. Beverly Jacobs reflects on this common sentiment: "[Indigenous people] get caught up in [the settler colonial criminal justice] system, saying, '[Offenders] need to be thrown in jail and throw away the key.' But does that address anything? Does that system *actually* work for anybody? Does it deal with any of the harms that have been done?" The answer for Christa Big Canoe is a definitive "No," which has led her to engage in public awareness raising that lays bare the facts about the "real lived experience of Indigenous people going through [the policing, legal, and carceral] systems and what harm it causes them."

For her part, Sarah Hunt describes engaging with the Canadian legal system as "usually a horrific, drawn out, racist, and violent process." She calls attention to a specifically gendered dimension of this conundrum evident in a markedly different approach to Indigenous struggles when they relate to MMIWGT2SQ versus land defence: "There's still this mentality that when it comes to issues of violence against our bodies, our loved ones at the intimate scale . . . that we still turn to state processes, like the National Inquiry. Whereas when it comes to protecting land, water, or questions of sovereignty at a larger scale, we are more likely to assert our rights in defiance of colonial systems."

During my exchange with Sarah, I realized I had never thought about that distinction, but it rings true. For example, all the solidarity actions with the Wet'suwet'en in British Columbia and across these lands called Canada focused on Wet'suwet'en hereditary leaders and laws and how the land is still under their jurisdiction since it was never ceded. However, there isn't the same focus on asserting traditional laws when it comes to gender-based violence. Instead, many look to the recommendations of study after study and now to the *Calls to Action* from the National Inquiry on Missing and Murdered Indigenous Women and Girls.

CAROL LYNNE: Given that the Canadian "justice" system is clearly not working for them, why do so many Indigenous people turn towards state-sanctioned, retributive justice solutions?

AUDREY: Sarah points to a very practical reason, that the Canadian "justice system is what we currently have. We haven't built up those other systems of justice or community processes." Not least, as several interviewees mention, for decades Indigenous communities have been living in crisis mode and struggling to survive. As Krysta indicates, "There isn't always the capacity to even engage because people are too overwhelmed or concerned with basic needs. You know? This idea that if we can't even get clean drinking water, how could we possibly build towards something more complex?" Sarah emphasizes, "When it comes to individual instances of violence, especially murder . . . many communities have no viable alternatives—just yet."

I heard other equally convincing explanations that I don't think are mutually exclusive. One comes from Alex Wilson, who believes that the desire for retribution is not unexpected. In saying this, Alex cautions against a binary approach: "Coming from an Indigenous paradigm . . . in reality, there's not this cut and dry binary around justice. And I think it just seems like a natural response to want some kind of vindication or retribution when somebody's loved one is harmed or hurt." I know my blood boiled and I felt so hurt and had so much rage when Tina Fontaine's and Colton Boushie's murderers received their innocent verdicts.

Krysta says much the same with respect to families' desires to seek justice for their missing and murdered Indigenous women, girls, Two-Spirit, and queer folks:

> I mean, by and large, what we heard from family members who decided to participate [in the National Inquiry] at various points in the process . . . was "this needs to be seen and this needs to be heard and this needs to be believed." That is a deep human need, not just in the face of violence, but just in general, in order to feel like we can exist in the world as ourselves. So, it's understandable that that was something that they were looking for from kind of the highest power.

Terri Monture also references the families of MMIWGT2SQ people: "They're looking somehow for that disruption to be healed. And I don't think it can ever be [healed] by sticking some asshole in jail, as much as it would be nice. That's not going to give you the peace you need." Speaking more generally, Sarah notes, "There is still a real willingness to believe in the Canadian government's capacity to do good, to finally deliver justice. Like, the government is going to save or heal us," despite evidence to the contrary.

CAROL LYNNE: That reminds me of something I witnessed in Guatemala in the late 1990s. The Indigenous population there felt vindicated when the Commission for Historical Clarification (the Guatemalan version of a truth commission) found the government guilty of genocide during the nation's civil war. Words can't describe the atmosphere in the room when this was announced.

AUDREY: We saw the same phenomenon happening in relation to the Truth and Reconciliation Commission here in Canada and the Harper apology, for that matter.[4] It seems to come down to the need to be visible and to hear truth spoken out loud. Referring to state apologies, Krysta affirms Alex's assessment of false binaries:

> Maybe those are actually steps on the way to divestment . . . I think we create a false binary when it's "either you're [for] abolition or you're participating in the system" and those are your only options. I think people need to experience what the state can offer and see if it meets their needs and, you know, come to the realization that it doesn't.

Krysta's statement meshes with one of the solutions Sarah proposes to resolve the tension we've been discussing. She advocates "being able to be honest about the stories we tell about how that system works, even when people choose to want to use it because it's what is available."

CAROL LYNNE: Sarah said there's a double standard when it comes to invoking Indigenous laws. What can be learned from traditional Indigenous governance and legal systems in relation to "violence against bodies," as Sarah puts it, that could help achieve decolonization and a real sense of justice for those who have been wronged?

AUDREY: People had more or less to say about this question depending on how connected they are to their homelands, Knowledge Keepers, and Elders. For example, Beverly, who is from Six Nations and has spent many years studying traditional Haudenosaunee law, describes the focal point of traditional justice as addressing harm:

> I think there's a huge difference between justice and punishment. According to our laws, Haudenosaunee Laws, there was no such thing as punishment. We didn't have jails. We didn't have police the way police are in the system that we have today. We had a system of checks and balances. We had a system where if somebody did harm to somebody else, everybody was involved in addressing the harm, whether it was the abuser or the person who caused harm, their whole family, their whole community, and also the victims. And having the support around them, whether it was family, community, there was a process to get to the root of the problem.

A recurring theme that came up in several conversations is the idea of restoring balance and harmony—even when punitive measures are taken to ensure people are safe and no further harm can be done. For instance, working with Hawaiian Elders and community members, Alex learned about a walled city that community members who had violated the collective trust would voluntarily move to, to remove the possibility of them doing further harm, and "so they could return to a kind of balance through hard work on whatever level, like spiritual or physical . . . They kind of were working for the community while they were there and kept away from others, so there was safety."

Sometimes traditional measures were simply retributive and did involve punishment. Terri discusses banishment as a common practice for many Indigenous nations in the past and one that still functions in a modified way today. For instance, Alex gave an example of banishment in reference to Cree communities today that take the form of Band Council resolutions. In the case of Tashina General's murder by a star lacrosse player in Six Nations of the Grand River First Nation, after being released from jail on appeal, he returned to his reserve and found that, although the community had once been divided in their loyalty to him, there was no longer any room for him, not on any lacrosse team nor in everyday interactions.

At another point in our conversation, Terri offered examples of how the principle of restitution was applied. If, for example, someone had taken the life of a person who was a provider for a family, they would then be responsible for taking care of and feeding the loved ones left behind. Adoption of noncommunity members was another common practice when there was a loss. When Terri shared that story, I was reminded of a story Angela Davis on the occasion of the twentieth anniversary of INCITE!, a US-based "network of radical feminists of color organizing to end state violence and violence in our homes and communities."[5] She talks about how a participant in the South African Truth and Reconciliation process, a mother who had lost both a son and a husband to police violence, asked the officer who committed the murder to spend time with her every couple of weeks so she could give him the love she could no longer share with her lost loved ones.

CAROL LYNNE: That's astounding and takes me to my next question: How does reconciliation or forgiveness figure into Indigenous traditional understandings of justice?

AUDREY: Well, the idea of forgiveness is rooted in Christian concepts and is not everyone's cup of tea, but Bev also sees the teachings of love and kindness as well as understanding and compassion for the person who committed the crime as foundational to traditional forms of Indigenous justice. What that means in practice is that you look at the context of what brought that person to cause harm, to act that way: Were they themselves subjected to violence? As children? Perhaps in foster care or because of intergenerational trauma related to residential school? Alex adds the important caveat that we need to look to the *principles* of traditional Indigenous law rather than focus on specific practices that may not work in today's world. She also stresses the importance of understanding these principles as land-based:

> And those "natural laws," those descriptions and philosophies and actions that came with them, didn't just pop out of nowhere. They were developed in relationship with land, with the [context and] environment at a local level. And then our languages built around that over millennia. There are ways of being that create and maintain balance and health with our environment. Those

are really important. And we can figure out how those principles translate today and reframe around those, which means that there couldn't be one universal system. Right now, we have one universal system across Canada.

Perhaps the most common traditional practice employed in community organizing around MMIWGT2SQ is ceremony. Elder Wanda Whitebird, founding member of No More Silence, has led a Strawberry Ceremony on February 14 in Toronto for more than fifteen years. Vancouver's Downtown Eastside community has been conducting the Memorial March on that day for over twenty-five years—it is led by Medicine women who burn medicines and smudge at various sites along the route.

According to Terri, ceremonies have always played an essential part in fostering individual—and I would add, collective—healing and restitution for those suffering from traumatic grief, citing the condolence rite as an example:

> At the heart of the condolence rite is removal of grief so that your mind is clear and you can be in balance and peace again. Perhaps that's part of what we're needing here in abolitionist circles, a way to remove grief, because that is the one thing that causes people to want revenge, right? Somebody kills your child; you want revenge on that person. Condolence rites were done in a way to temper that immediate desire to cause harm. I think that is the piece that's missing out of crime and punishment in most cultures. There's no ability to deal with grief.

Along these same lines, Sarah asks Indigenous communities to focus on their own practices rather than the state and to "really value the intimate interpersonal networks of care and sense of responsibility and accountability to each other that our systems of justice have always been built upon."

CAROL LYNNE: What did folks say about some of the challenges involved in applying these teachings, in particular, moving towards restitution and away from retribution?

AUDREY: I'll begin with a mundane but very real challenge that

Terri brought up, which is to not get co-opted by the colonial system. As Terri says, "Either you figure out a way to resist or you end up being co-opted. . . . You start getting seduced by that system . . . they start giving you fancy upgrades at hotels and flights and stuff. That's how they get you."

In other words, once people's livelihoods depend on the system, they are less likely to oppose it. I mentioned to Terri at the time that this reminds me of that adage by Audre Lorde that "the master's tools will never dismantle the master's house." The underlying factor of colonial dispossession has severed many Indigenous individuals and communities from much of their cultural wisdom and traditional laws. In addition to being separated from these practices and principles of Indigenous governance and legal systems, Christa cited "loss of language" as an integral part of what has "caused so much pain to our community." I think both loss of language and lack of understanding of traditional justice mechanisms can lead to their misapplication or misinterpretation, a glaringly apparent reality when it comes to the issue of gender-based violence in our communities. Alex spoke to this point, saying, "The Indigenous kind of approaches like healing circles and so-called alternative justice or Indigenous justice didn't work because the facilitators didn't have training or an understanding of domestic violence and how [these approaches] could end up revictimizing survivors." Put another way, there is a real risk that power dynamics between perpetrators and survivors will repeatedly play out. Survivors are forced to confront their perpetrators instead of having the necessary time and space to heal.

CAROL LYNNE: I know you have been involved in anti-violence, decolonizing work for decades. Have you seen anything similar play out in that time?

AUDREY: What immediately comes to mind is the participatory action research project, Journey for Justice, I was involved in when I worked for the Vancouver-based Aboriginal Women's Action Network in fall of 2000. A group of us rafted through eleven Fraser River communities to talk about the possible impacts of restorative justice reforms on women and children survivors of violence. We were motivated by the concern that the brand of reformative justice being introduced was a false model of justice that would end up benefiting the patriarchy and be misused by the male leaders in the community. For instance, there was a Band Council chief who got his son off on multiple rape charges by sitting in a circle and talking about how sorry he was. Our position was "we don't want restorative justice to be used in cases of violence against women and children because we don't believe that you can protect the survivor." Looking back, I am reminded that any kind of transformative justice or community accountability process we come up with must recognize the existing power structures they're working within.

My observations in BC and elsewhere resonate with a critical point made by Sarah, that some issues are taken more seriously than others in many Indigenous communities:

> I recently heard someone on the radio talking about reconciliation and police violence and a number of issues related to violent colonial systems, but then they tacked on "our MMIW" without any mention of the connection to colonization. It's like there's not really the full understanding of what we're actually talking about. [It] gets shortened to this kind of hashtag or add-on. I saw that with a lot of the Land Back actions, that people had this very in-depth way of understanding and talking about Indigenous jurisdiction and Indigenous law when it comes to land and decision-making and what that means. But then they reduce gendered violence to "women are being murdered because of the man camps." MMIW was sort of put in there, but it wasn't talked about in the same way—that we have the right to govern our bodies and that we have to build up those same systems of governance over ourselves. We have the inherent right to govern our bodies, our homes, and our lands.

I find Sarah's incredulity at the different responses to the Land Back movement versus the MMIWGT2SQ movement, often by the same people, especially relevant for our discussion. With Land Back, there's this embrace of traditional laws and practices, whereas when it comes to sexual and gender violence, people seem content to look to the settler colonial state for solutions. I'm thinking in part about all the National Inquiry recommendations. Krysta articulates one more perspective on the challenges of moving away from a state-centric retributive "justice" system. On the one hand, there is a romanticized notion of community that diverts attention away from an honest assessment of community capacity. On the other, there can be a lack of confidence in a community's ability to pursue alternatives. In Krysta's words:

> Not everybody experiences this romantic notion of community, especially people who have experienced harm. There isn't always that reciprocity that is needed for any sort of community accountability process. There isn't always the capacity to even engage because people are too overwhelmed or concerned with basic needs . . . I actually think that's a false binary. I think you can work on all of those things, and they're all connected . . . But in that perpetual motion, there's also a lot of possibility for change and transformation.

Summing it all up, Krysta declares, "Community is messy."

CAROL LYNNE: So, would an important way forward be to acknowledge that messiness as a starting point? More broadly, what did the women say about how Indigenous communities might overcome these challenges and move from retribution to restitution?

AUDREY: For starters, I agree with Krysta that it is critical to account for the messiness, to acknowledge just how complex it is for communities to navigate colonialism past and present. What I think Krysta and others are recommending is a reality check. As Bev ponders, "How do you incorporate [our own laws about kindness and compassion and love and healing and grieving] into something so horrific today? It takes a lot of work. And that's what I think we need to do, is to take on that work." Christa brings to bear a historical perspective: "As long as we've been sort of submerged in [settler colonialism], is as long as it'll take to heal from it completely. That doesn't mean that you can't have, like, revolutions or big changes in spurts and bursts. It's time we've had some big changes."

For both Christa and Bev, Indigenous communities are up to the challenge. Christa emphasizes that "one of the really important things to understand in terms of decolonization, in sort of putting the power back to the people, is [that] . . . Indigenous people are in the best place to understand their communities, to provide solutions . . . [that] already exist." Bev agrees, putting into sharp relief an advantage Indigenous people have over some of their non-Indigenous counterparts:

> What about the non-Indigenous peoples who came here . . . already colonized? How many more hundreds of years of healing do they have to do? For us, I think it's easy, as Indigenous people, because we still have our laws, we still have our languages, we still have our ceremonies, and we still have the connection to our lands and our territories . . . We still have the Knowledge Holders. We still have the Healers.

For Bev, Indigenous women are up to the task of doing the emotional, spiritual, and physical work of realizing Indigenous visions of justice "because we have been doing it. We have already started that healing process, probably for the last twenty-five, thirty years or more. Our women have been the leaders in that. So, I think that's where it's going to happen."

CAROL LYNNE: One of the central messages of It Starts With Us is that Indigenous communities are the experts on their own lives. Would you agree?

AUDREY: Absolutely! In fact, several people add the corollary that Indigenous communities can and should build on existing traditional knowledge and practices. For example, Terri suggests that when we find ourselves caught up in that tension (of seeking to dismantle the settler colonial state while equating justice with carceral punishment), we should rethink crime as a social breach and punishment as reparation, prevention, or reduction of harm:

> How do we heal [the perpetrators] and heal the families that have had harm done? . . . At the heart of these situations, it's a person putting their shit on another in a harmful fashion because that's what these breaches come to . . . It's always that cycle of "hurt people hurt people" . . . we need to get out of that, right? So, we need to be paying more attention to how . . . we heal that person and prevent them from ever doing that again.

When Sarah talks about the relationship between the police and some reserve communities in Northern BC, I think she is describing a community response that fits Terri's redefinition. As Sarah puts it:

> When people have called the police . . . it might take a day or five days for them to show up. There are other things that people call on instead, even those people who might trust the police. Out of necessity, those systems don't operate in the same way in our communities, especially smaller communities. I think that we can look at it as kind of learning from, building up, and expanding those networks.

Going further, Sarah believes that

> localized, small scale networks of people that have a shared kind of understanding or framework for how we respond together, how we act together, how we show up for each other . . . [make it] more possible to have other mechanisms for justice so that we don't end up, just out of default, going through a court process.

Sarah's advice makes me think of Bev's take on the question of how to move from retribution to restitution, which hinges on the potential of ceremony as a way not only to reconnect but also to enact Indigenous knowledges and practices. Not one to shy from a challenge, Bev tells me:

> The work that we need to do is to return to that legal system and understand what it means on a bigger scale. Not only language wise, ceremonial wise. Ceremony is just one of the tools and actions of practicing our laws . . . And that's the work that I was talking about in the beginning. That's a lot of work. It's a lot of work to understand the colonial system and what they've done to us, but also a lot of work for us to return to those principles of our laws.

CAROL LYNNE: I think Bev's point really helps explain why we consider the condolence ceremony described by Terri as a practice of governance.

AUDREY: I agree, and I think Alex would too. As I suggest above, for her, a lot hinges on repairing relationships with the land:

> I'm really passionate about and support land-based learning and land-based education in whatever form that takes. There's something that's happened in the colonization process that has intentionally but also inadvertently disconnected people from land-based knowledge and . . . so part of land-based [learning] is reconnecting or repairing those relationships with land and other beings as well. If there's any kind of intervention . . . that I see working for children at least, and youth that . . . are either survivors of violence or that have done violence . . . is that kind of land-based reconnection.

It's all about slowing down and learning from the land, which in turn reveals possibilities.

To me, this all links back to the importance of reviving Indigenous languages, something Christa, Bev, and Alex brought up explicitly as a way to implement Indigenous alternatives to retributive forms of justice that involve the carceral state.

Like Krysta, I too wonder "if we were to reframe for ourselves what justice looks like or what are the practices that lend themselves to creating it, would some of those structures already exist?" The movement that organizes around MMIWGT2SQ already has multiple ways of looking after those who are left behind when a loved one has gone missing or been murdered. Community is there to assist when it comes to supporting those observing court processes, providing food for families who are grieving, and organizing ceremony, as many cities do on February 14. I agree with Sarah, who points out that colonizer systems have not succeeded in breaking up collective responses:

> Those systems isolate us. That's partly what they are built to do. You become an individual going through the system instead of it being a collective, a sense of justice formed collectively. Thinking about things like showing up with food, going with people through the process, or if someone has been harmed, to not rely on state systems like policing or social workers or whatever, but to think about how we can listen to each other. We can ask, "What

would justice mean for you in this context, or what would help you to get through this time?" and then walk beside one another to prevent further harm. I mean, we've all always been doing that.

Many Indigenous people involved in their traditional ceremonies or who practice Indigenous spirituality already seek the wisdom of Elders to mediate strife and conflict and they are certainly at the forefront of creating alternatives to punitive models, such as the healing lodges that have been introduced in the prison system. In fact, Bev comments on the irony that for some folks, prison is the first time they have access to the wisdom of Elders and Knowledge Keepers, and one reason they end up back inside is that they no longer have that access once they are released. As Bev explains:

> The women and men who are inside are actually healing a lot more because they have access to [Elders] . . . Once they get outside, the reality sets in that, "Hey, not everybody's doing this" and they lose the connection. And that's when they end up back inside again.

Christa reminds us that "we have had governance and legal processes" from time immemorial:

> The Inaakonigewin, the Anishinaabe constitution: the rules of how we live that govern us. Whether it be the seven grandfather teachings or the law of respect, those are all things that help provide guidance. And they're very theoretical, but they're also very practical and most people who are non-Indigenous or even Indigenous people who don't practice them don't necessarily understand that those principles of living a good life are what creates harmony amongst people and amongst society.

I am most hopeful we can add a gendered perspective and be intentional about centring women, genderqueer, and nonbinary folks, as Sarah does. She makes a really good point about taking into account the impacts of patriarchy enacted through Indian Act policies when we look to traditional forms of governance and law:

> I don't really trust that the people being turned to for our laws,

our stories, our traditions of governance can account for gendered violence today. Also, we didn't need the same systems we need now because we have different forms of violence. So, instead, I'd rather be talking to small networks about how people see Indigenous law being enacted through the ways we take care of each other. My current work is asking: What does justice feel like for coastal people, especially women and Two-Spirit and queer people, our gender diverse relations? What does justice feel like in our collective work together? Which is a different question than "go find that Elder who knows a story about how we enacted justice," and it's centring, inspired by Patricia Monture, forms of law that put our relations at the centre.

CAROL LYNNE: Were there any major points of contention among the interviewees?

AUDREY: Well, I think the most unpopular opinion, not just necessarily among the folks I talked to for this chapter but for the movement, revolves around noncarceral solutions for settler perpetrators. For example, Krysta puts forward, and cites others who believe, that it makes sense on some level to use the Canadian legal system to hold settlers accountable:

> When we are talking about harm that's been done by mostly cisgender heterosexual men and white men versus harm that's done within our communities, I think those are actually pretty different scenarios. I've heard people say that, depending on the perpetrator you're dealing with, you have to use the system that they are accountable to.

Others, however, seem to go back to Angela Davis's appeal to start operating in the way that we envision our end game, in which case, I don't see two sets of systems. I fully agree with Bev that "if I really walk my talk that I don't want prisons, that I don't want police, that I don't want these things to impact our system, then I also have to do the work of healing when it comes to the offenders. And I'm talking about *all* offenders." Proponents of separate systems may also not agree with Christa, who says that "to achieve decolonization, we have to actually invest in Indigenous practices, Indigenous cultures.

And I don't just mean Indigenous people. I mean the entire society, right? The entire society has to recognize their value." I think there is a deep-seated fear of further loss due to hundreds of years of attempted genocide that has expressed itself in some insidious and violent ways, so there is an instinct to be protective of culture, land, and language; but I agree with Christa when she states:

> If you take that Indigenous knowledge and you share . . . I'm not talking about the most sacred or ceremonial stuff, but if you share those principles and you teach those principles and they're learned from a young age, it's going to benefit everyone, not just Indigenous people in terms of creating a better society.

CAROL LYNNE: How do we hold the state accountable while pushing for decolonization, abolishing prisons, or divesting from the state?

AUDREY: How organizers related to the demands for a National Inquiry and then how they positioned themselves once one was conducted is a good example of how some people grapple with this seeming contradiction. We've had to carefully measure how much energy and attention we devote to state-led initiatives or risk neglecting the work on the ground due to burn out and lack of capacity. For many years, No More Silence supported families' demands for an inquiry. In particular, demands coming out of Vancouver's Downtown Eastside. The obvious sham nature of the BC Missing Women Inquiry, which ended up absolving local police forces and was boycotted by most of the groups who had standing, confirmed our expectations that no government-led initiative will further our end goal of decolonization as much as our own efforts to build power from the grassroots. One outcome that we couldn't ignore, however, was that for the first time, a broad civil society discourse took place. Opportunities to educate the public opened up in a way that had never been seen before.

Once the Trudeau Government began pandering to Indigenous communities with the promise of an inquiry of national scope, we already knew that we would not be able to compete with the capacity of police to once again dominate the hearings, and that our energy would be best used elsewhere. That said, we did recognize the healing potential for families who were afforded the chance to speak their truths and supported where we could.

In my view, the best thing to come out of this most recent inquiry was the report's findings of genocide. This was a first for a government publication and provides a point of reference that can't be brushed off, as has occurred to those of us who have been defining the femicide of Indigenous women, girls, trans, Two-Spirit, and queer people in this way for decades. The implementation of these calls can now be measured. Unfortunately, most recommendations coming out of the plethora of studies on MMIWGT2SQ have not been implemented, which demonstrates a general lack of political will when it comes to making the changes needed to stop the violence.

In my conversations with Alex and Krysta, I appreciated their understanding that tensions can exist while we endeavour to end the settler colonial project and achieve abolition. They describe the binary between demanding state accountability and wanting to divest from the state as problematic. In fact, Krysta sees it as a process; the desire to have the state validate that harm has occurred is "a step on the way to divestment." Additionally, Alex points out that we will face criticism trying to balance holding the state accountable while at the same time trying to dismantle it:

> There will be contradictions and there will be both. We have to do work in the ways that we can. And that's always going to be a critique. I think people will say, "Well, what do you mean defund police? We need police." People will criticize Black Lives Matter, Idle No More, or any movement, really, and say things like, "'How do you mean save the environment? You're driving a car, you know?" But, you just have to keep doing what you can.

As Krysta notes, an important way to confront the state with the violence it produces is to bring the conversation back to the roots or systemic conditions that create the violence. It's that endless educational work to deconstruct and refute the victim blaming:

> I think it is about always circling back to what were the conditions under which that [harm] was allowed to happen. We place that at the feet of the state and those colonial ways of relating to

each other and all of these things that remove people's humanity and allow for violence to happen.

Even more important, I think, is the focus on building up our own community capacity with Indigenous-led processes that create our own programs and institutions that centre Indigenous knowledge. It is worth noting that these programs and institutions will differ across nations. Christa points out that along with Indigenous leadership, it is key to have adequate funding so these projects aren't set up to fail:

> The first thing we need is recognition by government actors. And this is part of their accountability that they have to invest some of those funding resources and supports so that there is actual Indigenous success, not so that programs are set up for failure or that all the criteria are set by the colonizer or the government, but by the people who are back in the best place to deliver that.

People may agree to varying extents that you can't dismantle the master's house with the master's tools, but they still consider these tools to be a powerful and transformative force when working within state institutions. Bev has recently become the Dean of Law at the University of Windsor and is using her position to incorporate Indigenous law and governance into the curriculum, exposing hundreds of scholars to traditional knowledge. As Bev argues, "If we have enough people infiltrating the system, then it will be easy to move. Because people will understand, based on the help, that healthy relationship and knowledge." Personally, I love how Indigenous women are doing this work of decolonizing and transformation from so many different vantage points and from both within and outside state institutions. There is no one way, and we are engaging with each other while we do it—working the system where we can and building our own structures and resources in the community.

CHAPTER 12

BABY BUNDLE PROJECT AND COMMUNITY BIRTH WORK JOURNEYS

Krysta Williams

I share these stories based on my personal experiences as a novice community birth worker, Indigenous full spectrum doula, and longtime sexual health educator—as well as an urban Indigenous community member in Tkaronto. At the time of writing, I was contracted as a survey interviewer for a research project that transformed into the Baby Bundle Program. The Baby Bundle Program started in June 2020 and provides ongoing wraparound care and support to Indigenous families who are pregnant or postpartum up to six months. In this chapter, I reflect on my experiences with the program and ask deep questions about its role in community, humbly speculating about future possibilities. Before you read further, I want to emphasize the importance of centring lived experiences from survivors of these systems and reading/listening to their experiences first and always. While some of what I discuss here is not my lived experience in a direct way in my lifetime, the spectre of the Children's Aid Society (CAS) is never far from Indigenous families or children and informs all aspects of our lives.

For me, getting involved in this work felt aligned with the birthwork resurgence that is happening across Indian Country, which has called on people to take up ancestral roles, skills, and knowledge and surround community members on their birthing journey, with a full spectrum of outcomes including loss, termination, apprehension, or parenting. The urban Indigenous community in Toronto has been identifying gaps and developing growing supports for perinatal care for years, including the creation of the Toronto Birth Centre.

When I was trying to get a sense of what I was going to write,

I reflected on a question posed during the creation of the Baby Bundle Project: Can a program, service, or organization (or a collection of them) have a shared goal of keeping families together and connected while also providing practical support that is lacking in social services? The primary fear for so many people is removal, intervention, separation, and loss. For example, it is has been made clear by survivors that CAS agencies (also called Child and Family Services [CFS] in other provinces) exist in a legislative framework that emphasizes funding of staff and foster parents over larger budgets for food, health care, child care, supplies, housing, transportation, and all the other extra expenses that come with living in a large urban centre as an Indigenous family.

To understand the need for projects like Baby Bundle, we need to take a closer look at how and why CAS intervention happens, including the circumstances under which children are removed and stolen from their families and communities. This includes realities of violence and abuse in addition to what is labelled as poverty and neglect. "Lack" is not inherent to families or individuals specifically but in the structures and systems that would support them to self-actualize their own goals, enact autonomy, and self-determine their needs. Families are forced to meet benchmarks and goals known only to their worker / supervisor / protection department / court, which are often punitive in nature and offer no room for error or growing pains as they adjust. This sets families up to fail. One toe out of line, one beer, one email to someone you are not supposed to be in contact with, and you risk being separated from your child. This is unreasonable.

WHAT IS NEGLECT TO CHILDREN'S AID SOCIETIES?

How do we come to understand neglect in the context of ongoing settler colonialism in combination with Indigenous families' encounters with CAS? How is it measured? By bank accounts? By spending? By how much food is in the fridge? By the quality of clothing a child is wearing? Without a deep understanding of how trauma, poverty, and mental health come together to influence financial "management" strategies for poor people, something that is basically impossible under capitalism, we punish families further for being trapped in a cycle of debt that did not originate with them. What about the parents that are going hungry to buy their child or infant clothes so it can *appear* to the social worker that they are a fit parent? When they get their social assistance cheque, do we judge them if the first thing they spend it on is not food but diapers or vice versa?

While I am not an expert on financial management, I bring up these questions to illustrate the central role that poverty plays in family separation via apprehension. Other chapters in this book, such as the one by Skeete and Bergen, speak to the connection between child apprehension and the never-ending cycle of poverty and debt. This context challenges us as community members and organizers to think differently about the redistribution of the little resources we do have, the role of "mutual" aid, and how to structure support programs to meet basic needs while validating and affirming to community members that accessing those supports is not a personal or moral failure but a systemic one. The relief I have seen among participants in our program when we have directly expressed this to them is palpable and results occasionally in surprise, as many folks have internalized the idea that they have failed as a parent simply for having consumer or student debt (which is widely encouraged by capitalism) and no strategy for managing it.

SUBVERTING THE CONTROL OF CHILDREN'S AID SOCIETIES

We cannot hope to tackle a large and powerful system such as Children's Aid Societies on our own (and there are others working on legislative changes), but I am hopeful that the severe harm and lack of trust in this system has primed us for transformation, experimentation, and community organizing in a way that can preventatively divert people away from these systems, build skills within our communities to mitigate harm and interrupt discrimination when forced interactions do occur, and support those for whom involvement in the system is already a reality intergenerationally and/or as a result of crisis. To achieve these goals, we need to start exposing the root reasons for people's involvement with CAS, be that material means (i.e., poverty or housing), interpersonal violence, or other basic needs that have become barriers (i.e., increasing access to parenting strategies in challenging situations, managing substance use, and healing from family violence).

We have so much to be justifiably angry for. As an emotion, anger points us towards a deep need that is not being met—not feeling heard, a boundary being crossed, or safety being threatened (even in a perceived way). For Indigenous peoples and many communities of colour, this anger becomes weaponized and quickly transforms into criminalization either through mental health language of emotional instability or dysregulation or through proving that someone is not interested in cooperating with CAS to meet the needs of their child(ren). We see this also in the medicalization of birth, treating each event in pregnancy and labour as a threat and interventions that need to be "complied" with to maintain a colonial order of operations over our bodies.

Anyone who has supported family, friends, clients, or community members in these systems knows—your attitude and emotions are also under surveillance and could be weaponized. Frustration or resistance can be dismissed easily as "unprofessional"—particularly when you are calling out actual unprofessional or harmful behaviours and decisions. Closeness and intimacy are also under scrutiny and navigating emotional vulnerability, connection, and disclosures becomes very treacherous.

Survivors and advocates alike agree that it is critical we demand transparency from the child welfare system. Getting things like expectations, case conference notes, and any other documentation in writing after each interaction is critical. Especially when cooperation feels like the only path forward—and to not comply would potentially result in more harm.

DIVERTING PEOPLE AWAY FROM CHILDEN'S AID SOCIETIES

Multiple studies have shown that the separation of an infant from the person who birthed them is traumatizing and affects immediate and long-term ability to heal, feed, soothe, and rest. Just the threat or fear of that possibility (however remote) can cause anxious thoughts and changed behaviour for both parent and child. For instance, if a pregnant person cannot obtain safe housing for themselves and their baby once they are born, apprehension will likely be at the top of the list of intervention strategies. Some shelters are considered unfit housing, and there are very limited spots in "family shelters" that offer more infrastructure and space. This forces people into system-run temporary housing options that offer up further opportunities for surveillance and intervention. In a city like Toronto, which is in a constant housing crisis, what does "safe and stable" housing even mean or look like? Should someone go into debt paying for an apartment they cannot afford or will this backfire in the long run? Without transparency, families get lost in the bureaucracy of it all, overwhelmed with vague requirements while simultaneously dealing with crises from a lack of structural supports.

We should question the decision to separate children from their parents precisely when the person who has birthed the child is experiencing the direst of circumstances. Why not divert the millions of dollars allocated to CAS agencies to support residency-based programs? While it seems culturally appropriate to centre children's needs, Children's Aid Services / Societies actually serve the interests of the state and the laws under which they were created. By utilizing language like "best interest of the child," any resistance or uncooperative behaviours are framed as not having the best interest of a child at the forefront. Indigenous children are integral and vital parts of our nations and communities. They exist in relationship to the people who care about and look after them, their families (however complicated), Nations, lands, and societies; they are not separate. Their health and interests are inextricably linked to the societal conditions we find ourselves in. They do not exist in a vacuum.

Framing birthing people as mere vessels to be forgotten and discarded after birth fails to understand these connections when the reality is that the birther's well-being is linked with that of the child and that of their community on multiple levels. Often the focus is so much on the baby's safety that the birthing person gets left behind. They are expected to take care of themselves. This contradiction intensifies when there has been suspicion about the person's ability to parent or whether they are "fit" to do so. Ask any prospective or current parent and they will openly discuss their own self-doubts about newborn and infant care, parenting, and general worries that they won't be good enough. Indigenous families are scrutinized on a whole other level with very real threats of separation or state surveillance—and with no oversight, supervision, or transparency about what considerations are considered. It is a subjective assessment on the part of a worker, and the family in question has little to no control.

MITIGATING HARM: INTERROGATING THE MYTH OF PARENTING SKILLS

It is a common misconception that caregiving comes "naturally" to everyone—or at least to certain people. While it may seem "natural," caregiving is an observed, learned, and experienced skill. We must first experience or witness parenting/caregiving and then be rewarded socially when we emulate or practice these behaviours. Even if someone experiences neglect or abuse, we innately know that we have needs. Having those needs met or acknowledged internally and then expressing those needs to others is critical to human relationships. Even if the experience of getting your needs met is unfamiliar to you, we each possess some baseline knowledge of its importance.

The idea that someone who hasn't experienced good caregiving can't themselves be a good parent is a fallacy. An external agency's investigation of a person's level of caregiving "skill" is often dripping with bias towards people who face multiple barriers. Meanwhile, many people with privilege who are able to become pregnant and parent do so without such state-sanctioned interference, despite not having strong caregiving skills. We see this in the prevalence of "mommy blogs" and parenting groups who express deep concern about feeling ready, making mistakes, or not knowing what they will need to do when the child is born. Some people are able to do so openly, to the point where it is now the stuff of memes, and indeed some can turn a profit as parents whose brand is expressing failure.

In an ideal situation, it can be the responsibility of everyone—community, health care providers, and kinship networks—to share information and knowledge about basic safety, normal infant behaviour, and how to navigate the many forces of harm in our worlds. Midwives regularly instruct new parents on what to expect from a neonate—not because there is a deficiency but because they have the benefit of interacting with many infants and have developed a confidence and comfort level through repetition. This is also found in the knowledge of community grandmas and aunties. There is so much we are not told or shown about how to care for a child! I remember learning about infant breathing patterns (regularly erratic and uneven) and being absolutely in awe of parents who must get used to observing these patterns and managing the panic about when their little one will take their next breath, all the while holding their own. And this is all considered normal!

Many people struggle to attend prenatal and parenting classes on top of all the other things going on in their lives. It can be like a part-time or sometimes full-time job to just attend medical appointments, go to meetings, gather supplies. On top of these necessary tasks are people's paid jobs, their search to secure housing in an increasingly expensive market, their work dealing with family dynamics or trying to build supportive relationships, all while under the threat of apprehension or surveillance by social workers.

BREAKING FROM INTERGENERATIONAL FORMS OF EXTRACTION

Clinical systems are by design complex and confusing, with various silos and separate departments that operate under massive bureaucracies governed at a distance by boards concerned with liability and the bottom line, not the well-being of service users. The quality of a person's experience within that system is directly linked to their ability to navigate these infrastructures with ease. For example, in hospital settings, if a patient doesn't know where to access a shower or toiletries (especially in an emergency where they could not pack), what assumptions will staff make if they are unkempt? If they forget a phone charger and cannot look up the names of their health providers on their device and are managing, say, chronic fatigue from pregnancy, how will this reflect on their preparedness? Part of our role as birthworkers, then, is to prepare and explain as much as possible what to expect, how to make enquiries about resources, and how to strategize when miscommunication and bias inevitably happen.

Alas, there are so many ways for this system to entrench itself in people's lives and in our communities: people who are under extended care (youth who grew up in foster care, formerly crown wards), adoptees and Sixties Scoop survivors and their extended relatives and descendants, and anyone who has had a previously closed file or police involvement for other reasons. For lots of community members, dealing with CAS is like negotiating with a colonial settler entity in your home—you fight and try to advocate, or cooperate and comply, or you try some combination of all these strategies. Like land defenders and water protectors, we demand a right to our own children while constantly dodging very real attacks and threats from those who would try to extract our children. For some, CAS is both real and imagined—they may not have had direct lived experience with the agency but the spectre of sudden separation is ever present, bringing fear to the forefront of decision-making and planning. How do I avoid interacting with biased clinical staff? How do I receive quality prenatal care without disclosing my food insecurity? Is the housing I am in adequate? What is the likelihood of a breach of trust with every person I talk to? These are the questions that haunt Indigenous families, especially while pregnant—a time that should be about resting, celebrating, and nesting becomes marred with these realities.

We rely on getting "one of the good ones," workers who will go through the motions and close the file quickly or refer on to voluntary services and offer up material resources. However, even this help is often coercive, especially as funding for CAS agencies increases over the provision of community care. The deliberate redirection of funding away from community agencies and into CAS is a direct attack on community safety and our ability to support ourselves through self-organizing.

Recently, a few provinces in Canada have announced they are eliminating the practice of "birth alerts" within the hospital and health care system. Previously, if an individual under a "birth alert" presented at any hospital or health care setting in that province, the CAS/CFS agency would be notified to enable apprehension or intervention. We have survivors of apprehension to thank for this important shift and recognition of harm. With this change, there is a renewed hope that other policies can be abolished as well—but in the vacuum of a clear alternative, I also fear what may replace it. How can we truly engage in consensual intercommunication among health care providers, social workers, and outside agencies? How do we respond in an accountable and relational way to crisis or harm? Why is the performance of compliance (informing your worker when labour is happening and birth is imminent) a marker of good behaviour?

BUILDING COMMUNITY-BASED SELF-DETERMINED SUPPORT PROGRAMS: A JOURNEY THROUGH CYCLES

Given our understanding of the conditions urban Indigenous people in Toronto face in the birthing process, we organized the Baby

Bundle Project into four phases we felt would help to create community self-determination through their journey. The four phases include: (1) the undoing, (2) the resurgence, (3) the rebuilding, and (4) the implementation/living our truths.

THE UNDOING

In the undoing phase of the Baby Bundle Project, we focus on the removal and dismantling of a colonial mindset. We focus on mindset because the actual structures of CAS, police, prisons, et cetera. still exist and our perspective is often the only thing we have control over at this time. This process is about weeding out the ways our behaviour, thought patterns, and feelings reinforce settler colonial control over our families. Reflection questions like, What if I trusted people fully to be their resilient survivor selves before, during, and after our relationship? What if my actions reflected the belief that the person receiving care and support is the expert of their lives and knows what's best for themselves given all the information and options? What if I trusted in myself and my team/community to hold space for needs that are otherwise ignored, suppressed, or left unaddressed? We remind ourselves that Maslow got it wrong in his "hierarchy of needs." In that system, there is an overfocus on meeting basic needs, which dehumanizes the dreams and goals "service users" have for themselves, their children, and their families. This is a missed opportunity to validate and support those dreams and goals and build trust through the acknowledgment of a whole person—not just their receipt of essential support services.

THE RESURGENCE

Understanding community in our current social context, the Baby Bundle Project asks us to dig deep into understanding longstanding cultural roles and about ancestral and "historic" ways of living, doing, and being. Reflection questions for us in this phase include, What systems were in place to make possible the work of traditional midwives? What enabled them to travel, be sought out, and hone their craft? Who were their helpers? What did labouring people do before they got there? How did we prepare, birth, and recover? What did trust and reciprocal care look like? From here we reflect and apply these principles to our present reality. What are my specific gifts and skills? Be specific, humble, and direct while centring your own self-worth. We can't be everything to everyone, but we can know ourselves.

Here I also think about who does this work and why, what permission or alignment do we seek? There is a strong pull to professionalization of roles, especially in a social service/clinical model, but what we are building towards is not more professionals—it is a restoration and resurgence of these roles as they contribute to our collective community well-being.

THE REBUILDING → IMPLEMENTATION/LIVING OUR TRUTHS

Action. The time of doing. The scary part!

In phase three of the Baby Bundle Project we start asking, offering, What do you need? How can I support you? Am I being honest with where I am at, that I am just learning and want to learn together? I had to know my own limits, not agree to providing care that I couldn't do. I had to be vulnerable and have relationships that I could lean on and trust. Listening to feedback, constantly adjusting and pivoting, I thought and still do think a lot about the transactional nature of professionalized caregiving; health care relationships where your cooperation and attendance is currency. The ability to state your needs and receive quality care lies in the hands of the provider rather than the service user. For folks with trauma from service providers (basically all of us), keeping providers at an arm's length, carefully controlling disclosures and the flow of information about your life are all techniques to build some kind of safety net in the absence of actual safety in these relationships. It's frustrating to see someone holding back, knowing there's more to their story and experience. That's a reminder of the need to show up and do the things you said you would. To demonstrate through actions these values that are professed. Don't push for more, but express yourself freely, show examples of our own humanity that are nonthreatening (I find swearing helps if that's the vibe), hold each disclosure with care and compassion, their tentative steps towards trusting you are precious.

In the fourth and final phase of the Baby Bundle Project we focus on centring power—theirs and yours. I've seen relationships where people are overjoyed to finally find a safer provider, a stable caring relationship, a grounding presence. And in our need to celebrate and validate/affirm, we may offer too much, cross a boundary, or fail to notice how we might be reinforcing that colonial mindset (this time in a saviourship or "positive" way). Freely offering suggestions, opinions, or life experiences may not align with the needs of the person you are working with. The relief from decision fatigue is a tempting one, to take the burden of making hard choices away from the person, but this is where caregiving can become toxic. At this point, we must go back through these phases and think about what it would be like to give someone their power back, to affirm that they have what is needed to decide *for themselves* and *be fully supported to do so—even if we don't agree!* This is where transformation can happen, where healing is possible.

I have so many teachers, aunties, chosen family, fellow birth workers, clients, and people to thank for literally pushing and birthing me into this role (often reluctantly). I acknowledge I have so much more learning and growing (gestating if you will!) to look forward to.

CHAPTER 13
SOCIAL WORK'S VERY COMPLICATED RELATIONSHIP WITH INDIGENOUS LANGUAGES

Rochelle Allan

Throughout my language-learning journey, I have had to re-evaluate what I am capable of, how I can integrate the language into my life, and to what extent I can pass it along to the next generation. The stories that we usually hear about Indigenous-language revitalization focus on resilience and reclamation, but it's often much more complicated—not to mention difficult and emotional—than that.

—SHELBY LISK, "FOR OUR CHILDREN"

I spend a lot of my time these days thinking about Indigenous language learning and social work.[1] It is an unusual combination, but one we should start paying more attention to if we are to imagine abolitionist and decolonizing possibilities and to reflect on and limit the harm we as social workers do to Indigenous communities and languages. I did not expect to be writing about this topic. I was not destined to be here—in fact, seven years ago, I was not involved in language learning at all. I was, however, looking for a way to support language development for my kids in Toronto.

I had recently gotten married and wanted my future children to have access to Anishinaabemowin in ways I did not have when I was a child. I thought the way to go about this was to connect with Indigenous organizations in my city and offer my assistance in developing programs. I could write grants or work behind-the-scenes to help get something going. I had heard about the success of immersion programs for children in Hawai'i (Kaiapuni schools), New Zealand, and more locally in the Ojibwe immersion program Waadookodaading. It seemed like immersion was the natural next step for my children and others seeking to learn Anishinaabemowin in the city.

I thought this would be an easy process. I had spent years listening to Toronto's Indigenous social service organizations talk about how much they valued language revitalization and how much they were doing for it, but when I approached these same organizations, I couldn't get anyone to even talk to me about it. I was shocked. I went around to language programs and events and was surprised that despite using buzz words like "language nest" and "immersion" there was actually very little language learning happening at the events and programs. And, as it turned out, there seemed to be little interest in doing more.

At that time, I was also in a Master of Social Work program and had the privilege of being around several fluent Anishinaabemowin speakers. These women were inspiring to me and hearing them speak encouraged me to study independently. I found online resources and books and started on my journey, thinking that the organizations I had first approached would eventually come around, and I would be better able to support them if I had at least some language skill. Unfortunately, a couple of years went by, and I was now ready to welcome children to our family, but the organizations had not come around. Feeling defeated, I complained to a stranger about the situation while attending an Anishinaabemowin language conference. This older woman advised me that I should not continue waiting for organizations to help me. If I wanted my kids to have access to language, I would have to be the one to provide it. This was quite the revelation. The suggestion to go on without the support of an organization was quite empowering.

I started with a goal to expose my kids to as much language as possible after reading a study suggesting this could assist with language learning later in life.[2] I covered my house in post-it notes with things to say to the kids, translated in Anishinaabemowin. I bought Anishinaabemowin books to read to them and played Anishinaabemowin audio in the house as much as possible. My language skills were not strong. I was still very much a beginner, but I felt like I had nothing to lose. I was so embarrassed of my language skills at that point that I have very little video footage of me speaking, but I spoke and read to the kids as much as possible and, as I did, I got better. I decided to continue trying as long as I could.

In the intervening five years, we have learned a lot of language together. We still only speak to the kids in Anishinaabemowin and they are quite competent speakers for their ages (four and five years old). I still want to support existing language programs, but I fear compromising the progress being made through my home language learning if I invest too much time in programs constrained by funders and colonial forms of bureaucracy.

THE INTERSECTIONS OF SOCIAL WORK AND LANGUAGE REVITALIZATION

Institutional language initiatives both contribute to and undermine Indigenous language revitalization. My social work education has given me tools to navigate language learning in a unique way. This education has helped me develop a framework to understand language learning as a form of healing, not just skill building. This education has also given me tools to discuss and navigate the underlying grief and trauma that comes from language loss.

But I am also painfully aware that the intrusion of social workers in the lives of my community is a main reason that I am having to learn my language now rather than growing up with it as a child. I am living the colonial impact of decisions of social workers and social service organizations to remove children from our communities and to implement assimilation policies that prioritized English and French. If families used an Indigenous language in their home, they could be targeted and have their children taken away. The result was language collapse and a near complete breakdown in intergenerational transmission as families tried to protect their children. Given this history, I see language learning and the active support of social workers in that as a process of both decolonization and abolition of the control mechanisms of the profession. Our active contribution to this process will affect the health and well-being of Indigenous communities today and in the future.

Anishinaabemowin has several thousand speakers, but most fluent speakers are from older generations, and so the language is considered severely endangered. It is imperative that we start developing child speakers to improve the likelihood of long-term survival and usage of our language. Teaching Indigenous languages is very challenging and if done poorly can recreate or cause more trauma for Indigenous learners. As Anton Treuer points out, "Reforming broken systems of oppression will not work. We have to build new systems of liberation."[3] These discussions are particularly important right now in Canada given the creation of the Office of the Commissioner of Indigenous Languages. This office has come with promised increases in federal funding for language revitalization and preservation. In this climate, it will be important for grassroots language advocates to be heard and engaged in this process. If the only people engaged in these discussions are academics and large organizations (who are already systematically privileged), we will not see the significant change we need.

I think social workers can assist in this effort. We are taught skills to navigate complex situations and to discuss and analyze things intersectionally. We can help create spaces where language learning is understood as not just skill building but as a process of healing and resurgence. Social workers can help nonprofit organizations offering language-learning initiatives to step back when needed and to work collaboratively with grassroots individuals establishing a more ambitious and sustainable path forward. As Anton Treuer reminds us:

> Our governance systems, languages and cultures, economies and bodies have been under assault systemically for generations. We face both internal and external threats. We have lost a lot, but we have retained a lot too. Rebuilding and revitalizing require a systemic response. We can't just send a few warriors over the hill and expect them to vanquish all political, economic, cultural and linguistic threats. We have to very consciously build up our people as individuals and as communities.[4]

If social workers are to play a role in language revitalization, it will be important for us to reckon with our history of undermining and eliminating Indigenous languages through coercion and control and understand how this relationship still affects Indigenous language learners today.

SOCIAL WORK AND THE UNDERMINING OF INDIGENOUS LANGUAGES

It is not uncommon in my experience for Indigenous social workers to feel something more complicated than pride in their profession.

For many of us, the desire to help our community is partnered with the knowledge or at least the suggestion that the paths available to assist our communities are not as beneficial as we thought they would be. One thing that draws many people to social work and other helping professions is the idea of making things better. Unfortunately, the singular focus on action, over reflection or communication, has caused a great deal of harm.

I often muse about the fact that, in English, when we speak about acting on another person, we usually mention the actor first (*I* help you, *she* saves you, *we* remember him). I don't know the impact this word order has on our ideas, goals, and actions, but when I started learning Anishinaabemowin, I realized that this is not a universal way to phrase people's interactions. I began to wonder if the English "to the actor goes the glory" structure was pushing me to social work in pursuit of a false sense of control in the world (I will help them) and an unnecessary drive to act. In contrast to English, Anishinaabemowin speakers start independent clauses first with *you* (the audience), and only if *you* (the audience) *is not in the story* can I mention myself first, regardless of who is acting. The below chart helps show what this looks like for each language.

English	Anishinaabemowin template	English translation of pronoun order with directional indicators
I help you	gi____in	You ____ ← me
You help me	gi____ (i)	You ____ → me
She saves you	gi____ig	You ____ ← she
We(incl) remember him	gi____aanaan	You ____ → him ← me and others as well
You see him	gi____aa	You ____ → him

No matter the impact of this difference in order of pronouns, when I think of social work, I am struck by how much our thinking is focused on *action and ourselves as actors*: a profession *I* wanted to enter so that *I* could help others and *I* could improve society, et cetera. I think back on all the trauma put on families (including my own) that might have been avoided if a social worker had decided not to act, not to intervene, if our profession was built on a slightly different understanding of what helping meant. What if the profession had been created *to love* rather than *to act upon and intervene?* Much like policing, social work is now an industry that thrives and grows more powerful, trying to solve problems it created, often without admitting fault or changing in any significant way.

> Indigenous people in Canada first encountered the social work profession as wards of the federal government through the Department of Indian Affairs. Social workers were tasked to accompany Indian agents onto reserves to remove children to residential schools and later, in the 1960s and 1970s, to apprehend children deemed to be in need of protection.[5]

These actions were historically significant in interrupting the transmission of Indigenous languages. The trauma done by institutions still haunts survivors and their descendants and the actions of social workers today continue to affect current efforts in language revitalization. Social work, as Nicole Penak notes, is not just about individual organizations or individuals who work there; they are (we are) part of the larger system of settler colonialism. Penak argues:

> I've both spent my life engaged in Indigenous social services in this city and witnessed the rise of the phenomena of "Indigenous social work," now rather comfortably discussed in university curricula. As settler colonialism is not an event but a structure, a process that continues to unfold over time (Wolfe, 2006), I can't help but ponder the implications of these developments. It's important to note that "social work" is not synonymous or generalizable to all helping traditions. It is a regulated profession, with its own system of governance, registration, principles, education, history, practices, values, limits, and jurisdictions.[6]

There is, of course, amazing work happening in Indigenous social work scholarship and teaching. There are discussions about reconciliation, responsibility, and sovereignty happening now that never happened before. But I fear that the desire to act, without investing in deep relationships, still resides in our profession and its organizations and policies. Left unchecked, that impulse could be very dangerous to the success of language initiatives. Social service organizations often throw language initiatives under the "culture" umbrella or bring in someone to do a one-off workshop without thought to the specific skills and needs of language learners and the language itself. These types of programs waste a staggering amount of time, money, and energy on the part of both the learners and teachers, and for all the effort and money spent, learners do not develop their language abilities.

Many people don't realize that we are lucky to have a fair number of Indigenous Language Keepers in the city. For instance, the Toronto Aboriginal Research Project (TARP) reports that 19 percent of the urban population *is able to converse* in their Indigenous language.[7] That number is in line with numbers across the country. According to Statistics Canada, "In 2016, 15.6% of the Aboriginal population reported being able to conduct a conversation in an Aboriginal language."[8] In Toronto, however, the Indigenous population is widely dispersed within the general population, and to my knowledge, we don't have any programs to support and connect speakers or learners with each other, so the "language communities" are often confined to people who are from the same home community or who are related. It often feels like we are disadvantaged in building a language community. We need to rely on organizations that serve a broad range of people from different backgrounds for programming and information. Communities that lie outside of the organizations and funding structures and are often overlooked.

INSTITUTIONAL BARRIERS TO LANGUAGE LEARNING

At the start of my journey, I expected that the best way to engage in language revitalization would be by reaching out to professionals at Indigenous-serving organizations. I didn't have any fluent family members, I thought that the organizations and their teachers would be the ones I'd listen to and learn from. But the further I went in my learning, the more I realized that if I wanted to really give my kids the language, I needed to refocus my energy on the individuals who were interested in supporting us. So, when my son was born, I started to take him to find *speakers*—not just those who are considered "teachers" by organizations, but those who are just living their lives using the language: the older women hanging out and chatting in our language, a friend hundreds of kilometres away trying to do the same thing with her family, et cetera. It was through informal networks that language learning began to open up for me and my children. One of the things that Kathy Absolon and many others reiterate in discussions of Indigenous social work is the importance of self-location.[9] I'm grateful that I didn't give up. In going around and visiting with language speakers, I was surprised by how useful my social work education skills were. People often told me about the guilt they felt not knowing the language or not passing it on to their children. I wonder if our organizations have reached a point where it is no longer possible for them to reflect on who they are and what they value. The pressures of funders, liability, and capitalism have led to the idea that *they* are, in fact, the community, rather than *being a member of the community* with specific skills, roles, and responsibilities. Each organization now tries to serve everyone, and they have limited desire to work together. Through this loss of self-reflection and self-location, they have lost the ability to move with the unique needs of community members, limiting their effectiveness.

Certainly, looking around Toronto, a city full of beginner Anishinaabemowin classes, many serving a surprisingly high percentage of non-Indigenous students, I wonder why these programs are not coordinating with each other? If revitalization was truly the goal, we would have access to various levels of classes seeking to further develop fluency in the community. These programs would be connected to language speakers and advocates. They would be working to create safe spaces for Indigenous people. Instead, language is discussed in the TARP report as something you add to other programs to make them better. That very common mindset does not actually imagine the creation of language communities and true revitalization, it only imagines what language can do for other programs. It commodifies language for exploitation and unfortunately it ignores revitalization altogether.

This mindset justifies pulling language warriors away from their language work in favour of one-off talks and workshops, or to find a name for a building, or to label some things in an office. It also creates a dependency on organizational support that limits the types of informal networks that might arise in their place. As Treuer suggests:

As a result of these historical and contemporary practices, tribal people are often acclimated to dependency. When we want to get something going, we look to our tribal, state, provincial, or federal governments to provide the impetus, the money and the skilled people, and the buildings, and to pay for the heat and make it happen. We expect this. And when our expectations are not met, we get discouraged and give up.[10]

This common mindset is typified by this quote from the TARP report: "Despite the unlikelihood of full language fluency for many urban Aboriginal people, organizations remain committed to providing opportunities for Aboriginal community members to learn their languages."[11] If this is the starting place, one can easily see why the organizational desire to support innovative educators and programs is so low.

THE FOCUS ON NAMING RATHER THAN LANGUAGE LEARNING

Using Indigenous languages in naming spaces and programs is quickly becoming a very popular gesture by social service organizations since the release of the Truth and Reconciliation of Canada's *Calls to Action*.[12] There are many funds and actions that aim to show recognition of the harms of colonialism. Unfortunately, many of these actions lack meaningful accountability or do not help reverse the harms of colonialism. Often social service organizations that take part in these processes are more focused on recognition than on reconciliation, what Eve Tuck and K. Wayne Yang call "a move to innocence."[13] For Tuck and Yang, "Settler moves to innocence are those strategies or positionings that attempt to relieve the settler of feelings of guilt or responsibility without giving up land or power or privilege, without having to change much at all."[14]

In my own life, I have had the responsibility to name very few things, and when I have, I've used it as an opportunity to reflect on the use of Indigenous languages in naming and the motivations and factors that underlie these decisions. This type of reflection is not always done by people who request Indigenous people's help in a (re)naming process. When is it appropriate to use Indigenous words to name programs and things? Who should do the naming? What purpose does this naming serve? Who most benefits from this effort? By taking a deeper look into the trend towards Indigenous language naming as a response to the TRC *Calls to Action*, we are better able to understand its connection to language revitalization. Using Tuck and Yang's moves to innocence, I hope to open discussions and paths of reflection for organizations considering (re)naming and help ensure that these efforts don't undermine true progress for Indigenous-serving organizations, language revitalization efforts, and the well-being of language speakers and advocates.

MOVES TO INNOCENCE: SETTLER NATIVISM

When I started to become more actively involved in Indigenous language learning, I became aware of the growing number of requests for Indigenous language speakers to give names to things. People ask to translate names for programs or job titles, things they can put on signs, and even tattoos. While it may be very well intentioned, this rush to use Anishinaabemowin words or translations for signs, documents, advertisements, city streets, and all sorts of other things places undue pressure on language speakers and learners and has the unintended effect of disrupting the work of revitalization. When thinking about this process, I reflected on the first "move to innocence" identified by Tuck and Yang, "settler nativism." Settler nativism describes the common scenario of a settler "locating or inventing" a long-lost ancestor who has "Indian blood" to then mark themselves as blameless in the process of the eradication of Indigenous peoples. I feel as though this can also apply to organizations and institutions, such as social service organizations, who had a hand in eradicating Indigenous languages but now believe that a sign or pamphlet translated into Anishinaabemowin marks them as safe/blameless.

The motivation for requesting a name in an Indigenous language may be very different for the front-line staff person versus the executive director, and the motivations may change over time. There are many examples of organizations that started out community—or Indigenous—led but now have very different stakeholders and a very different composition and trajectory, and so it is important to step back and reflect on where the organization's motivation to adopt an Indigenous language name or signage comes from. Is this a commitment to building relationships with Indigenous communities, trusting our knowledge and experiences, and working more closely with us to address the harms of settler colonialism? Or is this a public relations move to maintain the organization's reputation as "progressive"? Exploring this topic in relation to social work organizations is particularly important because of the role the profession has played in the destruction of Indigenous languages, the continued role these organizations play in disrupting Indigenous family lines, and the potential danger that the solitary focus on Indigenous language names and signs poses to language revitalization. Is there reason to expect that this use of Indigenous language will make the Indigenous community more comfortable in that space? When a social work organization or a school labels offices, rooms, and maps in an Indigenous language but doesn't commit to supporting the growth of a language community—of people who can read or use these signs—they have (consciously or unconsciously) chosen to divert money to signage rather than language work. Often, these changes allow organizations to avoid difficult conversations about the ineffectiveness or inability of the organization to lead necessary transformative change. For instance, if you give a child protection office an Indigenous language name but don't do anything to give the kids you apprehend access to language, and don't give families credit for providing kids access to intergenerational language transmission, your agency's net impact on language is still negative. An abolitionist approach to language learning would refocus our energy on healing and away from these continued forms of coercion and dispossession.

MOVES TO INNOCENCE: COLONIAL EQUIVOCATION

Tuck and Yang also discuss a move to innocence they describe as "colonial equivocation," which basically means we have a habit of making it seem that all forms of oppression or loss are experienced in the same way and can be considered colonialism. They note, "calling different groups 'colonized' without describing their relationship to settler colonialism is an equivocation."[15] In relation to language learning, there is a practice of equivocation in which courses for Indigenous languages are funded, run, set up, and practiced in the same way as other language-learning opportunities. There is this sense from the government, universities, and even Indigenous organizations that beginner classes in Anishinaabemowin can be done in the same way as a program that offers French or Mandarin or Arabic classes.

Learning any language is challenging, but when Indigenous people seek to learn their languages, they are also contending with the colonial violence that undermined the passing on of these languages to children, the shame that was placed on language speakers, and the indifference of the Canadian government to rectifying this harm. There are issues of racism, inclusion, and lateral violence that need to be carefully considered and tended to if we are to build a truly safe program for Indigenous students and teachers. This is especially challenging because very few spaces are specific to Indigenous people. Community centres and postsecondary institutions, where a lot of Indigenous languages are taught, are often not allowed to exclude non-Indigenous people from classes. And teachers are rarely prepared to talk about the differences in motivation, capacity, and emotional investment in language learning for Indigenous and non-Indigenous students.

Often, non-Indigenous students, who want to be allies by learning Indigenous languages, come into these spaces unaware of their responsibility to create an environment that promotes and supports the capacity of Indigenous students to work towards language revitalization. This, as I've witnessed on numerous occasions, can lead to Indigenous learners having negative experiences and leaving language learning. If you are a non-Indigenous student of an Indigenous language, be sure you know that you are responsible to understand what your presence and behaviour in that class might mean for Indigenous people in those spaces.

MOVES TO INNOCENCE: FREE YOUR MIND AND THE REST WILL FOLLOW

The final move to innocence is what Tuck and Yang call "free your mind and the rest will follow."[16] Drawing on the work of Frantz Fanon, the authors affirm that while freeing one's mind from internalized colonialism is a step towards decolonization, it is not the only step. In social work spaces, settlers like to stay at the "free your mind" stage and don't like to move towards the next stages, which often require real tangible restitution.

There is no doubt that Indigenous people want to see their languages thrive, but inviting us to help in renaming places and things or funding beginner classes is not sufficient to revitalize our languages. We are all responsible for moving towards more tangible support for language revitalization, including advocating that more resources be available for grassroots teachers and learners. I often muse that one of the reasons my family has had some level of success with Anishinaabemowin as our home language is because it is *not* my job; I am free to do what is best for the language at every intersection. I don't need to justify it to others who are not involved in language work. I don't have to convince others to support me. I don't need to take on other tasks to benefit funders, boards, new learners, my detractors, or non-Indigenous people. We need more spaces where people can always do what is best for the language.

Social service organizations that offer language classes need to coordinate so they are not all offering the same class every week, year after year. Plans need to be made to move each language community's learning forward. If you work with an organization that offers language classes or is considering it, you can have these difficult conversations and get an honest sense of where you are at and what your organization can responsibly take on.

CONCLUSION

As both a social worker and an Indigenous person trying to learn my language, I am inspired by a piece of advice that comes from the *The Language Warrior's Manifesto*:

> Do the work even if you are the only one doing the work. You can't wait. Do treasure any partners who join you. Do accept help. Do find the money. But don't wait for any of those things. You can't convince everyone. And you don't need to. Take a triage approach. If someone needs convincing, they will take too much of your precious time. Send them a YouTube link to an inspiring language video or send them a book. Then get back to work.[17]

As Robyn Maynard and Leanne Betasamosake Simpson note in their book *Rehearsals for Living*, the work of abolition and decolonization is deeply entwined.[18] We need social workers working in organizations that engage in Indigenous language programming to talk with their peers about how to engage in this work in a responsible and sustainable way. Putting Anishinaabemowin names and signs on organizations can be of value to my family—as we raise our young children speaking Anishinaabemowin, the opportunity to read signage in the language is really fun!—but the question of whether these signs genuinely represent/respect the population and serve a need is rarely explored. Sometimes those signs are a false commitment to language work and reconciliation. Some organizations use naming and signage to be seen as "acting," but at the same time, they hold back language advocates' efforts to incorporate language into the same space in meaningful ways—which continues the carceral violence of social workers towards Indigenous language speakers.

Difficult conversations need to be had. There is value in the tools social workers bring to the table and they can assist in leading these conversations—they can insist that their organizations use Indigenous language with integrity and to benefit the community, not just as a symbolic action. Language advocates are given many roles. If social workers can take on facilitating organizational self-reflection and the difficult conversations needed to support Indigenous language learners, it will free up time to move language reclamation forward more effectively and show language warriors that we see the value of their work and we want our profession to be allies. We don't want to hide from our role in creating this crisis, but we do want to work now to change our path going forward.

CHAPTER 14
TORONTO INDIGENOUS HARM REDUCTION
Solidarity with Indigenous Encampment Residents

Brianna Olson Pitawanakwat

Toronto Indigenous Harm Reduction emerged in the spring of 2020 when Two-Spirit Inuk artist and land defender Nanook Gordon walked through their Parkdale community and witnessed the desolation and neglect faced by the houseless Indigenous community.[1] Fears were high during this first wave of the global COVID-19 pandemic. Many front-line services had shut down and a painful avoidance of houseless residents of the community was visible. Nanook commented on how people would literally walk across the street to avoid Indigenous people who were panhandling. Local businesses and drop-in shelters had shut down, creating a lack of access to essential supplies, public washrooms, and running water for people who were unhoused. This suffering and the inhumane conditions that were further exposed after the pandemic began is what motivated them to begin Toronto Indigenous Harm Reduction and the radical care it provided. A couple of months later, I joined. Wearing my jingle dress, carrying our drums, and singing our songs, Nanook and I, now engaged, are the co-organizers of Toronto Indigenous Harm Reduction.

Fast forward to spring 2021, almost a year later, and another crisis emerged as Indigenous people experiencing the houselessness crisis in Toronto found themselves further displaced and criminalized by the state after police began mass evictions of tents in public parks. On March 27, 2021, Toronto Indigenous Harm Reduction raised a teepee in Toronto. Three days later we took it down. While it was up, it created a space of ceremony, healing, and community at Allan Gardens Park, a gathering place for many houseless Indigenous people in the city.

It was also medicine to strengthen people against the coming displacement. *This teepee stood as a symbol of unconditional love, support, and the unconquered spirit of our people in the face of colonization.* The teepee, a traditional home of Plains Cree people, had been lent to the people in this space to lift their spirits at a time of suffering. On April 6, 2021, mass evictions were set to unfold against encampment residents at Moss Park, Scadding Court, Trinity Bellwoods, and other parks throughout the city—part of a new campaign of displacement.

The land and territory in which Toronto resides has a long history of Indigenous resistance and front-line movements on behalf of Indigenous peoples. As this land is governed by the One Dish One Spoon Wampum Belt Covenant, Indigenous peoples and subsequent nations are called to share peaceably and to steward the land and waters here. Grassroots movements, led by Indigenous individuals, have organized rallies, sit-ins, occupations, marches, and other acts of resistance to protest ongoing colonization and imbalances in the treaty relationships. We have come together around land and water defense, missing and murdered Indigenous women, girls, trans and Two-Spirit people, lack of clean drinking water in Indigenous communities, police brutality, and most recently, the houselessness crisis and encampment evictions.

The systemic displacement of Indigenous people in urban centres, specifically Toronto, is always happening. According to the Canadian Observatory on Homelessness, Indigenous Peoples in this city "constitute around 15 percent of those expe-

Construction of Toronto Indigenous Harm Reduction Teepee, 2021. Image by author.

riencing homelessness in the city, even though they make up only around 0.5 of the total population."[2] Indigenous people who are forcibly removed from treaty lands are then displaced and pushed around in the cities—this country's longest standing tradition. Many of the Indigenous houseless are residential school and Sixties Scoop survivors.

As the third wave of COVID-19 emerged, Indigenous folks who found themselves unhoused were being threatened with violence to clear encampments, with no promise of safety or permanent housing. Instead, they were being coerced inside spaces where people's lives were dismal. Overwhelmed shelter programs, many of which were over capacity on a given night, were also rife with COVID-19 outbreaks. Shelter hotels, which were a revolving door due to harsh guidelines and often had no capacity to support or tolerate the trauma that our people live with, were inadequately proposed by the city to deal with the tent evictions. Almost no options for permanent stable housing existed. A stark contrast to the enormous wealth and resources that exist in the City of Toronto.

We need more permanent solutions. Our people deserve better. This was all so tragic. What is hopeful, though, is the ways that Indigenous peoples make community wherever we go and show up for one another. We mark our grief and loss in feast and ceremony. We carry our Indigeneity with us wherever we go. But as we said at a recent rally in support of encampment residents: this situation is the criminalization of Indigenous place-making and care. And everyone's watching it. The state is criminalizing people for not having homes. And the reason we come out here to do what we do—we drum and we sing and we practice our cultures—is because many of the people in these camps are Indigenous. They speak their languages, they know their songs, they are brilliant Knowledge Holders. Many are Elders themselves. And we practice our cultures because guess what else is criminalized in this country? Being Indigenous is criminalized. So, if they're going to come in and they're going to arrest everybody, they can do it while we are practising our cultures, just like they've done for hundreds of years in this country.

CHAPTER 15
BLACK CREEK COMMUNITY FARM
Mutual Aid, Abolition, and Food Justice in Jane and Finch

Suzanne Narain, Sabrina "Butterfly" Gopaul, Sam Tecle, Zakisha Brown, Rosie Mishaiel, Anan Lololi, and Leticia Ama Deawuo

During a Zoom discussion with other members of the Black Creek Community Farm (BCCF), Zakisha Brown leans back in her chair in reflection, but as the conversation begins to centre on what is at the heart of their organization, she finally jumps in, "We communicate with a different form of language. That's what growing food is about. That's what food justice and food sovereignty is about. What I learned from the Black Creek Community Farm, is that there is no culture without agriculture."[1] Food is at the centre of life, it is a human right, a basic need, yet not everyone is granted the privilege of having access to healthy and affordable food.

The neighbourhood of Jane and Finch in Toronto, where BCCF is situated, is known as a food desert, a place where there is little access to affordable and nutritious food. Like so many lower-income communities in North America, the neighbourhood is filled with a surplus of fast-food chains and predatory grocery stores seeking to capitalize on a captive clientele who live in high rise apartments and don't always have access to a vehicle for shopping.

Zakisha continues:

> What I learned from Black Creek Community Farm really baffled my mind, the reality of food injustice and racism existing within our community. But, it was true, when I go to Richmond Hill [a suburb north of Toronto] and go to Shoppers Drug Mart there, they have so many more options, so much variety.

Given that deserts occur naturally and there is nothing natural about being denied access to food, it is perhaps more appropriate to use the term "food apartheid" to describe the social conditions in Jane and Finch.[2] Apartheid is planned and governed by the state and the capitalist system. Food apartheid makes it possible for wealthier communities in Toronto, like Richmond Hill or Yorkville, to have access to more affordable healthy food than others, like Jane and Finch.

A 2009 Heart and Stroke Foundation study revealed that prices for groceries in Jane and Finch were higher than those of higher income suburban areas.[3] Drawing on that research and the Three Cities Within Toronto study, the activist group Jane and Finch Action Against Poverty (JFAAP) led the The Right Food: Right to Food campaign that raised awareness of these disparities.[4] Focused not only on the high price of food in the neighbourhood but also the quality of produce that was available, this campaign created opportunities for on-the-ground conversations that put this inequality into the context of everyday life for the residents of Jane and Finch.

This disparity has grown more rampant with hypersurveillance and criminalization of residents at grocery stores. As a result, Jane and Finch residents suffer disproportionately from dietary health issues, including higher rates of diabetes and higher cholesterol levels. Over 80 percent of the residents in the Jane and Finch area, many of whom are immigrants or newcomers, are living below the poverty line.[5] BCCF is a space of possibility amidst these harsh realities. In the last ten years, as Jane and Finch residents began to take control of an organization that was largely run by white folks with little knowledge of or connection to the community, BCCF transformed from an ineffective community farm into a site of food justice.

HISTORY OF THE FARM

BCCF was preceded by Solomon Boye, who ran the farm under the Toronto Urban Farms. For this current iteration of BCCF leaders, it is important to honour the work of Solomon Boye, a Black farmer, who laid the foundation of the farm in the community. At that time, Solomon worked closely with the City of Toronto, but the farm was later taken over by Everdale, a primarily white-led organization from Hillsburgh, Ontario.

Everdale launched the eight-acre urban farm at the southeast corner of Jane Street and Steeles Avenue in 2012. In its early days, many community residents were unaware that a farm even existed in the area. Everdale held several consultations to try to involve the community, but without much connection to the neighbourhood, they operated with very little knowledge of working in low-income racialized communities. As Leticia reflects, "This included a lack of understanding of some of the key issues that residents faced, especially anti-Black racism." It quickly became apparent that a community presence was needed at the farm, and through these consultations, the BCCF resident's council and steering committee were formed.

Many members of the resident's council were also members of JFAAP, who had long been doing work on food justice in the community. They identified a major disconnect between the white liberal community organization operating the farm and the needs of the wider community and invited Connect the Dots, a coalition of organizers and community residents in Jane and Finch, to conduct several anti-oppression trainings at the farm. Later, mediations were held with Everdale, the farmers, and the community around the conflicts that had arisen. Leticia Deawuo, who became the inaugural executive director, reflects back to this time: "It took a lot of effort from a lot of people who are on this call today and those that are not even here: people who got burnt, people who were traumatized, all of it, to really make sure that we were creating a community farm."

While the BCCF started as a project led by Everdale, community residents organized around it, and Afri-Can Food Basket, the Black Farmers Collective, Food Share, and JFAAP played a huge role in its development, vibrancy, and sustainability. Butterfly Gopaul, a resident's council and steering committee member, remarked, "Our ideas got co-opted by this organization and we had to fight tooth-and-nail to try to get it back or try to make it be a community space again." The early days at the farm were difficult for many farmers, workers, and residents with the ongoing racism, white supremacy, and discrimination experienced from Everdale; however, the site in and of itself was a space for healing and growth for the community, which is why we fought so hard to make it ours.

Residents of the community were involved in building the

greenhouses, getting the soil prepared, harvesting vegetables, and running programs. Some of the key stakeholders at the farm were Afri-Can Food Basket, Food Share, the Black Farmers Collective, York University, and the Toronto Regional Conservatory Authority (TRCA). This coalition worked with the resident's council to transition Everdale out of its leadership role so the farm could be community-led. While there were a lot of struggles, heartaches, and much labour to envision and bring these goals to fruition, everyone stayed the course and remained committed to the project.

URBAN FARM LIFE

The farm has become a second home to many in the community. It is a space for public education, healing, and growth. In 2020, in the midst of the COVID-19 pandemic, the farm harvested over twenty thousand pounds of produce to be distributed in the community. The farm runs various programs such as outdoor education for elementary school children, mentorship programs for youth, and programs for seniors. People who have been through these programs have commented that they have made life-long friendships and relationships at the farm.

The farm has held our community's young people, creating meaningful employment opportunities and providing people with mentorship and tangible skills. As Suzanne Narain recounts:

> One day, I walked into the farm and saw one of the first students I ever taught when I was in teacher's college ten years prior. She was doing a mentorship program at the farm and had been struggling a bit since the passing of her mom but was getting a lot of support from the folks at the farm.

While in no way does the farm replace therapy or other vital social work programming, it offers an alternative site of demonstrating "care." For the past decade, it has become a makeshift drop-in centre, where people in the community can go almost anytime, walk in nature, find someone to chat with, and organize free meetings and events.

BCCF prioritizes people in the community who are in socioeconomic need. The process of outlining the terms of reference for the farm, its definitions of "marginalized" and "community" took a great deal of time and effort. We needed to ensure no one would be left behind in the employment and organizing of the farm. As Rosie Mensah describes, "The farm is based on intergenerational learning. Right from the very beginning, we prioritized drawing upon the knowledge of farmers in our community who are coming from different places around the world." Rosie links the work of the farm with the politics of abolition, explaining that this form of intergenerational learning also means quite literally creating access to space for Black and other racialized folks in the community to create new worlds. By doing so, she suggests, the farm isn't just about planting and seeding, but about recognizing the importance of "getting police officers out of our grocery stores, making things like baby formula and food free for folks who need it, taking over green spaces and corridors to plant food, and imagining access to quality food outside of the capitalist economy." Zakisha Brown, who was one of the first youth involved in the mentorship program at the farm, affirmed what Rosie was saying:

> [BCCF] really gave me peace of mind and connected me with nature. It helped me be more present in life. I feel like being in a space that grounds you, and makes you realize the important aspects of life ... taught me that letting your food be your medicine and your medicine be food is not just a saying, it's an active part of your life. [At the farm] we cry of happiness, cry of sadness, we purge, we have bonfires, have conversations, we have walks, and all of that really made me look at Toronto different. To look at my community and what can be created if you harness that energy in this beautiful environment. I had the opportunity to help build the greenhouses when I was in the mentorship program. And that right there made me like, "Is this real life? Who am I, at twenty, twenty-one years old, helping to build a greenhouse and learning about greenhouses and the importance of it?" I think being around that environment opened my eyes to so much, especially as an artist, to help implement more substance in my lyrics too.

Zakisha's reflections embody what is at the heart of the farm as a BIPOC and community-led space for learning, growing, and belonging. Butterfly remarked that "we came to the table to resist, to build, and to dream [together]." The farm provides a place where new possibilities for learning about food and food processes exists, a place for us to push back against large food corporations and demand more green space in our community. Additionally, it allows the community to become its own educators, to shift from traditionally trained teachers, community farmers who are normatively white, and social workers, to elders in our community who had been farming for generations to share their knowledge and mentor their neighbours.

Sam Tecle, a member of the resident's council, also brought forward that "the farm provides a space to dream and to ask questions like: Why doesn't everybody have what they need to eat? How do we find different ways of taking care of each other beyond the paradigms that we have?" The workers, residents, organizers, and people behind the development of the farm have dedicated time, energy, and resources to think about how to intervene in the systemic oppression within the food system, how to ensure our community has more access to fresh and affordable food, and maybe most significantly how to address the multiple factors of poverty and discrimination that many people in the community face.

BLACK CREEK FOOD JUSTICE NETWORK

Butterfly Gopaul recalled that this type of organizing and struggling to imagine food justice for Jane and Finch was instrumental in developing the political orientation of the farm. She recounts, "After Everdale left, the work of implementing our politics—around pay grades, job equity, access to organic food . . . having those hard conversations . . . birthed the Black Creek Food Justice Network." Black Creek Food Justice Network (BCFJN) was a working group that emerged out of the farm in the early 2010s. BCFJN hosts meetings on the first Monday of every month to discuss issues of food justice and to plan actions and events. In their report *Fighting for Food Justice in the Black Creek Community*, BCFJN states:

> Food justice means many things at once to the community. It means being able to access affordable, culturally relevant, and healthy food. It means being able to easily get to and from gro-

cery stores. It means not having food locked away from your access and not being policed by virtue of your race and socioeconomic status.[6]

BCFJN garnered a lot of community interest and brought together organizations across the province to mobilize for "farm to table" food justice. BCFJN has partnered with organizations such as JFAAP, Justicia for Migrant Workers, Food Not Bombs, Workers Action Centre, the Network for the Elimination of Police Violence, and the National Farmers Union. Over the course of the past decade, BCFJN has organized many events and programs, such as the Food Frequency radio program on CHRY 105.5FM (York University and Jane and Finch's community radio station).[7] One of the most significant actions that the BCFJN has carried out is the annual Food Justice Day of Action. The Food Justice Day of Action involves a series of community consultations and conversations on food justice that culminate in direct actions, panels, and reports. On a recent Day of Action, over a hundred protestors and allies gathered at the corner of Jane and Finch to support the following demands: (a) improve growing spaces and support urban growing, (b) make food more affordable by raising wages and social safety nets, (c) fight for justice for the people that work to feed us, (d) stop criminalizing our communities, and (e) connect food and health.

Under each of these demands are more detailed visions that the network put forward.[8] During the Day of Action, participants engaged in guerilla gardening where members of the BCFJN built beds and planted vegetable along two kilometers of the southeast side of Jane Street from Finch Avenue to Driftwood Avenue, a stretch of road that is car-centric, with lots of concrete and little green space. Rally-goers met at the intersection, some dressed up as broccoli, carrots, and other vegetables, and marched up Jane Street, singing, dancing, and giving speeches about food justice while planting kale, beets, radishes, callaloo, and peas. The purpose of the guerilla gardening was to take over green space in our community left abandoned by the city and to demonstrate how food planting and growing could be more accessible in the neighbourhood. This action was meant to be both symbolic and pragmatic by demonstrating to the different levels of government how we could make green spaces more agriculturally friendly. It was also meant to show community members that we can cultivate food in public spaces and grow culturally relevant food in our neighbourhood without waiting for the government, outside organizations, or private companies to do it.

FOOD JUSTICE AS ABOLITIONIST POLITICS

Sam Tecle reminded the group during the Zoom chat that the farm has become a "site of imagination." Leticia Deawuo identified the campaign to get Toronto police out of local grocery stores as an example of the type of political work that emerged out of conversations at the farm. Grocery stores in Jane and Finch may not have the freshest produce, but they are well stocked with undercover police and security guards.

For over a decade, undercover police officers have been patrolling the aisles of the grocery stores in our neighbourhood, charging people with theft under $5,000 for stealing food. A charge of this nature goes on someone's record and prevents them from being able to apply to certain jobs, keeping people stuck in the web of poverty, unable to access employment and food. BCCF members argued that it was the doling out charges and fines for stealing food in a grocery store that was, in fact, *the criminal act*. People should be able to access food. No one steals food for fun, people steal food because they are hungry. Yet, in Jane and Finch, baby formula, cough and allergy medication, and other necessities are locked away in cages. People who need them must pay for the product first and then be escorted to these cages to get their product—these measures only take place in communities like ours and it is completely dehumanizing. BCCF encountered young people and elders alike who have been charged and banned from the local malls for taking food from the grocery stores.

JFAAP and BCCF started working with youth and elders in our community to ensure that they are still able to access services at the mall after these punitive measures. In April 2019, the No Frills grocery store at the Yorkgate Mall banned strollers, personal trolleys, backpacks, or reusable bags as part of a new policy aimed at preventing food theft. JFAAP and BCFJN quickly responded to this blatant act of discrimination by writing an open letter and shared it across social media.[9] This letter garnered significant attention and No Frills revoked the ban. No Frills, owned by Loblaws, the largest grocery chain in Canada, then released a statement claiming the policy banned trolleys and backpacks in all of their stores; however, activists charged that there is no implementation of this policy in their downtown stores or elsewhere in the city. The ban and policy were discriminatory in nature: classist, racist, sexist, ableist, and misogynistic. BCFJN and JFAAP's speedy response put pressure on No Frills and Loblaws to reverse this discriminatory policy.

This political engagement is an example of what social work might look like if it were community-led and oriented around a transformative rather than reparational framework. Members of the community had space to conceptualize what abolition could look like in our food system through these actions. A lot of conversations went into creating an equitable and accessible model at the farm; for example, a sliding scale option for produce, work opportunities for folks in the community, the opening of greenspace to community where access is often restricted, and a space where people can escape the constant surveillance and monitoring experienced in stores, social work agencies, workplaces, and other institutions in the neighbourhood. On a broader scale, this engaged community work is centred around the desire to abolish capitalism and imagine new kinds of economic and social systems, quite literally from the soil up and directly on the land.

Our dream of abolition is centred around space and imagining what could be possible if we started to grow food, share land, and exchange knowledge differently. "It is also looking at knowledge sharing, about the way that farmers were originally farmer to farmer, sharing seeds, and exchanging knowledge," said Leticia. In addition to thinking about how knowledge sharing models can be different, the BCCF also offers a food share program, where folks from the community are able to freely access fresh produce as well as canned and boxed goods. Zakisha commented, "The BCCF was the first organization that I've come across where it says: 'We trust you. Here, take your bag of veggies and put the amount here in this jar.' No one's really overseeing you, watching you, all that. It creates an environment of trust ... and an abundance mentality instead of scarcity." The farm values treating people with dignity and accessing food as a basic human right not as a charitable act or a community service.

FOOD JUSTICE AS MUTUAL AID

On the Zoom call, we spent a lot of time talking about our most recent work in response to the COVID-19 pandemic, examining how we seemed to be ahead of a lot of organizations in the city in terms of identifying needs and mobilizing to support community. When asked about practicing mutual aid, Suzanne Narain reflected:

> We were doing mutual aid before mutual aid became a thing, right? Like this has been a part of our life at BCCF. We're so connected to each other. That is how we were able to mobilize on so many different fronts for so long. It's not just COVID. It's not just getting police out of schools. It has been decades and decades of struggle that we have been able to mobilize and often win.

When the World Health Organization declared a global pandemic in March 2020 and we went into lockdown, many people lost their jobs or were forced to work on the front lines in grocery stores, cleaning hospitals, doing gig work like deliveries without the proper personal protective equipment. Many seniors in our neighbourhood were unable to travel to get groceries and some families were in financial distress and unable to afford groceries because of lost income. The emergency social assistance program offered by the federal government during the COVID-19 pandemic had not yet started.

We quickly saw the disparity between those who could access and stockpile resources and those who could not. In the beginning of the pandemic, some people were spending hundreds of dollars on groceries; however, people in our community did not have that kind of disposable income available. The idea of the "Good Box" came out of knowing that the elders, aunties, and single parent households in our community were even more limited in their ability to access food. The pandemic, in addition to the loss of jobs, people getting severely sick and dying, and the lack of governmental assistance, really exasperated the food insecurity that already existed in the community. With no budget to offer emergency food boxes, we started to make phone calls, hoping to be able to support about two hundred families. The need was so high that we had to start an online fundraiser to support more families. Even people without online access would come to the farm to donate money after hearing about the fundraiser. As of August 2021, the farm distributed over twenty-eight thousand food boxes to approximately twenty-thousand people. The food boxes were delivered to people's door and did not require them to come and stand in line like they do at a food bank. The farm has always been committed to providing food to families in a dignified way, and for us this is not charity but a form of mutual aid—any one of us could be in precarious financial circumstances, and we want to make sure there are established relationships and practices that help our community help ourselves. The demand for food boxes was really high, with requests from people outside the catchment area, and we tried to reach as many people as possible with the generous support and organization of Food Share, something that typical social service or social work organizations aren't able to do with such flexibility. The success of the emergency food box was a result of people coming together to support and take care of each other. It was also a reflection of the kind of support and mutual aid work that has been the cornerstone of the Jane and Finch community. When COVID-19 happened, our response was immediate because we had already been looking out for and taking care of each other. BCCF, JFAAP, BCFJN, to name a few organizations in the Jane and Finch area, have been on the ground and on the front lines supporting families in material and meaningful ways, and we were able to provide more immediate support than any government aid could. While we continued—and continue—to push for the government to take seriously their commitment to social welfare, we mobilized through a labour of love focused on each other's survival despite this state abandonment.

Our community takes mutual aid seriously. It isn't a fad or a novel activist strategy that emerges in crises and then disappears. It's not social work–style charity where people are surveilled, moralized to, burdened with unnecessary bureaucracy, or made to feel shame. We have been connected to each other and have been mobilizing together on multiple fronts *as community*. We operate through a neighbourliness that is reminiscent of the communal bonds found in many of the places that folks in Jane and Finch migrate from. We listen and act. Through getting police out of schools and grocery stores, fighting for affordable housing, responding to crises of food insecurity, and so much more, we take care of each other.

NOTES

INTRODUCTION

1. Carrie Freshour and Brian Williams, "Abolition in the Time of COVID-19," *Antipode Online*, April 9, 2020, antipodeonline.org.
2. Sparrow A. Preston, "Abolitionist Disjuncture: Reducing Police Violence in Frontline Social Work," *Intersectionalities: A Global Journal of Social Work, Analysis, Research, Polity, and Practice* 9 no. 1 (2021): 142–53; Vava Tampa, "As Social Workers, We Must Do More Than Stand in Solidarity with Black People," *The Guardian*, October 20, 2020, theguardian.com.
3. Christine A. Walsh, Kimberly Van Patten, Natalie St-Denis, and Les Jerome, "Towards Decolonization and Indigenization of Social Work Research: Responding to the Truth and Reconciliation Commission's Calls to Action," *Canadian Journal of Native Education* 40 no. 1 (2018): 144–63.
4. In 2021, due to personal reasons, Nicole Penak stepped away from the project, but her fingerprints are felt throughout the work, and we are grateful for her contributions to the conceptualization of the project and the contributors she brought into the process.
5. Dean Spade, *Mutual Aid: Building Solidarity During this Crisis (and the next)* (London: Verso, 2020).
6. Chris Chapman and A. J. Withers, *A Violent History of Benevolence: Interlocking Oppressions in the Moral Economies of Social Working* (Toronto: University of Toronto Press, 2019); Craig Fortier and Edward Hon-Sing Wong, "The Settler Colonialism of Social Work and the Social Work of Settler Colonialism," *Settler Colonial Studies* 9 no. 4 (2019): 437–56.
7. Chapman and Withers, *Violent History of Benevolence*.
8. David M. Austin, "The Flexner Myth and the History of Social Work," *Social Service Review* 57 no. 3 (1983): 361.
9. Therese Jennissen and Colleen Lundy, *One Hundred Years of Social Work: A History of the Profession in English Canada, 1900-2000* (Waterloo, ON: Wilfrid Laurier University Press, 2011), 21.
10. Malcolm Carey and Victoria Foster, "Social Work, Ideology, Discourse and the Limits of Post-Hegemony," *Journal of Social Work* 13 no. 3 (2013): 248–66; Jennissen and Lundy, *One Hundred Years*.
11. Edward Said, "Professional and Amateurs," in *Representations of the Intellectual: The 1993 Reith Lectures* (New York: Vintage, 1994), 68.

12. Uzo Anucha, "Exploring a New Direction for Social Work Education and Training in Nigeria," *Social Work Education* 27 no. 3 (2008): 229–42.
13. Richard L. Edwards, Wes Shera, P. Nelson Reid, and Reginald York, "Social Work Practice and Education in the US and Canada," *Social Work Education* 25 no. 1 (2006), 28.
14. Therese Jennissen and Colleen Lundy, *Keeping Sight of Social Justice: 80 Years of Building CASW* (Canadian Association of Social Workers, 2006), casw-acts.ca.
15. Jennissen and Lundy, *One Hundred Years*, 30.
16. Jennissen and Lundy, *One Hundred Years*, 31.
17. Jennissen and Lundy, *One Hundred Years*, 157.
18. Bonnie Burstow, *Psychiatry and the Business of Madness: An Ethical and Epistemological Accounting* (Toronto: Springer, 2015).
19. Sharma, Nandita, and Cynthia Wright (2008–2009). "Decolonizing Resistance, Challenging Colonial States," *Social Justice* 35(3): 120–138.
20. Patricia Johnston and Frank Tester, "Breaking the Colonial Role: Changing Social Work Practice in Nunavut," *The Canadian Journal of Native Studies* 34 no. 1 (2014): 115.
21. Chapman and Withers, *Violent History of Benevolence*.
22. Joshua R. Gregory, "The Imperative and Promise of Neo-abolitionism in Social Work," *Journal of Social Work* 21 no. 5 (2021): 1211.
23. Fortier and Wong, "Settler Colonialism of Social Work."
24. Johnston and Tester, "Breaking the Colonial Role."
25. Johnston and Tester, "Breaking the Colonial Role."
26. Robyn Maynard, *Policing Black Lives: State Violence in Canada from Slavery to the Present* (Halifax, NS: Fernwood, 2017).
27. Maynard, *Policing Black Lives*, 129.
28. Maynard, *Policing Black Lives*, 191.
29. Saidiya Hartman, *Wayward Lives, Beautiful Experiments* (New York: W.W. Norton, 2019).
30. Said "Professional and Amateurs," 2.
31. Karen Healy, *Social Work Theories in Context: Creating Frameworks for Practice* (London: MacMillan International Higher Education, 2014).
32. Carol Baines, "Women's Professions and an Ethic of Care," in *Women's Caring: Feminist Perspectives on Social Welfare* 2nd ed., eds. Carol Baines, Patricia Marie Evans, and Sheila M. Neysmith (Oxford, UK: Oxford University Press, 1998), 23–46.
33. Edward Hon-Sing Wong, "An Arm of the Carceral State: Mental Health Social Worker Complicity in Police Violence" (PhD diss., York University, 2023).
34. Hartman, *Wayward Lives*.

35. W. E. B. Du Bois, *Black Reconstruction in America: An Essay Toward a History of the Part Which Black Folk Played in the Attempt to Reconstruct Democracy in America, 1860–1880* (New York: Free Press, 1935).
36. Hartman, *Wayward Lives*.
37. INCITE! Women of Color Against Violence, *Color of Violence: The INCITE! Anthology* (Cambridge, MA: South End Press, 2006); INCITE! Women of Color Against Violence, *The Revolution Will Not Be Funded: Beyond the Non-Profit Industrial Complex* (Cambridge, MA: South End Press, 2007).
38. Edward Ou Jin Lee and Ilyan Ferrer, "Examining Social Work as a Canadian Settler Colonial Project: Colonial Continuities of Circles of Reform, Civilization, and In/visibility," *CAOS: The Journal of Critical Anti-Oppressive Social Inquiry* 1 no. 1 (2014): 1–20; Jackie Wang, *Carceral Capitalism* (Cambridge, MA: MIT Press, 2018).
39. Angela Y. Davis, *Are Prisons Obsolete?* (New York: Seven Stories Press, 2011).
40. Davis, *Are Prisons Obsolete?*, 37.
41. Davis, *Are Prisons Obsolete?*, 96.
42. Wang, *Carceral Capitalism*, 83.
43. Tia Dafnos, "Pacification and Indigenous Struggles in Canada," *Socialist Studies* 9 no. 2 (2013): 57–77; Dylan Rodriguez, "The Political Logic of the Non-Profit Industrial Complex," in *Revolution Will Not Be Funded*, eds. INCITE! Women of Color Against Violence, 21–40.
44. Leah A. Jacobs, Mimi E. Kim, Darren L. Whitfield, Rachel E. Gartner, Meg Panichelli, Shanna K. Kattari, Margaret Mary Downey, Shante Stuart McQueen, and Sarah E. Mountz, "Defund the Police: Moving towards an Anti-carceral Social Work," *Journal of Progressive Human Services* 32 no. 1 (2021): 37–38.
45. Fortier and Wong, "Settler Colonialism of Social Work."
46. We draw on the term "Weapons of the Weak" from anthropologist James C. Scott, who, in his book *Weapons of the Weak* (New Haven, CT: Yale University Press, 1987), describes the small-scale forms of resistance that relatively powerless groups might engage in to slow down, obfuscate, or subtly resist authority figures. Scott describes these as "foot dragging, dissimulation, false compliance, pilfering, feigned ignorance, slander, arson, sabotage, and so forth," 29.
47. Beth E. Richie and Kayla M. Martensen, "Resisting Carcerality, Embracing Abolition: Implications for Feminist Social Work Practice," *Affilia: Journal of Women and Social Work* 35 no. 1 (2020): 12–16.
48. Preston, *Abolitionist Disjuncture*.
49. Autumn Asher BlackDeer and Maria Grandilla Ocampo, "#SocialWorkSoWhite: A Critical Perspective on Settler Colonialism, White

Supremacy, and Social Justice in Social Work," *Advances in Social Work* 22 no. 2 (2022): 720–40.
50. Daphne Jeyapal, "The Evolving Politics of Race and Social Work Activism: A Call across Borders," *Social Work* 62 no. 1 (2017): 45–52.

CHAPTER 1: TOWARDS ABOLITIONIST SOCIAL WORK

1. Chris Chapman and A. J. Withers, *A Violent History of Benevolence: Interlocking Oppression in the Moral Economies of Social Working* (Toronto: University of Toronto Press, 2019).
2. Ruth Wilson Gilmore, *Abolition Geography: Essays towards Liberation* (London: Verso, 2023).
3. Bethany Jo Murray, Victoria Copeland, and Alan J. Dettlaff, "Reflections on the Ethical Possibilities and Limitations of Abolitionist Praxis in Social Work," *Affilia* 38 no. 4 (December 2023); Network to Advance Abolitionist Social Work, *Challenging Carceral Social Work and the Struggle for Abolition*, March 2022, naasw.com.
4. There has likely always been resistance to oppressive social work in the US, most notably from Black social workers and the National Association of Black Social Workers in the US.
5. Mimi Abramovitz, "Theorising the Neoliberal Welfare State for Social Work," in *The SAGE Handbook of Social Work*, eds. Mel Gray, James Midgley, and Stephen Webb (Los Angeles: SAGE Publications, 2012), 33–50, doi.org/10.4135/9781446247648.n3.
6. Mimi E. Kim, "Challenging the Pursuit of Criminalization: The Limitations to Social Work Responses to Violence in the USA," *British Journal of Social Work* 43 no. 7 (2012): 1276–93.
7. Mimi E. Kim, "Anti-Carceral Feminism: The Contradictions of Progress and the Possibilities of Counter Hegemonic Struggle" *Affilia* 35 no. 3 (2020): 309–26.
8. Dorothy Roberts, *Shattered Bonds: The Color of Child Welfare* (New York: Basic Books, 2002).
9. Maya Schenwar and Victoria Law, *Prison By Any Other Name: The Harmful Consequences of Popular Reforms* (New York: New Press, 2020).
10. Leah A. Jacobs, Mimi E. Kim, Darren L. Whitfield, Rachel E. Gartner, Meg Panichelli, Shanna K. Kattari, Margaret Mary Downey, Shanté Stuart McQueen, and Sarah E. Mountz, "Defund the Police: Moving towards an Anti-carceral Social Work," *Journal of Progressive Human Services* 32 no. 1 (2020): 40.
11. Beth Richie and Kayla Martinsen "Resisting Carcerality, Embracing Abolition: Implications for Feminist Social Work Practice," *Affilia* 35 no. 1 (2020): 14.

12. Cameron Rasmussen and Kirk "Jae" James, "Trading Cops for Social Workers Isn't the Solution to Police Violence," *Truthout*, July 17, 2020.
13. Edward Hon-Sing Wong, MJ Rwigema, Nicole Penak, and Craig Fortier, "Abolishing Carceral Social Work," in *Disarm, Defund, Dismantle: Police Abolition in Canada*, eds. Shiri Pasternak, Kevin Walby, and Abby Standyk (Toronto: Between the Lines, 2022), 145–53.
14. Ruth Wilson Gilmore, "The Case for Prison Abolition: Ruth Wilson Gilmore on COVID-19, Racial Capitalism & Decarceration," interview by Amy Goodman, *Democracy Now*, May 5, 2020, democracynow.org.
15. Jacobs et al., "Defund the Police," 40.
16. bell hooks, *From the Margins to the Center* (Boston: Southend Press, 1984).
17. Leah Lakshmi Piepzna-Samarasinha, *Care Work: Dreaming Disability Justice* (Vancouver: Arsenal Pulp Press, 2018).
18. Ejeris Dixon and Leah Lakshmi Piepzna-Samarasinha, eds., *Beyond Survival: Strategies and Stories from the Transformative Justice Movement* (Oakland, CA: AK Press, 2020).
19. Big Door Brigade, bigdoorbrigade.com.
20. Mia Mingus, "Transformative Justice: A Brief Description," *Leaving Evidence*, January 9, 2019, leavingevidence.wordpress.com.
21. See "Race, The War on Drugs and Reparative Justice," Colorofpain.org.
22. Non-reformist reforms is a term, coined by Andre Gonz, that has been taken up by Critical Resistance and other abolitionist organizations to discern which reforms are more likely to advance abolition.
23. Dean Spade. *Mutual Aid: Building Solidarity during this Crisis (and the Next)*, (London: Verso, 2020).
24. Spade, *Mutual Aid*; Rasmussen and James, "Trading Cops for Social Workers."
25. This framework is likely an evolution of Antonio Gramsci's conception of the War of Position. Antonio Gramsci, *Selections from the Prison Notebooks*, eds. Q. Hoare, and G. Nowell Smith (New York: International Publishers, 2003).
26. Interrupting Criminalization, *Abolition and the State: A Discussion Tool*, 2022, interruptingcriminalization.com; Mijente, "Sin el que?" March 10, 2020, mijente.net.
27. Mariame Kaba, *We Do This 'Til We Free Us: Abolitionist Organizing and Transforming Justice*, (Chicago: Haymarket, 2021).
28. See Bay Area Transformative Justice Collective, batjc.wordpress.com.
29. See Mandatory Reporting is Not Neutral, mandatoryreportingisnotneutral.com.

CHAPTER 2: MENTAL HEALTH WORKERS HAVE NEVER BEEN THE SOLUTION TO RACIAL VIOLENCE BY POLICE

1. "CAMH Statement on Police Interactions with People in Mental Health Crisis," *CAMH*, accessed June 15, 2021, camh.ca.
2. Liat Ben-Moshe, *Decarcerating Disability: Deinstitutionalization and Prison Abolition* (Minneapolis: University of Minnesota Press, 2020); Liat Ben-Moshe, Chris Chapman, and Allison C. Carey, eds., *Disability Incarcerated: Imprisonment and Disability in the United States and Canada* (New York: Springer, 2014); Edward Hon-Sing Wong, "An Arm of the Carceral State: Mental Health Social Worker Complicity in Police Violence" (PhD diss., York University, 2023); Maya Schenwar and Victoria Law, *Prison by Any Other Name: The Harmful Consequences of Popular Reforms* (New York: The New Press, 2020).
3. Timothy Lenoir, "Kant, Blumenbach, and Vital Materialism in German Biology," *Isis* 71, no. 1 (1980): 77–108.
4. Emil Kraepelin, *Dementia Praecox and Paraphrenia* (Pennsylvania Furnace: Lippincott, William, and Wilkins, 1921).
5. A. J. Withers, *Disability Politics and Theory* (Winnipeg. MB: Fernwood, 2012).
6. Philippa Levine, "Anthropology, Colonialism, and Eugenics," in *The Oxford Handbook of the History of Eugenics*, eds. Alison Bashford and Philippa Levine (Oxford, UK: Oxford University Press, 2010), 43–61.
7. Amina Mama, *Beyond the Masks: Race, Gender and Subjectivity* (London: Routledge, 2002).
8. Ian R. Dowbiggin, *Keeping America Sane: Psychiatry and Eugenics in the United States and Canada, 1880-1940*, (Ithaca, NY: Cornell University Press, 1997); Ameil J. Joseph, *Deportation and the Confluence of Violence within Forensic Mental Health and Immigration Systems* (New York: Springer, 2016); Ameil J. Joseph, "Ancestries of Racial and Eugenic Systems of Violence in the Mental Health Sector," in *Third International Conference on Violence in the Health Sector*, Vancouver, BC, (October 25, 2012); David MacLennan, "Beyond the Asylum: Professionalization and the Mental Hygiene Movement in Canada, 1914–1928," in *Canadian Bulletin of Medical History*, 4 (1987): 7–23; Angus McLaren, "The Creation of a Haven for 'Human Thoroughbreds': The Sterilization of the Feeble-Minded and the Mentally Ill in British Columbia," *Canadian Historical Review* 67 no. 2 (1986): 127–50; Robert Menzies, "Governing Mentalities: The Deportation of Insane and Feebleminded Immigrants out of British Columbia from Confederation to World War II," *Can. JL & Soc.* 13 (1998): 135; Edward Hon-Sing Wong, "'The Brains of a Nation': The Eugenicist Roots of Canada's Mental Health Field and the Building of a White

Non-Disabled Nation," *Canadian Review of Social Policy/Revue Canadienne de Politique Sociale* 75 (2016): 1–29.
9. Clarence M. Hincks, "The Scope and Aims of the Mental Hygiene Movement in Canada," *Canadian Journal of Mental Hygiene* 1 no. 1 (1919): 20.
10. Stephanie May McKenzie, "Canada's Day of Atonement, the Contemporary Native Literary Renaissance, the Native Cultural Renaissance and Post-Centenary Canadian Mythology," (PhD diss., University of Toronto, 2001).
11. J. D. Page, "Immigration and the Canadian National Committee for Mental Hygiene," *Canadian Journal of Mental Hygiene* 1 no. 1 (1919): 59.
12. Neil Smith, *The New Urban Frontier: Gentrification and the Revanchist City* (London: Routledge, 2005).
13. W. G. Smith, "Immigration Past and Present," *Canadian Journal of Mental Hygiene* 1 no. 1 (1919): 47.
14. It is also important to note that this definition of white, in terms of whom it encompasses, was more specific and limited when compared to contemporary understandings that might include Eastern Europeans and other groups.
15. Jasper Halpenny, "One Phase of the Foreign Invasion of Canada," *Canadian Journal of Mental Hygiene* 1 no. 3 (1919): 225.
16. "Mental Hygiene Survey of the Province of British Columbia," *Canadian Journal of Mental Hygiene* 2 no. 1 (1920): 48.
17. Hincks, "Mental Hygiene Movement," 25.
18. "Mental Hygiene Survey," 48.
19. Jessie Taft, "Supervision of the Feebleminded in the Community," *Canadian Journal of Mental Hygiene* 1 no. 2 (1919): 166.
20. Karen Stote, "The Coercive Sterilization of Aboriginal Women in Canada," *American Indian Culture and Research Journal* 36 no. 3 (2012): 117–50.
21. Amy Samson, "Eugenics in the Community: Gendered Professions and Eugenic Sterilization in Alberta, 1928–1972," *Canadian Bulletin of Medical History* 31 no. 1 (2014): 146.
22. Amanda Oliveira, "The Coming and Going of Eugenics in Alberta: A Discarded History, 1928 to 1972" (PhD diss., Lakehead University, 2016), 79.
23. Amy Samson, "Guidance Clinics," Eugenics Archive, May 14, 2015, eugenicsarchive.ca.
24. Samson, "Eugenics in the Community."
25. Oliveira, *Eugenics in Alberta.*
26. Ashifa Kassam, "Canada Indigenous Women Were Coerced into Sterilisations, Lawsuit Says," *The Guardian*, October 27, 2017, theguardian.com.

27. Kassam, "Canada Indigenous Women."
28. Yvonne Boyer and Judith Bartlett, *External Review: Tubal Ligation in the Saskatoon Health Region: The Lived Experience of Aboriginal Women* (Saskatoon, SK: Saskatoon Health Region, 2017).
29. Kristy Kirkup, "Indigenous Women Coerced into Sterilizations across Canada: Senator." *CBC News*, December 11, 2018, cbc.ca.
30. Jorge Barrera, "MPs Call for Criminal Probe of Coerced Sterilization Cases of Indigenous Women," *CBC News*, February 1, 2019, cbc.ca.
31. Fakiha Baig, "Forced and Coerced Sterilization of Indigenous Women Ongoing, Senate Report Reveals," *Canadian Press*, March 6, 2021, winnipegfreepress.com.
32. Debra E. Thompson, "Racial Ideas and Gendered Intimacies: The Regulation of Interracial Relationships in North America," *Social & Legal Studies* 18 no. 3 (2009): 353–71.
33. Thompson, "Racial Ideas," 360.
34. Michael Valpy, "A Dark Passage in Ontario's Past," *Globe and Mail*, March 22, 2002, theglobeandmail.com.
35. Velma Demerson, *Incorrigible* (Waterloo, ON: Wilfrid Laurier University Press, 2006).
36. Debra Jeffery, Sarah Clement, Elizabeth Corker, Luise M. Howard, Joanna Murray, and Graham Thornicroft, "Discrimination in Relation to Parenthood Reported by Community Psychiatric Service Users in the UK: A Framework Analysis," *BMC Psychiatry* 13 no. 1 (2013): 1–9.
37. "Abstracts," *Canadian Journal of Mental Hygiene* 1 no. 3 (1919): 242–58.
38. Taft, "Supervision of the Feebleminded," 34.
39. "Immigration Act, 1869," *Canadian Museum of Immigration at Pier 21*, 2018, pier21.ca.
40. Roy Hanes, "None Is Still Too Many: An Historical Exploration of Canadian Immigration Legislation as It Pertains to People with Disabilities," *Developmental Disabilities Bulletin* 37 (2009): 91–126.
41. Amy L. Fairchild, *Science at the Borders: Immigrant Medical Inspection and the Shaping of the Modern Industrial Labor Force* (Baltimore, ML: Johns Hopkins University Press, 2003), 146.
42. Ninette Kelley and Michael Trebilcock, *The Making of the Mosaic: A History of Canadian Immigration Policy* (Toronto: University of Toronto Press, 1998).
43. Brian Hill, "Father of Son with Autism Calls Canada's New Immigration Policy a 'Blessing for All of Us,'" *Global News*, April 17, 2018, globalnews.ca.
44. Constance MacIntosh, "Medical Inadmissibility, and Physically and Mentally Disabled Would-Be Immigrants: Canada's Story Continues," *Dalhousie Law Journal* 42 no. 1 (2019).

45. Yahya El-Lahib and Samantha Wehbi, "Immigration and Disability: Ableism in the Policies of the Canadian State," *International Social Work* 55 no. 1 (2012): 4; Rachel Gorman, "Empire of Rights: The Convergence of Neoliberal Governance, 'States of Exception,' and the Disability Rights Movement," paper presented at *Cripping Neoliberalism: Interdisciplinary Perspectives on Governing and Imagining Dis/Ability and Bodily Difference*, October 8, 2010, Charles University, Prague; Rachel Gorman, "Disablement in and for Itself: Toward a 'Global' Idea of Disability," *Somatechnics* 6 no. 2 (2016): 249–61.
46. Ann De Shalit, Adrian Guta, Camisha Sibblis, Emily van der Meulen, and Jijian Voronka, "Troubling Police and Social Work Collaborations," in *Disarm Defund Dismantle: Police Abolition in Canada*, eds. Shiri Pasternak, Kevin Walby, and Abby Stadnyk (Toronto: Between the Lines, 2022).
47. F. M. Baker and Carl C. Bell, "Issues in the Psychiatric Treatment of African Americans," *Psychiatric Services* 50, no. 3 (1999): 362–68; Robert C. Schwartz and Kevin P. Feisthamel, "Disproportionate Diagnosis of Mental Disorders among African American versus European American Clients: Implications for Counseling Theory, Research, and Practice," *Journal of Counseling & Development* 87, no. 3 (2009): 295–301; Rebecca Pinto, Mark Ashworth, and Roger Jones, "Schizophrenia in Black Caribbeans Living in the UK: An Exploration of Underlying Causes of the High Incidence Rate," *British Journal of General Practice* 58, no. 551 (2008): 429–34; Shula Minsky, William Vega, and Theresa Miskimen, "Diagnostic Patterns in Latino, African American, and European American Psychiatric Patients," *Archives of General Psychiatry* 60, no. 6 (2003): 637–44; Robert C. Schwartz and David M. Blankenship, "Racial Disparities in Psychotic Disorder Diagnosis: A Review of Empirical Literature," *World Journal of Psychiatry* 4, no. 4 (2014): 133; Joseph P. Gone and Joseph E. Trimble, "American Indian and Alaska Native Mental Health: Diverse Perspectives on Enduring Disparities," *Annual Review of Clinical Psychology* 8 (2012): 131–60; Lin Zhan, *Asian Americans: Vulnerable Populations, Model Interventions, and Clarifying Agendas* (Burlington, MA: Jones & Bartlett Learning, 2003).
48. Apu Chakraborty, Lance Patrick, and Maria Lambra, "Racism and Mental Illness in the UK," in *Mental Disorders: Theoretical and Empirical Perspectives*, eds. Robert Woolfolk and Lesley Allen (London: IntechOpen, 2013).
49. "Hold Your Fire," Firsthand, CBC, August 25, 2016, http:/cbc.ca/firsthand/episodes/hold-your-fire.
50. Jennifer Skeem and Lynne Bibeau, "How Does Violence Potential

Relate to Crisis Intervention Team Responses to Emergencies?," *Psychiatric Services* 59, no. 2 (2008): 202.

51. American Public Health Association, "Law Enforcement Violence as a Public Health Issue," *American Public Health Association Policy* No LB-16-02, 2016; Samuel R. Aymer, "'I Can't Breathe': A Case Study—Helping Black Men Cope with Race-Related Trauma Stemming from Police Killing and Brutality," *Journal of Human Behavior in the Social Environment* 26, nos. 3–4 (2016): 367–76.
52. Jillian Boyce, Cristine Rotenberg, and Maisie Karam, "Mental Health and Contact with Police in Canada, 2012," *Juristat: Canadian Centre for Justice Statistics*, 2015, 1; Frank Iacobucci, "Police Encounters with People in Crisis" (Toronto Police Service, 2014); Tim Szkopek-Szkopowski et al., *Vancouver's Mental Health Crisis: An Update Report* (Vancouver Police Department, 2013).
53. Katharine Byrick and Barbara Walker-Renshaw, *A Practical Guide to Mental Health and the Law in Ontario* (Ontario Hospital Association, 2016). Note: Police officers also have the authority to use their own discretion to apprehend someone for transportation to a psychiatric facility for an assessment by a physician under Section 17 of the Mental Health Act, should the police officers deem the person to have engaged in "disorderly conduct" and fulfil the criteria outlined in Box A.
54. John Dawson, "Community Treatment Orders," in *Law and Mind: Mental Health Law and Policy in Canada*, eds. Jennifer A. Chandler and Colleen M. Flood (Toronto: Lexis Nexis Canada, 2016).
55. Dawson, "Community Treatment Orders."
56. Dawson, "Community Treatment Orders."
57. "Success in Reintegration: The Potential Application of Situation Tables to Community Corrections," Correctional Service Canada, July 13, 2017, csc-scc.gc.ca.
58. Nathan Munn, "Police in Canada Are Tracking People's 'Negative' Behavior In a 'Risk' Database," *Vice*, February 27, 2019, vice.com.
59. Citizen Lab, "To Surveil and Predict: A Human Rights Analysis of Algorithmic Policing in Canada," *Ontario Law Commission*, Retrieved November 11 (2020): 2020, ssrn.com.
60. Munn, "Police in Canada."
61. Munn, "Police in Canada."
62. Citizen Lab, "To Surveil and Predict."
63. Edward Hon-Sing Wong, personal communication, May 11, 2020.
64. Bonnie Burstow, *Psychiatry and the Business of Madness: An Ethical and Epistemological Accounting* (New York: Springer, 2015).
65. Edward Hon-Sing Wong, personal communication, May 5, 2020.

CHAPTER 3: FOR BLACK WOMEN, HEALTH CARE IS AN ABOLITION ISSUE

1. For examples, see Josephine B. Etowa, Brenda L. Beagan, Felicia Eghan, and Wanda Thomas Bernard, "'You Feel You Have to Be Made of Steel': The Strong Black Woman, Health, and Well-being in Nova Scotia," *Health Care for Women International* 38 no. 4 (2017): 379–93; Onye Nnorom, Nicole Findlay, Nakia K. Lee-Foon, Ankur A. Jain, Carolyn P. Ziegler, Fran E. Scott, Patricia Rodney, and Aisha K. Lofters, "Dying to Learn: A Scoping Review of Breast and Cervical Cancer Studies Focusing on Black Canadian Women," *Journal of Health Care for the Poor and Underserved* 30 no. 4 (2019): 1331–59; Esther Tharao and Notisha Massaquoi, "Black Women and HIV/AIDS: Contextualizing their Realities, their Silence and Proposing Solutions," *Canadian Woman Studies* 21 no. 2 (2001): 72.
2. See Ruth Wilson Gilmore, "Globalisation and US Prison Growth: From Military Keynesianism to Post-Keynesian Militarism," *Race & Class* 40 nos. 2–3 (1999): 171–88; James Kilgore, "Mass Incarceration: Examining and Moving Beyond the New Jim Crow," *Critical Sociology* 41 no. 2 (2015): 283–95.
3. Anthony N. Morgan, "Black Canadians and the Justice System," *Policy Options*, May 18, 2018, irpp.org.
4. Ontario Human Rights Commission, "New OHRC Report Confirms Black People Disproportionately Arrested, Charged, Subjected to Use of Force by Toronto Police, *OHRC News Centre*, August 10, 2020, ohrc.on.ca.
5. Davis, *Are Prisons Obsolete?*
6. Katherine Beckett and Naomi Murakawa, "Mapping the Shadow Carceral State: Toward an Institutionally Capacious Approach to Punishment," *Theoretical Criminology* 16 no. 2 (2012): 221–44.
7. For more details, see Robyn Maynard, *Policing Black Lives: State Violence in Canada from Slavery to the Present* (Halifax, NS: Fernwood Publishing, 2017).
8. "Ontario's Action Plan for Healthcare," Ontario Ministry of Health and Long Term Care, 2023, ontario.ca.
9. Bryan M. Evans and Carlo Fanelli, eds, *The Public Sector in an Age of Austerity: Perspectives from Canada's Provinces and Territories* (Montreal: McGill-Queen's Press, 2018).
10. Mary E. Wiktowicz, "Restructuring Mental Health Policy in Ontario: Deconstructing the Evolving Welfare State," *Canadian Public Administration* 48 no. 3 (2005): 386–412.
11. Alexandra Swigger and Tim Heinmiller, "Advocacy Coalitions and Mental Health Policy: The Adoption of Community Treatment Orders in Ontario," *Politics & Policy* 42 no. 2 (2014): 246–70.

12. De Lissovoy, "Conceptualizing the Carceral Turn," 740.
13. Barbara Beardwood, Vivienne Walters, John Eyles, and Susan French, "Complaints against Nurses: A Reflection of 'the New Managerialism' and Consumerism in Health Care?," *Social Science & Medicine* 48 no. 3 (1999): 363–74.
14. See Keisha Jefferies, Lisa Goldberg, Megan Aston, and Gail Tomblin Murphy, "Understanding the Invisibility of Black Nurse Leaders Using a Black Feminist Poststructuralist Framework," *Journal of Clinical Nursing* 27 nos. 15–16 (2018): 3225–34; Agnes Calliste, "Race, Gender and Canadian Immigration Policy: Blacks from the Caribbean, 1900–1932," *Journal of Canadian Studies* 28 no. 4 (1993–94): 131–48; Agnes Calliste, "Antiracism Organizing and Resistance in Nursing: African Canadian Women," *The Canadian Review of Sociology* 33 no. 3 (1996): 361–90; Najja Nwofia Modibo, "The Shattered Dreams of African Canadian Nurses," *Canadian Woman Studies* 23 no. 2 (2004): 1101.
15. Tania Das Gupta, "Anti-Black Racism in Nursing in Ontario," *Studies in Political Economy* 51 no. 1 (1996): 97–116.
16. Jefferies, et al., "Understanding the Invisibility"; Calliste, "Race, Gender and Canadian Immigration Policy"; Calliste, "Antiracism Organizing and Resistance"; Modibo, "Shattered Dreams."
17. Keisha Jefferies, Chelsea States, Vanessa MacLennan, Melissa Helwig, Jacqueline Gahagan, Wanda Thomas Bernard, Marilyn Macdonald, Gail Tomblin Murphy, and Ruth Martin-Misener, "Black Nurses in the Nursing Profession in Canada: A Scoping Review," *International Journal of Equity in Health* 21 (2022): 102.
18. For the early history of institutionalization in Canada, see Frances Frankenburg, "The 1978 Ontario Mental Health Act in Historical Context," *HSTC Bulletin* 6 no. 3 (1982): 172; for the role of deinstitutionalization in CTO development, see Swigger and Heinmiller, "Advocacy Coalitions."
19. Michel Foucault, l. *Discipline and Punish: The Birth of the Prison* (New York: Vintage Books, 1979).
20. Manuel Vega, "A Trans Woman Died in Toronto Police Custody. After Public Pressure, the SIU Has Corrected the Report That Misgendered Her," *Toronto Star*, November 4, 2020, thestar.com.
21. Annette Bailey, Manoj Sharma, and Michelle Jubin, "The Mediating Role of Social Support, Cognitive Appraisal, and Quality Health Care in Black Mothers' Stress-Resilience Process Following Loss to Gun Violence," *Violence and Victims* 28 no. 2 (2013): 233–47.
22. Bailey, Sharma, and Jubin, "Mediating Role of Social Support."

23. Ruth Wilson Gilmore and James Kilgore, "The Case for Abolition," *Marshall Project*, June 19, 2019, themarshallproject.org.
24. "Code of Ethics and Scope of Practice," *CASW*, accessed February 1, 2021, casw-acts.ca.
25. "COVID-19—What We Know So Far About... Social Determinants of Health," *Public Health Ontario*, May 24, 2020, publichealthontario.ca.
26. Rinaldo Walcott, "The Problem of the Human: Black Ontologies and the Coloniality of Our Being," in *Postcoloniality - Decoloniality - Black Critique: Joints and Fissures*, eds. Sabine Broeck and Carsten Junker (Frankfurt: Campus Verlag, 2014).
27. Paula Maurutto, "Charity and Public Welfare in History: A Look at Ontario, 1830–1950," *Philanthropist* 19 no. 3 (2005): 159.
28. Raven Sinclair, "Bridging the Past and the Future: An Introduction to Indigenous Social Work Issues, in *Wícihitowin: Aboriginal Social Work in Canada*, eds. Gord Bruyere, Michael Anthony Hart, and Raven Sinclair (Winnipeg, MB: Fernwood Publishing, 2009), 27–41.
29. See Gordon Pon, Kevin Gosine, and Doret Phillip, "Immediate Response: Addressing Anti-Native and Anti-Black Racism in Child Welfare," *International Journal of Child, Youth & Family Studies IJCYFS* 2 nos. 3/4 (2011): 385; Doret Phillips and Gordon Pon, "Anti-Black Racism, Bio-Power, and Governmentality: Deconstructing the Suffering of Black Families Involved with Child Welfare," *JL & Soc. Pol'y* 28 (2018): 81.
30. Marie-Jolie Rwigema, Onyinyechukwu Udegbe, and David Lewis-Peart, "We Are Expected to Work as if We Are Not Who We Are": Reflections on Working with Queer Black Youth," in *LGBT People and Social Work: Intersectional Perspectives*, eds. Brian J O'Neill, Tracy A. Swan, and Nick J. Mule (Toronto: Canadian Scholars Press, 2015), 37–52.
31. Akua Benjamin, "Doing Anti-Oppressive Social Work: The Importance of Resistance, History and Strategy," in *Doing Anti-Oppressive Practice*, ed. Donna Baines (Winnipeg, MB: Fernwood, 2007), 196–204.
32. Wanda Thomas Bernard, Lydia Lucas-White, and Dorothy E. Moore, "Triple Jeopardy: Assessing Life Experiences of Black Nova Scotian Women from a Social Work Perspective," *Canadian Social Work Review* 10 no. 2 (1993): 256–74.
33. Eve Tuck, "Suspending Damage: A Letter to Communities," *Harvard Educational Review* 79 no. 3 (2009): 409–28.
34. Carl E. James and Akua Benjamin, *Race & Well-Being: The Lives, Hopes, and Activism of African Canadians* (Halifax, NS: Fernwood Publishing, 2010), 27.

CHAPTER 4: "KEEP THIS UP AND THEY'LL BE PULLING YOU FROM THE RED"

1. The author of this chapter has chosen a pseudonym.
2. Marni Brownell, "Canada Has One of the Highest Rates of Kids in Care in the World," *New News Ledger*, November 7, 2015, netnewsledger.com.
3. Statistics Canada, "2011 Census," *Statistics Canada Catalogue* no. 98-312-XWE2011001, statcan.gc.ca.
4. CFS Manitoba is made up of twenty-three agencies responsible for child protective services. These agencies are largely distinguished by region, with recent efforts to create child welfare services and CFS agencies specifically for Indigenous families.
5. Statistics Canada, "2011 Census."
6. Marni Brownell, Mariette Chartier, Wendy Au, Leonard MacWilliam, Jeffrey Schultz, Wendy Guenette, Jeff Valdivia, *The Educational Outcomes of Children in Care in Manitoba* (Winnipeg: Manitoba Centre for Health Policy, 2015), umanitoba.ca.
7. Ruth Gilbert, John Fluke, Melissa O'Donnell, Arturo Gonzalez-Izquierdo, Marni Brownwell, Pauline Gulliver, Staffan Janson, and Peter Sidebotham, "Child Maltreatment: Variation in Trends and Policies in Six Developed Countries," *The Lancet* 379 no. 9817 (2012): 758–72.
8. Chinta Puxley, "CFS Seizes a Manitoba Newborn a Day, First Nations Advocate Says," *CBC Manitoba*, September 1, 2015, cbc.ca.
9. Marni Brownell, Maritte Chartier, Ron Santos, Okechukwu Ekuma, Wendy Au, Joykrishna Sarkar, Leonard MacWilliam, Elaine Burland, Ina Koseva, and Wendy Guenette, *How Are Manitoba's Children Doing?* (Winnipeg: Manitoba Centre for Health Policy, 2012), umanitoba.ca.
10. Brownell et al., *Educational Outcomes*.
11. Pamela Palmater, "From Foster Care to Missing or Murdered: Canada's Other Tragic Pipeline," *Macleans*, April 12, 2017, macleans.ca.
12. *Annual Report for the Department of Families 2016–2017* (Winnipeg: Manitoba Department of Families, 2017), gov.mb.ca.
13. Chinta Puxley, "Manitoba Changes How It Counts Kids in Care, Abruptly Reducing Number," *CBC Manitoba*, February 10, 2016, cbc.ca.
14. Puxley, "Manitoba Changes How."
15. Kristin Annable, "Province Reports 1st Decrease in Child Welfare Numbers in 15 Years," *CBC Manitoba*, September 25, 2018, cbc.ca.
16. Aidan Geary, "Number of Manitoba Kids in CFS Care Down 4 Per Cent from Last Year," *CBC Manitoba*, October 1, 2020, cbc.ca .
17. Laurence Y. Katz, Wendy Au, Deepa Singal, Marni Brownell, Noralou

Roos, Patricia J. Martens, Dan Chateau, Murray W. Enns, Anita L. Kozyrskyj, Jitender Sareen, "Suicide and Suicide Attempts in Children and Adolescents in the Child Welfare System," *Canadian Medical Association Journal* 183 no. 17 (2011): 1977–81.
18. Brownell et al., *Educational Outcomes*.
19. Brownell et al., *Educational Outcomes*.
20. Katie May, "'Crossover Kids': Teens Caught between Child Welfare and Criminal Justice Institutions," *Winnipeg Free Press*, December 31, 2017, winnipegfreepress.com.
21. *2nd Quarter Update: Indigenous Women—Safety & Protection* (Winnipeg Police Board, 2015), documentcloud.org.
22. Annable, "Province Reports 1st Decrease."
23. Jill Macyshon, "Manitoba CFS Increasingly Used Hotels to House Vulnerable Children, Documents Show," *CTV News*, April 8, 2015, ctvnews.ca.
24. Macyshon, "Manitoba CFS Increasingly."
25. Jill Macyshon, "CFS Stops Using Winnipeg Hotel That Housed Hundreds of Children," *CTV News*, April 7, 2015, ctvnews.ca.
26. Kelvin Goertzen, "Rural CFS Kids Still in Hotels," *My Steinbach*, June 4, 2015, mysteinbach.ca.
27. Steve Lampert, "Manitoba Stops Tracking CFS Wards in Hotels," *CBC Manitoba*, April 6, 2017, cbc.ca
28. Chanti Puxley "Lack of Foster Spots Keeps Manitoba Kids in Jails," *Globe and Mail*, April 14, 2015, theglobeandmail.com.
29. Jill Macyshon, "Manitoba Accused of Violating Rights of Foster Children Stuck in Jail," *CTV News*, April 15, 2015, ctvnews.ca.
30. "Family of Teen Who Hanged Herself in Jail Cell Sues Manitoba Child and Family Services," *CBC News*, October 7, 2015, cbc.ca.
31. "Manitoba Family Services Minister Warned about Jail Time for CFS Kid," *Global News*, April 22, 2015, globalnews.ca.
32. Erin Brohman, "Teen Killed Herself at Foster Home, Mother Wishes She Hadn't Obeyed 'Their Rules,'" *CBC Manitoba*, January 24, 2018, cbc.c.
33. Karen Pauls, "Plan to Give Indigenous Governments Control over Child Welfare Draws Mixed Reviews," *CBC Manitoba*, December 1, 2018, cbc.ca.
34. Megan Rowney, "A Life Discarded: Child Deaths in Care across Canada" *Global News*, October 22, 2015, globalnews.ca; Pauls, "Plan to Give Indigenous Governments."
35. Rowney, "A Life Discarded"; Pauls, "Plan to Give Indigenous Governments."
36. Kenneth Jackson, "Death As Expected: Inside a Child Welfare System

Where 102 Indigenous Kids Died over 5 Years," *APTN News*, September 25, 2019, aptnnews.ca.

CHAPTER 5: NOT CRIMINALLY RESPONSIBLE

1. *Annual Report: Fiscal Reporting Period April 1, 2019—March 31, 2020*, Ontario Review Board, 2020, on.ca.
2. "Mental Health and Addictions Legislation," Canadian Mental Health Association of Ontario, 2022, ontario.cmha.ca.
3. Shannon Bettridge and Howard Barbaree, *The Forensic Mental Health System in Ontario: An Information Guide* (Toronto: Centre for Addiction and Mental Health, 2004).
4. Bettridge and Barbaree, *Forensic Mental Health System*.
5. ORB, *Annual Report*.
6. A file or a medical chart is a written or electronic record of patient notes by doctors, social workers, and other service providers. Service providers are required to write clinical notes about their interactions with and assessments of patients. These are permanent records not able to be altered.
7. Erick Fabris and Katie Aubrecht, "Chemical Constraint: Experiences of Psychiatric Coercion, Restraint, and Detention as Carceratory Techniques," in *Disability Incarcerated: Imprisonment and Disability in the United States and Canada*, eds. Liat Ben-Moshe, Chris Chapman, and Allison C. Carey (New York: Palgrave Macmillan, 2014), 185–99.
8. *Abolish the Psych Ward*, Disability Justice Network of Ontario, July 20, 2021, YouTube video, 1:25:39, youtube.com
9. Merrick D. Pilling, Andrea Daley, Margaret F. Gibson, Lori E. Ross, and Juveria Zaheer, "Assessing 'Insight,' Determining Agency and Autonomy: Implicating Social Identities," in *Containing Madness: Gender and "Psy" in Instituional Contexts*, eds. Jennifer M. Kilty and Erin Dej (Toronto: Palgrave, 2018), 191–213.
10. Canadian Mental Health Association, "Early Psychosis Intervention Program (MOD)," August 21, 2012, toronto.cmha.ca.
11. Ann De Shalit, Adrian Guta, Camisha Sibblis, Emily van der Meulen, and Jijian Voronka, "Troubling Police and Social Work Collaborations," in *Disarm, Defund, Dismantle: Police Abolition in Canada*, eds. Shiri Pasternak, Kevin Walby, and Abby Standy (Toronto: Between the Lines, 2021), 140–45.
12. ohrc.on.ca.
13. "Mental Health Mobile Crisis Intervention Teams (MCIT)," Toronto Police Service, 2022, torontopolice.on.ca.
14. The ORB annually reviews the status of every person who has been found not criminally responsible or unfit to stand trial for criminal

offences on account of a mental disorder. The ORB is established under the Criminal Code of Canada. We further elaborate on how the ORB works later in the chapter.

15. NCR means you committed a crime but because of your mental disorder you are not responsible for what you did. The Criminal Code of Canada states that you are NCR for an offence if a mental disorder prevents you from appreciating the nature of your actions OR knowing that your actions were wrong.
16. Alexander I. F. Simpson, Sumeeta Chatterjee, Padraig Darby, Roland M. Jones, Margaret Maheandiran, Stephanie R. Penney, Tania Saccoccio, Vicky Stergiopoulos, and Treena Wilkie, "Management of COVID-19 Response in a Secure Forensic Mental Health Setting," *Canadian Journal of Psychiatry* 65 no. 10 (2020): 695–700.
17. Simpson et al., "Management of COVID-19 Response."
18. ORB, *Annual Report*.
19. Radovan Radisic and Nathan J. Kolla, "Right to Appeal, Non-Treatment, and Violence Among Forensic and Civil Inpatients Awaiting Incapacity Appeal Decisions in Ontario" *Frontiers in Psychiatry* 10 (2019): 752.
20. Centre for Addiction and Mental Health, Privacy Officer, email message to author, September 9, 2021.
21. Waypoint Centre for Mental Health Care, Privacy Officer, email message to author, November 27, 2020.
22. Rebecca Zandbergen, "Man Remains Stuck in a Forensic Mental Health System Some Say is Biased against Black People," *CBC London*, July 27, 2020, cbc.ca.
23. CAMH quoted us $2,775 for our FOI, later reducing it to $1,387. Waypoint quoted us $300 and reduced it to $100.
24. Nadine Yousif, "CAMH Unveils 'Aggressive' Plan to Tackle Systemic Anti-Black Racism in the Mental Health Hospital," *Toronto Star*, February 10, 2021.
25. Yousif, "CAMH Unveils 'Aggressive' Plan."
26. Anita Szigeti (blog), "Dawson College Commissioned Short Film on Race and NCR/ORB," September 16, 2020, anitaszigeti.wordpress.com.
27. *Re: Sim*, 2020 ONCA 563.
28. As per CAMH's website, seclusion is the confinement of a client/patient in a locked room designated as a seclusion room to restrict movement from one location to another (also referred to as environmental restraint). The person cannot exit freely. The room often has two-way mirrors and only a bed and toilet. Restraints include the use of physical force, mechanical devices, or chemicals to immobilize a person.

29. Erick Fabris, *Tranquil Prisons: Chemical Incarceration under Community Treatment Orders* (Toronto: University of Toronto Press, 2011).
30. *Final Report on Alternative Crisis Response Models for Toronto*, Reach Out Response Network, November 2020, squarespace.com.
31. Krystle Martin and Erica Martin, "Factors Influencing Treatment Team Recommendations to Review Tribunals for Forensic Psychiatric Patients," *Behavioral Sciences & the Law* 34 no. 4 (2016): 551–63.
32. Martin and Martin, "Factors Influencing Treatment Team."
33. Meaghan McMahon, "Significant Risk of Significant Harm: An Onerous Threshold for Ongoing Review Board Jurisdiction," paper presented at the 30th Annual Criminal Law Conference, October 14, 2018, Toronto, ON.
34. Radisic and Kolla, "Right to Appeal."
35. Alexandra I. F. Simpson, Irene Boldt, Stephanie Penney, Roland Jones, Sean Kidd, Arash Nakhost, and Treena Wilkie, "Perceptions of Procedural Justice and Coercion among Forensic Psychiatric Patients: A Study Protocol for a Prospective, Mixed-Methods Investigation," *BMC Psychiatry* 20 no. 1 (2020): 230.
36. Szigeti, "Dawson College Commissioned."
37. Nadine Yousif, "Toronto's First-Ever Mental Health Crisis Response Teams—Without Police—to Launch in March," *The Star*, January 19, 2022, thestar.com.
38. Ted Rutland, "Police See Major Budget Increases Despite Majority Support for Defunding," Breach Media, February 1, 2022, breachmedia.ca.

CHAPTER 6: SHIFTING PRAXIS

1. INCITE! Women of Color Against Violence, *Color of Violence: The INCITE! Anthology* (Cambridge, MA: South End Press, 2006).
2. *Family policing system* is a term developed by grassroots groups such as Movement for Family Power, RISE, and the upEND Movement and Dr. Dorothy Roberts. The FPS is also known as the child "welfare" or "protection" system. This alternative phrasing has been developed to more appropriately describe how the system functions, through policing, surveillance, investigation, and even family separation.
3. I want to take a moment to spotlight Andrew, who was the beacon of the project, ensuring we always grounded FF in the community. He was a photographer and a huge advocate for creating spaces for youth. He had a vision for FF and the community. He always wanted to capture it in its best light. May he Rest in Paradise.
4. *Community Profile: Black Creek*, City of Toronto, 2006.
5. The community healing project is a prevention and intervention

project led by the City of Toronto that aims to address the root cause of trauma as resulting from community exposure to violence, toronto.ca.
6. *Someone to Turn to: A Vision for Creating Networks of Parent Peer Care*, Rise Insights, May 2021, risemagazine.org; Fearless R2W, fearlessr2w.ca.
7. The MotherRisk Commission was a public inquiry into how substandard hair strand testing for drug use was performed by the Hospital for Sick Children in Toronto and how their findings, including tests they knew to have a percentage of false positives, were used as the basis for separating families, archives.gov.on.ca.
8. bell hooks, *Yearning: Race, Gender, and Cultural Politics* (London: Routledge, 2014), 227.
9. Mariame Kaba, "We Do This 'Til We Free Us: Abolitionist Organizing and Transforming Justice," Haymarket Books (blog), February 23, 2021, haymarketbooks.org.
10. *Code of Ethics*, Canadian Association of Social Workers, 2005, casw-acts.ca.
11. INCITE! Women of Color Against Violence, *The Revolution Will Not Be Funded: Beyond the Non-Profit Industrial Complex* (Durham, NC: Duke University Press, 2017).

CHAPTER 7: THE ANTITRAFFICKING MOVEMENT IS NOT ABOLITIONIST

1. Depending on the municipality, massage parlours are called and licensed as body rub parlours, holistic centres, or personal wellness centres. I use the term "massage worker" because this is how the workers self-identify.
2. The dissertation from which this chapter emerges is informed by the methodological approaches of institutional ethnography and participatory action research as complementary modes of social inquiry. This work also inquires into how the anti–sex work and racist ideologies of the antitrafficking movement are embedded in such laws and policies. This research is approved by the McMaster Research Ethics Board (MREB) and supported by the Social Sciences and Humanities Research Council (SSHRC).
3. Personal communication, July 12, 2021.
4. Many feminists are involved in social work. Some of them provide direct services, such as programs, and advocacy work. I use the term "social work" broadly to include everyone in the social services, from community workers, organizers, counsellors, clinicians, and advocates to policymakers, regardless of training or licences.

5. Elene Lam, "Behind the Rescue: How Anti-Trafficking Investigation and Policies Harm Migrant Sex Workers," Butterfly Asian and Migrant Sex Workers Support Network, June 2018, filesusr.com; Elene Lam, "Survey on Toronto Holistic Practitioners' Experiences with Bylaw Enforcement and Police," Butterfly Asian and Migrant Sex Workers Support Network, May 2018, filesusr.com.
6. Theresa Anasti, "Officers Are Doing the Best They Can: Concerns around Law Enforcement and Social Service Collaboration in Service Provision to Sex Workers," *Affilia* 35, no. 1 (December 2019): 49–72, doi.org/10.1177/0886109919889034.
7. "Do No Harm When Working with Trafficked Victims," Government of British Columbia, accessed September 1, 2020, gov.bc.ca.
8. Kamala Kempadoo, "Prostitution and Sex Work Studies," in *A Companion to Gender Studies*, eds. Philomena Essed, David Theo Goldberg, and Audrey Kobayashi (Hoboken, NJ: Wiley-Blackwell, 2005), 255–56; Kamala Kempadoo, "Abolitionism, Criminal Justice, and Transnational Feminism: Twenty-First-Century Perspectives on Human Trafficking," in *Trafficking and Prostitution Reconsidered: New Perspectives on Migration, Sex Work, and Human Rights*, eds. Kamala Kempadoo, Jyoit Sanghera, and Bandana Pattanaik (London: Routledge, 2012) vii–xiii; Kamala Kempadoo, "The Modern-Day White (Wo)Man's Burden: Trends in Anti-Trafficking and Anti-Slavery Campaigns," *Journal of Human Trafficking* 1, no. 1 (2015): 8–20; Jennifer K. Lobasz, "Contemporary Approaches to Human Trafficking," in *Constructing Human Trafficking* (London: Palgrave Macmillan, 2019), 29–68; Nandita Sharma, "Anti-trafficking Rhetoric and the Making of a Global Apartheid," *NWSA Journal* 17, no. 3 (2005): 88–111; Julie Kaye, *Responding to Human Trafficking: Dispossession, Colonial Violence, and Resistance among Indigenous and Racialized Women* (Toronto: University of Toronto Press, 2017); Ronald Weitzer, "The Social Construction of Sex Trafficking: Ideology and Institutionalization of a Moral Crusade," *Politics & Society* 35, no. 3 (2007): 447–45.
9. Elizabeth Bernstein, "Militarized Humanitarianism Meets Carceral Feminism: The Politics of Sex, Rights, and Freedom in Contemporary Antitrafficking Campaigns," *Signs: Journal of Women in Culture and Society* 36, no. 1 (2010): 45–71.
10. Elizabeth Bernstein, "Carceral Politics as Gender Justice? The 'Traffic in Women' and Neoliberal Circuits of Crime, Sex, and Rights," *Theory and Society* 41, no. 3 (2012): 233.
11. Leah A. Jacobs, Mimi E. Kim, Darren L. Whitfield, Rachel E. Gartner, Meg Panichelli, Shana K. Kattari, Margaret Mary Downey, Shanté Stuart McQueen, and Sarah E. Mountz, "Defund the Police: Moving

Towards an Anti-Carceral Social Work," *Journal of Progressive Human Services* 32, no. 1 (2021): 37–62.

12. See Elizabeth Bernstein, "Militarized Humanitarianism"; Kamala Kempadoo, "Women of Color and the Global Sex Trade: Transnational Feminist Perspectives," *Meridians: Feminism, Race, Transnationalism* 1, no. 2 (2001): 28–51; Jo Doezema, *Sex Slaves and Discourse Masters: The Construction of Trafficking*, (London: Bloomsbury Publishing, 2010); Jo Doezema, "Ouch! Western Feminists 'Wounded Attachment' to the 'Third World Prostitute,'" *Feminist Review* 67, no. 1 (2001): 16–38.
13. Robyn Maynard, "Carceral Feminism: The Failure of Sex Work Prohibition," *FUSE Magazine* 35, no. 3 (2012): 28–32; Mechthild Nagel, "Trafficking with Abolitionism: An Examination of Anti-Slavery Discourses," *Champ pénal/Penal field*, 12 (2015).
14. Nagel, "Trafficking with Abolitionism," par 3.
15. Nagel, "Trafficking with Abolitionism," par 3.
16. Nagel, "Trafficking with Abolitionism," par 3.
17. Canadian Association of Social Workers, "Decriminalization, Exit Strategies, and the Social Determinants of Health: A Three-Pronged Approach to Health, Safety and Dignity for Sex Workers", August 2019, casw-acts.ca.
18. Stephanie Wahab, "For Their Own Good: Sex Work, Social Control and Social Workers, a Historical Perspective," J. Soc. & Soc. Welfare, 29 (2002): 53–54.
19. Ann De Shalit, Emily van der Meulen, and Adrian Guta, "Social Service Responses to Human Trafficking: The Making of a Public Health Problem," *Culture, Health & Sexuality* 23, no. 2 (2020): 12.
20. Jennifer Musto, "Transing Critical Criminology: A Critical Unsettling and Transformative Anti-Carceral Feminist Reframing," *Critical Criminology* 27, no. 1 (2019): 37–54.
21. Imagining Abolition, ep. 1, "It Started with Organizing," directed by Patrisse Cullors, aired July 16, 2021, YouTube, blacklivesmatter.com; "Stop Racism against Asian Migrant Massage Workers and Sex Workers," Toronto Solidarity Rally Against Anti-Asian Racism, Butterfly Asian and Migrant Sex Workers Support Network, last modified March 28, 2021, facebook.com; Carol Tosone and Kirk James, "Black Lives, Mass Incarceration, and the Perpetuity of Trauma in the Era of COVID-19: The Road to Abolition Social Work," in *Shared Trauma, Shared Resilience During a Pandemic: Social Work in the Time of COVID-19*, ed. Carol Tosone (Cham, Switzerland: Springer, 2020), 281–90.
22. Donna Baines, "Soft Cops or Social Justice Activists: Social Work's

Relationship to the State in the Context of BLM and Neoliberalism," *The British Journal of Social Work* 52, no. 5 (July 2021): 1–19.
23. Patricia O'Brien, Mimi Kim, Elizabeth Beck, and Rupaleem Bhuyan, "Introduction to Special Topic on Anticarceral Feminisms: Imagining a World Without Prisons," *Affilia* 35, no. 1 (2020): 8.
24. Sandra M. Leotti, "Social Work with Criminalized Women: Governance or Resistance in the Carceral State?" *Affilia* 36, no. 3 (2021).
25. Robyn Maynard, "Fighting Wrongs with Wrongs? How Canadian Anti-Trafficking Crusades Have Failed Sex Workers, Migrants, and Indigenous Communities," *Atlantis: Critical Studies in Gender, Culture & Social Justice* 37, no. 2 (2016): 40.
26. See Operation Northern Spotlight, Project Orphan, and Project Crediton Canada.
27. Lam, "Behind the Rescue"; Lam, "Survey on Toronto"; Canadian Alliance for Sex Work Law Reform (press release), "Sex Workers Groups Oppose Police Operation Northern Spotlight," October 9, 2018, sexworklawreform.com; Annalee Lepp, "Canada," in *Sex Workers Organising for Change: Self Representation, Community Mobilisation, and Working Conditions* (Global Alliance Against Traffic in Women, 2018), 151–95; Toronto Network Against Trafficking in Women, "Multicultural History Society of Ontario, and Metro Toronto Chinese and Southeast Asian Legal Clinic," in *Trafficking in Women including Thai Migrant Sex Workers in Canada* (Toronto: TNATW, June 2000), mhso.ca.
28. Nandita Sharma, "On Being Not Canadian: The Social Organization of 'Migrant Workers' in Canada," *Canadian Review of Sociology* 38, no. 4 (2001): 415–39.
29. Sharma, "Anti-trafficking Rhetoric"; Eithne Luibheid, *Entry Denied: Controlling Sexuality at the Border* (Minneapolis: University of Minnesota Press, 2002).
30. Chris Chapman and A. J. Withers, *A Violent History of Benevolence: Interlocking Oppression in the Moral Economies of Social Working* (Toronto: University of Toronto Press, 2019); Craig Fortier and Edward Hon-Sing Wong, "The Settler Colonialism of Social Work and the Social Work of Settler Colonialism," *Settler Colonial Studies* 9, no. 4 (2019): 437–56.
31. Philip Hughes, "Religion and Volunteering through Groups and Organisations," *Journal of Contemporary Ministry*, no. 4 (2018): 120–29.
32. Marilyn F. Whiteley, "'Allee Samee Melican Lady:' Imperialism and Negotiation at the Chinese Rescue Home (Women Missionary Societies Set Up the Chinese Rescue Home to Save Chinese Women from Prostitution)," *Resources for Feminist Research* 22, nos. 3/4 (1992): 45.

33. Maynard, "Fighting Wrongs with Wrongs?," 41.
34. Nagel, "Trafficking with Abolitionism."
35. Factum of the Interveners, Canadian Association of Sexual Assault Centres, Native Women's Association of Canada, Canadian Association of Elizabeth Fry Societies, Action Ontarienne Contre La Violence Faite Aux Femmes, La Concertation des Luttes Contre L'exploitation Sexuelle, Le Regroupement Québécois des Centres D'aide et de lutte Contre les Agressions À Caractère Sexuel, and Vancouver Rape Relief Society, Intervening as the Women's Coalition for the Abolition of Prostitution, May 30, 2013, 9.
36. O'Brien et al., "Special Topic on Anticarceral Feminisms," 6.
37. Maynard, "Carceral Feminism," par 24.
38. Mimi E. Kim, "Anti-Carceral Feminism: The Contradictions of Progress and the Possibilities of Counter-Hegemonic Struggle," *Affilia* 35, no. 3 (2020): 309–26; Mimi E. Kim, "Transformative Justice and Restorative Justice: Gender-Based Violence and Alternative Visions of Justice in the United States," *International Review of Victimology* 27, no. 2 (2021): 162–72.
39. Butterfly Asian and Migrant Sex Workers Support Network, "Rally Against Anti-Asian Racism."

CHAPTER 9: SOCIAL WORK ABOLITION IN UNSETTLING TIMES

1. *Truth and Reconciliation Commission of Canada, Calls to Action* (Winnipeg, MB: TRCC, 2015).
2. Dylan Rodriguez, "The Political Logic of the Non-Profit Industrial Complex," in *The Revolution Will Not Be Funded: Beyond the Non-Profit Industrial Complex*, eds. INCITE! Women of Color Against Violence (Cambridge, MA: South End Press, 2007), 21–40.
3. Rodriguez, "Political Logic."
4. Chris Chapman and A. J. Withers, *A Violent History of Benevolence: Interlocking Oppression in the Moral Economies of Social Working* (Toronto: University of Toronto Press, 2019).
5. Edward Hon-Sing Wong, MJ Rwigema, Nicole Penak, and Craig Fortier, "Abolishing Carceral Social Work" in *Disarm, Defund, Dismantle: Police Abolition In Canada*, eds. Shiri Pasternak, Kevin Walby, and Abby Stadnyk (Toronto, Between the Lines, 2021), 145–53.
6. Anna Lowenhaupt Tsing, *The Mushroom at the End of the World: On the Possibility of Life in Capitalist Ruin* (Princeton, NJ: Princeton University Press, 2017).
7. Gordon Pon, "Cultural Competency as New Racism: An Ontology of Forgetting, *Journal of Progressive Human Services* 20 no. 1 (2009): 149–67.

8. Craig Fortier and Edward HS Wong, "The Settler Colonialism of Social Work and the Social Work of Settler Colonialism," *Settler Colonial Studies* 9, no. 4 (2018): 437–56.
9. Fortier and Wong, "Settler Colonialism of Social Work"; Raven Sinclair, "Aboriginal Social Work Education in Canada: Decolonizing Pedagogy for the Seventh Generation," *First Peoples Child & Family Review* 1, no. 1 (2004): 49–61.
10. Chapman and Withers, *Violent History of Benevolence*.
11. Fortier and Wong, "Settler Colonialism of Social Work," 4.
12. INCITE! Women of Color Against Violence, *Revolution Will Not Be Funded*.
13. Eve Tuck and K. Wayne Yang, "Decolonization Is Not a Metaphor," *Decolonization: Indigeneity, Education & Society* 1, no. 1 (2012): 1–40.
14. Klee Benally, "Accomplices Not Allies: Abolishing the Ally Industrial Complex – An Indigenous Perspective & Provocation," *Indigenous Action Media*, 2014, indigenousaction.org.
15. Bindi Bennett, Joanna Zubrzycki, and Violet Bacon, "'What Do We Know?' The Experiences of Social Workers Working Alongside Aboriginal People," *Australian Social Work* 1, no. 64 (2011): 20–37.
16. Tuck and Yang, "Decolonization Is Not a Metaphor," 31.
17. Alexis Shotwell, *Against Purity: Living Ethically in Compromised Times* (Minneapolis: University of Minnesota Press, 2016), 36.
18. INCITE! Women of Color Against Violence, *Community Accountability: How Do We Address Violence in Our Communities?* INCITE! 2019, incite-national.org.
19. Nilan Yu, "Rights, Justice, the Law, and Extralegal Action," in *Subversive Action: Extralegal Practices for Social Justice*, eds. Nilan Yu and Deena Mandell (Waterloo, ON: WLU Press, 2015), 169.
20. Yu, "Rights, Justice, the Law," 169.
21. INCITE! Women of Color Against Violence, *Revolution Will Not Be Funded*, 3.
22. Ruth Wilson Gilmore, "In the Shadow of the Shadow State," in *Revolution Will Not Be Funded*, eds. INCITE! Women of Color Against Violence, 41–52; Glen S. Coulthard, *Red Skin, White Masks: Rejecting the Colonial Politics of Recognition* (Minneapolis: University of Minnesota Press, 2014).
23. Alexandra Crampton, "Decolonizing Social Work 'Best Practices' through a Philosophy of Impermanence," *Journal of Indigenous Social Development* 4, no. 1 (2015): 1–11.
24. Claire Norris and Christopher A. Faircloth, "Medicalization of Deviance," in *Encyclopedia of Social Deviance*, eds. Craig J. Forsyth and Heith Copes (Thousand Oaks: Sage Publications 2014).

25. Colin Barnes, "Understanding the Social Model of Disability," in *Routledge Handbook of Disability Studies*, eds. Nick Watson, Alan Roulstone, and Carol Thomas (New York: Taylor & Francis Group, 2012).
26. Crampton, "Decolonizing Social Work."
27. Amy Rossiter, "Innocence Lost and Suspicion Found: Do We Educate for or against Social Work?," *Critical Social Work*, 2(1), 2001. uwindsor.ca
28. Jen Preston, "Racial Extractivism and White Settler Colonialism: An Examination of the Canadian Tar Sands Mega-projects," *Cultural Studies* 31, nos. 2–3 (2017): 1–23.
29. Coulthard, *Red Skins*, 108–109.
30. Kimberly M. Blaeser, *Gerald Vizenor: Writing in the Oral Tradition* (Norman: University of Oklahoma Press, 1996).

CHAPTER 10: THE ONLY GOOD SOCIAL WORKER IS A CRIMINAL SOCIAL WORKER

1. In this essay, I'll be using social work in the "small s" sense to refer to all of those who labour in the social work sector, not only those who are registered and licensed social workers, though I recognize that there are significant differences between social workers and social service workers.
2. See Dorothy Roberts, *Torn Apart: How the Child Welfare System Destroys Black Families—and How Abolition Can Build a Safer World* (New York: Basic Books, 2022) and Chris Chapman and A.J. Withers, *A Violent History of Benevolence: Interlocking Oppression in the Moral Economies of Social Working* (Toronto: University of Toronto Press, 2019).
3. However, the governing bodies of social workers have participated in the development of oppressive criminal code legislation, and biased research conducted by social work researchers has sometimes played a role in racist, classist, and colonial court decisions.
4. For more information on the project, see ohtn.on.ca.
5. "Barring" refers to when social service agencies refuse to provide service to someone who has been banned from the space, typically for a specified period. This barring could be twenty-four hours, a few days, a week, a year, or permanent.
6. Quoted from Everyday Abolition/Abolition Everyday, "How Drug Users and Street Based Folks Are Transforming Harm into Community," September 15, 2015, everydayabolition.com.
7. Everyday Abolition/Abolition Everyday, "How Drug Users."

CHAPTER 11: CONVERSATIONS ON DECOLONIZING JUSTICE

1. Audrey identifies as being of mixed settler and Indigenous ancestry

and is a bisexual cis woman that uses she/her pronouns. Carol Lynne identifies as a white settler cis woman ally and also uses she/her pronouns.
2. itstartswithus-mmiw.com.
3. We hope to make the transcripts of these conversations available on the It Starts With Us website as well.
4. On June 11, 2008, then prime minister of Canada Stephen Harper issued a public apology to survivors of residential schools in Canada. The text of that apology can be read here: rcaanc-cirnac.gc.ca.
5. Angela Y. Davis, *Abolition Feminism: Celebrating 20 Years of INCITE!*, Hosted by the Interrupting Criminalization Initiative of the Barnard Center for Research on Women, April 30, 2020, virtual, incite-national.org.

CHAPTER 13: SOCIAL WORK'S VERY COMPLICATED RELATIONSHIP WITH INDIGENOUS LANGUAGES

1. Gratitude to Richard (Giibwanisi) Peters, a fellow Anishinaabemowin language learner, for reviewing an early draft of this chapter. The Lisk quote comes from "'For Our Children': How Families Are Passing Down Indigenous Languages," *TVO Today*, November 25, 2020, tvo.org.
2. Jiyoun Choi, Anne Cutler, and Mirjam Broersma, "Early Development of Abstract Language Knowledge: Evidence from Perception - Production Transfer of Birth-Language Memory," *Royal Society Open Science* 4, no. 1 (2017), doi.org/10.1098/rsos.160660.
3. Anton Treuer, *The Language Warrior's Manifesto: How to Keep Our Languages Alive No Matter the Odds* (Saint Paul: Minnesota Historical Society Press, 2020), 80.
4. Treuer, *Language Warrior's Manifesto*, 102.
5. Raven Sinclair, "Bridging the Past and the Future: An Introduction to Indigenous Social Work Issues" in *Wicihitowin: Aboriginal Social Work in Canada*, eds. Gord Bruyere, Michael Anthony Hart, and Raven Sinclair (Winnipeg, MB: Fernwood Publishing, 2009), 20.
6. Nicole Penak, "Walking Toronto's Red Road: The Story Pathways of Indigenous Social Workers" (PhD diss., OISE/University of Toronto, 2019), 5.
7. According to the Toronto Aboriginal Research report, "81% of respondents were unable to converse in their Aboriginal language." When I read this, I deduced that this meant 19 percent of the urban population is able to converse in their Indigenous language. Don McCaskill, Kevin FitzMaurice, and Jaime Cidro, *Toronto Aboriginal*

Research Project, Final Report, Commissioned by Toronto Aboriginal Support Services Council (TASSC), 2006, toronto.ca.
8. Statistics Canada, "The Aboriginal Languages of First Nations People, Metis, and Inuit," October 25, 2017, statcan.gc.ca.
9. Kathy Absolon King, *Kaandossiwin How We Come to Know* (Winnipeg, MB: Fernwood Publishing, 2011).
10. Treuer, *Language Warrior's Manifesto*, 72.
11. TARP, 303.
12. This chapter will not be discussing "traditional" or "spiritual" names given to organizations. This seems to be happening more and more in urban areas, and often these names include Indigenous languages, but there are more complicated cultural and political issues at play in these situations. While they do need to be discussed, they are beyond the scope of this chapter.
13. Eve Tuck and K. Wayne Yang, "Decolonization Is Not a Metaphor," *Decolonization: Indigeneity, Education & Society* 1, no. 1 (2012): 1–40.
14. Tuck and Yang, "Decolonization Is Not a Metaphor," 10.
15. Tuck and Yang, "Decolonization Is Not a Metaphor," 17.
16. Tuck and Yang, "Decolonization Is Not a Metaphor," 19.
17. Treuer, *Language Warrior's Manifesto*, 79
18. Robyn Maynard and Leanne Betasamosake Simpson, *Rehearsals for Living* (Toronto: Penguin Random House, 2022).

CHAPTER 14: TORONTO INDIGENOUS HARM REDUCTION

1. We would like to acknowledge the support of Elder Wanda Whitebird, Dashmaawaan Bemadzinjin (They Feed the People), Holy Trinity TO, all the youth, Fire Keepers, Knowledge Keepers, singers, and dancers who made this ceremony a reality and who also stand behind our community in solidarity. A version of this writing appeared on the Yellowhead Institute blog in 2021.
2. Peter Menzies, "Aboriginal Homelessness," paper presented at the Rethinking Homelessness: Theoretical and Methodological Challenges conference, University of Montreal, Montreal, Canada, October 28, 2010, homelesshub.ca.

CHAPTER 15: BLACK CREEK COMMUNITY FARM

1. The BCCF Roundtable took place over Zoom on September 29, 2020. Unless otherwise indicated, all quotes from participants in this chapter come from this roundtable.
2. Sara Thomas Black, "Abolitionist Food Justice: Theories of Change Rooted in Place—and Life-Making," *Food and Foodways: Explorations*

in the *History and Culture of Human Nourishment* 30, nos. 1–2 (2022): 123–41, doi.org/10.1080/07409710.2022.2030942.
3. "Canadians Pay Wide Range of Prices for Healthy Foods, Report," *CBC*, February 9, 2009, cbc.ca.
4. David Hulchanski, *The Three Cities within Toronto: Income Polarization among Toronto's Neighbourhoods, 1970–2005* (Toronto, Cities Centre Press, 2010), neighbourhoodchange.ca.
5. D. Ahmadi, "Diversity and Social Cohesion: The Case of Jane-Finch, a Highly Diverse Lower-Income Toronto Neighbourhood," *Urban Research & Practice* 2 (2018): 139–57.
6. Black Creek Food Justice Network (BCFJN), *Fighting for Food Justice in the Black Creek Community: Report, Analyses and Steps Forward*, Toronto, Black Creek Community Health Centre, December 13, 2017, bcchc.com.
7. Shortly after the radio program launched in 2015, CHRY got rebranded under VIBE 105.5 and all the community radio programs were cancelled.
8. BCFJN, *Fighting for Food Justice*.
9. Jane Finch Action Against Poverty, "Jane Finch Letter to No Frills," April 2, 2019, jfaap.wordpress.com.

INDEX

Abdi, Abdirahman, 40
Abolition Convergence, 1–2
abolition of social work: overview, 9, 11–12, 115–16; and abolitionism, 130–1; accountability, 118–20; building community, 12; and community leadership, 12 (*see also* leadership); divesting power, 10, 12 (*see also* power); and enforcing rules, 128; five principles of, 12; and funding, 12 (*see also* funding); mutual aid, 120–1 (*see also* mutual aid); pedagogy transformation, 12 (*see also* education); as process, 126; reckoning, 117–18; respectful relationships, 122; and solidarity, 126–9, 131–3; unsettling, 121–2. *See also* community-based approaches; resistance
abolitionism: overview, 20–1, 130–1; and abolition of social work, 130–1; as binary, 139; as Black women support, 49; and building structures, 22–3, 82; and carceral collaboration, 10; and contradictions, 90–1; defined, 54; defining social work, 22; disinvesting own power, 10; and Du Bois, 8; and enslavement, 9; and food security, 189–90; and forensic mental health system, 79; four principles of, 10; and INCITE! 8–9, 90, 141; and justice, 25; mental health care as therapeutic, 80–1; and noncooperation, 10; and people, 24; and policing within, 10; and power, 24–5; principles/frameworks, 23–7; as process, 126; against the state, 28–30; usage in anti-trafficking, 93, 95; and youth, 108. *See also* community-based approaches
Absolon, Kathy, 172
"Accomplices not Allies" pamphlet, 118
accountability: and abolition of social work, 118–20; and *Calls to Action*, 173; and liberatory reforms, 27; and settler colonialism, 119, 151–3, 173–7; as transformative justice, 29
Action Plan for Health Care, 46
activism and counselling, 89–90. *See also* abolition of social work; community-based approaches
Afri-Can Food Basket, 184
Against Purity (Shotwell), 119
agency, 25, 27, 57, 81, 95, 98
agriculture, 182–92
Allan, Rochelle, 165–78
Amara, Zakaria, 104, 108–13
anger, 156–7
Anishinaabe constitution, 149
Anishinaabemowin, 165–7, 169, 172, 174, 177–8

anti-Asian racism, 98, 102
anti-miscegenation, 32, 36, 38
antitrafficking, 92–102
antiviolence organizing, 24, 26
Asian people, 92, 97–8, 102
assimilation, 167, 168
Attah, Prince "Classiko," 83
autonomy, 119–20, 132

Baby Bundle Program, 154, 161–4
Bacon, Violet, 119
Bailey, Annette, 49
balance, 140, 141–2
Barr, James, 34
barring, 129, 217n5
Bay Area Transformative Justice Collective, 29
BC Missing Women Inquiry, 151
Beckett, Katherine, 45
Bedford v Canada Supreme Court, 100
Benjamin, Akua, 52–3, 54
Bennett, Bindi, 119
Bergen, Heather, 82–91
Bernstein, Elizabeth, 94
Beutin, Lyndsey, 97–8
Big Canoe, Christa, 135–6, 137, 143, 145–6, 150–1, 153
Bill 251, 100–1
BIPOC (Black, Indigenous, People of Colour), 6, 19, 24, 26. *See also* Black people; INCITE!; Indigenous languages; Indigenous Peoples; marginalization; racism
Birth Alert System, 58, 161
birthing people, 157–8. *See also* Child and Family Services; Children's Aid Societies
birthwork, 154, 160, 161–4
Black Creek Community Farm (BCCF), 182, 183–92
Black Creek Food Justice Network (BCFJN), 187–90, 192
Black Farmers Collective, 184
Black feminism, 24
Black Lives Matter (BLM), 1, 21
Black people: and abolition of social work, 119; and Child and Family Services, 56–7, 58, 59, 67; containment as "care," 7; and drapetomania, 33–4; and Du Bois's work, 8; and forensic mental health system, 76; National Association of Black Social Workers, 196n4; and out-of-placeness, 51; as overrepresented in carceral system, 44–5; pacification of, 120; and police, 45, 131; in social work, 52–3. *See also* BIPOC; Black Creek Community Farm; Black women; marginalization; racism
Black women: and carceral system, 45; coerced sterilization of, 37; and health care system, 47–9; as slut shamed, 65; in social work, 53–4, 196n4; as stigmatized, 7
BlackDeer, Autumn Asher, 11
Blaeser, Kimberly M., 122
book overview, 1–2, 12–15
border control, 39, 98

INDEX 223

Boushie, Colton, 138
"The Boy and His Sandcastle" (Amara), 108–11
Boye, Solomon, 183
Brown, Michael, 21
Brown, Zakisha, 182–92
building structures, 22–3
burnout, 89–90, 112
Burstow, Bonnie, 5, 43
Butterfly (Asian and migrant sex workers organization), 92, 100

Cabrera, Felix "Flex of all Trades," 83
Calls to Action (TRC), 1, 115, 173
Canadian Alliance of Sex Work Network, 101
Canadian Association of Elizabeth Fry Societies, 97, 99–100, 102
Canadian Association of Social Workers (CASW), 5, 6, 95
Canadian Association of Social Workers Code of Ethics and Scope or Practice, 50
Canadian Centre to End Human Trafficking, 97
Canadian Citizenship Act, 38
Canadian Mental Health Association (CMHA), 34–6, 38
Canadian National Committee of Mental Hygiene (CNCMH), 34
Canadian Welfare Council (CWC), 6
Canadian Women's Foundation, 97, 102

capitalism, 51, 116, 190. *See also* neoliberalism
carceral social work, defined, 19
carceral system: overview, 11, 17–19; and Black women, 45; and Black Lives Matter mobilizations, 1, 21; border control, 39, 98; and child welfare survivors, 61; and Elders/Knowledge Keepers, 149; ending all partnerships, 23; expanding, 19; and feminism, 18, 94–5, 96, 97; as foster care, 63–4; as guiding frameworks, 23; vs. Indigenous justice, 135–9, 142–3, 144–5, 148, 150–3; and individual behaviours, 20; isolation tactics, 130 (*see also* solitary confinement); as justice, 135–6; mandated reporting, 29–30; and Not Criminally Responsible, 75–7, 79–80, 208n14–15; and programming, 106, 107, 108; as radicalizing social workers, 21; shadow carceral state, 45; and slavery, 9; solitary confinement, 107; and support, 112 (*see also* programming); working directly with, 30. *See also* abolitionism; *Cell Count*; forensic mental health; law enforcement; punishment
"care and protection," 56–7. *See also* Child and Family Services
caregiving skills, 159–60
Cell Count (newsletter), 103–13

Centre for Addiction and Mental Health (CAMH), 32, 75–6, 77–9, 209n23, 209n28
Chapman, Chris, 6
charity, 24, 51, 192
Child and Family Services (CFS) (Manitoba), 59; overview, 56–7, 67–8, 206n4; abuse and violence, 62, 66–8; Black and Indigenous Peoples, 58–9; bureaucracy of, 59–60, 63; deaths "in care," 64–5; and detention centres, 63–4; foster home availability, 61–3; hotel/motel placements, 62–3; impacts of, 60–1; manipulated data, 60; and missing persons, 61; percentile of youth, 58; and Red River, 55–6, 67; and suicides, 63, 64. *See also* Children's Aid Societies
child welfare system (general): overview, 57–9; deaths "in care," 64–5; and residential schools, 58–9; Roberts's work, 18; Turcotte's experiences, 105–7, 108
children, 7, 105, 132
Children's Aid Societies (CAS), 96, 154, 155–61. *See also* Child and Family Services
Chinese people, 36, 38
Chinese Rescue Home, 98
choices, 55–6, 65, 67
Choudry, Ejaz, 32
Chrisjohn, Roland, 43
Christians, 96–7, 98–9, 127–8, 141
coerced sterilization, 36–8

colonial equivocation, 175–6
colonialism. *See* settler colonialism
Color of Violence (INCITE!), 8–9
Combating Human Trafficking Act, 100–1
Commission for Historical Clarification (Guatemala), 139
the commons, 5
communicating needs, 163–4
community accountability. *See* accountability
Community Action for Families (CAF), 86–8, 91
community befriending, 43
Community Healing Project, 85, 210–211n5
community practices of care, 3
Community Treatment Order (CTOs), 41, 77–8
community-based approaches: overview, 82, 88–9, 115; Baby Bundle Program, 154, 161–4; Black Creek Community Farm, 182, 183–4; caregiving skills, 159–60; *Cell Count*, 103–13; Community Action for Families, 86–8, 91; drop-in centres, 128–9; Freedom Fridayz, 83–5, 89, 91, 210n3; INCITE! 8–9, 90, 141; as messy, 145–6; peer support, 129–30; romanticizing community, 145; and sex workers, 101–2; sharing, 84; as small scale networks, 147; Toronto Indigenous Harm Reduction, 179–81.

See also Indigenous Peoples; justice; MMIWGT2SQ; social working
compassion, 69, 141, 145, 163
condolence rites, 142
Connect the Dots, 184
containment, 3, 71, 117–18. *See also* carceral system
co-option, 120, 142–3, 184
Coulthard, Glen, 121–2
counselling and activism, 89–90; and conflict de-escalation, 43. *See also* abolition of social work; community-based approaches
COVID-19 pandemic: and Black Creek Community Farm, 185; and food security, 191–2; and houselessness, 179, 181; and limits of institutions, 1; and mutual aid, 28–9; social determinants of health, 50–1
Crampton, Alexandra, 120–1
crime: as social breaches, 146
criminal justice systems. *See* carceral system
criminalization: anti-Black racism, 7; avoiding, 128–9; and hospitalization, 73–4; and houselessness, 181; of Indigenous Peoples, 181; and mental health, 35–6, 45; and peer support, 129–30; "protection" reinforcing, 18; street kids, 67 (*see also* street kids)
crossover kids, 61

Daniel, Karen, 130
Daniels, Roberta "Gracie," 63
D'Arcangelis, Carol Lynne, 134–53, 218n1
Das Gupta, Tania, 47
Davis, Angela, 9, 45, 141, 150
Dawson, John, 41
De Lessovoy, Noah, 46
De Shalit, Ann, 95
death penalty, 135–6
Deawuo, Leticia Ama, 182–92
decolonization: overview, 115; Baby Bundle Program, 162; vs. carceral punishment, 135; and divesting own power, 10; and entire society, 150–1; freeing mind, 176; and Indigenous power, 145–6; Indigenous women's work, 153; mutual aid, 120–1 (*see also* mutual aid); reckoning, 117–18. *See also* accountability; D'Arcangelis, Carol Lynne; Huntley, Audrey; Indigenous Peoples: Indigenous justice/law
decriminalization, 101, 128–9
Defend Dignity, 96–7
"Defund the Police" (Jacobs et al.), 10
degeneration, 33, 34
dichotomies, 20, 27
disabilities, 33, 39
disability justice, 24
drapetomania, 33
Drug Policy Alliance, 26
drug use, 105–6, 128–9
Du Bois, W. E. B., 7–8

Early Psychosis Intervention (EPI), 74
education, 8, 12, 53, 88, 97, 153
Edwards, Richard, 4–5
Elders, 139–40, 149
emergency food boxes, 191–2
encampments, 179–80
eugenics, 32, 33–4, 36, 38–9
Eurocentrism, 135–9, 142–3, 148, 150–3, 160–1
Evangelical Fellowship of Canada, 96–7
Evans, Bryan M., 46
Everdale, 183–5

false binaries, 139
Families of Sisters in Spirit, 134–5
family policing system (FPS), 86–7, 210n2. *See also* Child and Family Services; child welfare system; Children's Aid Societies
Fanelli, Carlo, 46
Fanon, Frantz, 176
fascism, 27
Federici, Silvia, 5
Female Refuges Act, 38
feminism: and antitrafficking, 93, 94–5, 96, 97; Black feminism, 24; carceral feminists, 18, 94–5, 96, 97; freedom for people, 24; and power, 24; and sex work, 101; and social workers, 211n4
Ferguson, Renée Nichole, 44–54
Fighting for Food Justice in the Black Creek Community (report), 187–8

Fontaine, Tina, 62, 138
food apartheid, 183
food justice, 182–92
Food Justice Day of Action, 188–9
Food Share, 184, 192
forensic mental health: overview, 80–1; Canadian Mental Health Association medium-secure unit, 77–9; discharge from hospital, 74–5, 79; entering hospital, 71–4; Not Criminally Responsible, 75–7, 79–80, 209nn14–15; Ontario Review Board review, 78–9; social workers influence, 71, 77, 81; system as distressing, 72, 73
forensic social work, 19
forgiveness, 111, 141
Forms 1 and 2, 40–1, 72
Fortier, Craig, 1–15, 115–23
foster care. *See* Child and Family Services; child welfare system; Children's Aid Societies
foundational myths of Canada, 34
Frederique, Kassandra, 26
Freedom Fridayz (FF), 83–5, 89, 91, 210n3
Freedom of Information Act (FOI), 75–6, 209n23
"#FreeTheYouth" (Turcotte), 104–8
Frempong, Kofi, 83
"frequent flyers," 61. *See also* street kids
Frost, Mary, 37

funding, 10, 12, 90–1, 95, 153

Gallant, Chanelle, 124–33
Galton, Francis, 33
Gandarilla Ocampo, Maria, 11
gender nonconforming people, 7. *See also* LGBTQ+
General, Tashina, 140
genetics. *See* eugenics
genocide, 51, 59, 135, 139, 151–2
Gilmore, Ruth Wilson, 17, 23, 44, 49–50
Gonz, Andre, 197n22
Gopaul, Sabrina "Butterfly," 182–92
Gordon, Nanook, 179
Grand River First Nation, 140
Grassy Narrows River Run, 122
Gray, Byron "B Grizzy," 83
grief, 49, 61, 127, 142, 167, 181
guerilla gardening, 188–9
Guta, Adrian, 95

Hall, Prescott F., 38
Halpenny, Jasper, 35
harm: action vs. communication, 169; carceral system's perspective, 93–4; and Eurocentric legal system, 136–7; and feminism, 102; and healing, 146; Indigenous justice/law, 140; and justice, 25–6, 29; perpetuators of, 150; as present, 119, 121–2; vs. rule violation, 132; and situation table, 42. *See also* punishment; violence
harm reduction, 128–9, 179–81
Harper, Stephen, 139, 218n4
Harris, Mike, 46

Hartman, Saidiya, 7
healing, 146, 149, 168, 211n5
health, 45–9, 50–1, 183. *See also* mental health
hierarchies of humanity, 20, 27
hierarchy of needs, 162
high risk, 56, 58, 59
Hincks, Clarence M., 34, 35
hooks, bell, 88
Hospital for Sick Children, 211n7
hospitalization, 40–2, 72–3
hospitals, 37, 41, 46, 68, 72, 74, 76–9, 160–1
hotels/motels, 62–3
houseless people, 179–81
human rights violations, 63, 64
human trafficking, 92–102
Hunt, Sarah, 137–9, 142, 144, 147, 148, 149–50
Huntley, Audrey, 134–53, 218n1
Hussain, Sena, 103–4, 111–12
Hussen, Ahmed, 39

identities, 50–1
immigration, 34, 35–6, 38–9, 117. *See also* migrant sex workers
Immigration and Refugee Protection Act, 99
impermanence, 121
Inaakonigewin, 149
incarceration. *See* carceral system
INCITE! Women of Color Against Violence, 8–9, 90, 141
Indian Act, 38
Indian agents, 3, 6
Indigenous languages: overview, 176–8; Allen's journey,

165–7, 171–2, 177; and assimilation, 167, 168; as gesture, 173; and guilt, 172; as healing, 168; Indigenous vs. settler students, 176; Lisk's journey, 165; loss of, 143; naming vs. learning, 173–5, 178; reality of programs, 165–6, 167, 171, 172–3; (re)naming, 173–5, 178, 219n12; reviving for justice, 148; speakers vs. teachers, 171–2; Toronto Aboriginal Research Project, 171, 172–3; threats to, 168

Indigenous Peoples: and abolition of social work, 119; anger as weaponized, 157; assimilation, 167, 168; and birthwork resurgence, 154; ceremony, 142, 147; and Child and Family Services, 56–7, 58, 59, 67; and child welfare system, 58–9, 117, 160–1 (*see also* Child and Family Services; Children's Aid Societies); and children, 158, 160–1; coerced sterilization of, 36–7; commerce of pain, 118; displacement, 179–81; Elders, 139–40, 149; and Eurocentric system, 135–9, 142–3, 144–5, 148, 150–3, 160–1 (*see also* Indigenous languages); and forensic mental health system, 76; grassroots movements in Toronto, 180; Grassy Narrows River Run, 122; harm reduction, 179–81; healing tools, 146, 149; houseless people, 179–81; Inaakonigewin, 149; Indian Act, 38, 149–50; and Indian agents, 3, 6, 51, 117; Indigenous justice/law, 139–43, 144–6, 153; Land Back movement, 137, 144, 148; and mental hygiene movement, 34–5; Millennial Scoop, 117; pacification of, 120; and patriarchy, 149–50; and police, 131; rebuilding, 168; recognition vs. reconciliation, 173; residential schools, 1, 121, 218n4; and settler nativism, 174; Sixties Scoop, 117, 121, 160; as slut shamed, 65; and social work abolition, 115; teepees, 179–80; Traditional Knowledge, 6–7, 149, 151, 153, 168; Turcotte's experiences (*see* Turcotte, Nolan). *See also* BIPOC; *Calls to Action*; marginalization; MMIWGT2SQ; settler colonialism; truth and reconciliation; Truth and Reconciliation of Canada

individualism, 20, 25

informal social work. *See* social working

"An Institutional Ethnography Inquiry into the Policing and Investigation of Migrant Sex Workers in Canada" (Lam), 92

interconnectedness, 52, 53

intersectionality, 9, 28, 102

interracial relations, 38

interventions, 42. *See also* involuntary hospitalization

INDEX

Inuit, 6–7
involuntary hospitalization, 40–2, 72–3
Iraq War, 110
Irvin-Ross, Kerri, 61, 64
Islam, 109, 110
It Starts With Us, 135, 146

Jacobs, Beverly, 137, 139–40, 141, 145–6, 149, 150, 153
Jacobs, Leah A., 10, 19, 23
James, Carl, 54
James, Kirk "Jae," 20
Jane and Finch Action Against Poverty (JFAAP), 183, 184, 189–90, 192
Jane and Finch neighbourhood, 83–5, 182–92
Jane's Walk, 88
Jarvis, Sheryl, 86
Jefferies, Keisha, 48
Jeyapal, Daphne, 11
Johnston, Patricia, 6
Journey for Justice, 143
Jubin, Michelle, 49
justice: and abolitionism, 25; carceral system as, 135–6; and compassion, 141; disability justice, 24; and language, 148; meaning of, 148–9, 150; social justice, 89; transformative/reparative, 25, 26, 28–9, 143–4. *See also* Indigenous Peoples
justice of the peace, 40–1
Juvie, 55–69

Kaba, Mariame, 28, 88–9
Kilgore, James, 44, 49–50
Kim, Mimi, 18, 23

knowledge, 4–5, 6–8, 120, 133. *See also* Indigenous Peoples: Traditional Knowledge
Korchinski-Paquet, Regis, 40, 48–9
Kraepelin, Emil, 33

Lam, Elene, 92–102
Land Back movement, 137, 144, 148
language learning. *See* Indigenous languages
The Language Warrior's Manifesto (Treue), 177
Law, Vikki, 19
law enforcement: antitrafficking, 92–3, 96, 102; and Black people, 45, 131; defunding, 10; and encampments, 179–80; and grocery stores, 189; and Indigenous Peoples, 131; Mobile Crisis Intervention Team, 74–5; and mental health, 32, 39–43, 48–9, 202n53; and MMIWGT2SQ, 151; policing within, 10; protection from, 130–1; and reserve communities, 147; and sex workers drop-in, 128; and street kids, 66–7; as targeting communities, 9–10; violence used, 40, 45, 48–9, 85. *See also* carceral system
leadership, 12, 24
Lewis-Peart, David, 52
LGBTQ+, 24, 49. *See also* gender nonconforming people
liability, 29, 71, 86, 160, 172
liberatory reforms, 26–7

Lisk, Shelby, 165
lived experience, 55–69, 154
Loblaws, 190
Loku, Andrew, 40
Lololi, Anan, 182–92
Lorde, Audre, 143
Lucas-White, Lydia, 53

mad literacy, 43
mad movement activists, 43
Maggie's, 101
mandated reporting, 29–30
Manitoba. *See* Child and Family Services
Manitoba Youth Centre, 63–4
Manning, Al, 107
marginalization: and carceral system, 18; as choice, 55–6, 65, 67; and leadership, 24; and resistance, 11; and transformative justice, 26
Martensen, Kayla, 11, 19–20
Maslow, Abraham, 162
Maynard, Robyn, 7, 97, 101, 177
medication, 72, 73, 77–8
Memorial March, 142
Mensah, Rosie, 186
mental health: Centre for Addiction and Mental Health police statement, 32; of child welfare survivors, 61; clinical notes, 208n6; and forensic social work, 19; generational trauma, 61; history of mental hygiene movement, 34–9; labelling, 72–3; and law enforcement, 32, 39–43, 48–9, 202n53; and Mi'kmaw society, 6; and neoliberalism, 46; Not Criminally Responsible, 209nn14–15; and racism, 32–4, 38, 39–40; records, 208n6; solitary confinement, 209–10n28; as therapeutic, 80–1. *See also* forensic mental health
Mental Health Act (Ontario), 48–9, 72, 202n53
mental hygiene movement, 34
Mi (sex worker), 97–8
midwives, 159, 162–3. *See also* Baby Bundle Program; birthwork
migrant sex workers, 92–102
Mi'kmaw society, 3
Millennial Scoop, 117
miscegenation, 38
Mishaiel, Rosie, 182–92
MMIWGT2SQ (missing and murdered Indigenous women, girls, trans, Two-Spirit, and queer people): and colonization, 144; and community support, 148; and death penalty, 135–6; as genocide, 152; vs. land rights, 137, 144; responses to, 134–5; and retribution, 138. *See also* National Inquiry into Missing and Murdered Indigenous Women and Girls
Mobile Crisis Intervention Team (MCIT), 74–5
money, withholding, 125
Monture, Patricia, 150
Monture, Terri, 138, 140–1, 142–3, 146
Moon/Water Song (Tammaro), v–vi

Moore, Dorothy E., 53
moral panic, 95, 96–8
MotherRisk Commission, 88, 211n7
Movement for Black Lives, 21
moves to innocence, 173–8
Murakawa, Naomi, 45
Musto, Jennifer, 96
mutual aid: overview, 25, 28–9; as African/diasporic interconnectedness, 52, 53–4; and the commons, 5; and food security, 191–2; and history of social work, 3; and nonprofit industrial complex, 120; as outside the state, 2–3, 28–9; and relationality, 121; and social work abolition, 120–1; as social working, 2–3

Nagel, Mechthild, 95
Nair, Sethu, 22
Narain, Suzanne, 182–92
National Association of Black Social Workers, 196n4
National Inquiry into Missing and Murdered Indigenous Women and Girls, 135, 137, 138, 144–5, 151–2. *See also* MMIWGT2SQ
Native Youth Sexual Health Network, 134–5
navigation of infrastructures, 160
neglect, 155–6
neoliberalism, 18, 20, 45–7, 94
Newsom, Andrew "Uncle Drew," 83, 210n3
No Frills, 189–90

No More Silence, 151. *See also* D'Arcangelis, Carol Lynne; Huntley, Audrey
nongovernmental organizations (NGOs), 95–6
nonprofit industrial complex (NPIC), 118, 120, 121
Northwest Territories Child Welfare Ordinance, 7
Not Criminally Responsible (NCR), 75–7, 79–80, 209nn14–15
nursing, 47–8

O'Brien, Patricia, 96
Office of the Commissioner of Indigenous Languages, 168
Olson Pitawanakwat, Brianna, 179–81
Ontario Review Board (ORB), 70, 73, 75–7, 78–9, 209n14

Page, J. D., 34
Palmer, Lue, 70–81
parenting skills, 159–60
parents, 157–8. *See also* Child and Family Services; Children's Aid Societies
patriarchy, 149–50
Paul Dojack Youth Centre (PDYC), 106–7
peer-led, 91, 129–30, 133. *See also* abolition of social work; community-based approaches
Penak, Nicole, 1–2, 170, 193n4
pod-mapping processes, 29
police. *See* law enforcement

Policing Black Lives (Maynard), 7
political homes, 30–1
poverty, 155–6, 183. See also houseless people
power: building, 24–5; centring, 163–4; for communities, 127; divesting, 10; monopolization of, 6; power over vs. power with, 24, 81; and professionalization, 4, 125; recognizing existing, 144; withholding money/necessities, 125
Preston, Sparrow, 11
principles/frameworks, 23–4
Prison By Any Other Name (Schenwar and Law), 19
prison industrial complex (PCI), 9, 17–19. See carceral system
professionalization, 4–6, 7, 116–17, 120, 121, 125, 127
Protection of Communities and Exploited Persons Act, 100
psychiatric survivors, 38, 41
punishment: overview, 52; anti-trafficking, 93–4; banishment as, 140; and Black women, 45, 47–9; and budget cuts, 46–7; as distressing, 74, 75, 77; in health care, 47–8; and Indigenous justice/law, 140; Mental Health Act, 72; and race, 76; restriction of liberty, 72; rethinking, 53; of social workers, 132

Qaujimajatuqangit, 6–7

racial capitalism, 51
racial equity, 6
racial identity, 50–1
racial profiling, 52–3, 97
racialized people. See BIPOC; Black people; Indigenous languages; Indigenous Peoples
racism: anti-Asian racism, 98, 102; anti-miscegenation, 38; and antitrafficking, 97–9; as central to social work, 18; and child welfare system, 7; Community Healing Project, 85; and disability, 33–4, 35, 39; and eugenics, 32, 33–4, 36, 38–9; and Everdale, 184; and forensic mental health system, 76, 80; and hospitalization, 73–4; and Jane and Finch neighbourhood, 84; in language learning context, 176; and mental health, 32–4, 38, 39–40; in nursing, 47–8; in school, 105; scientific racism, 32, 33–8, 43; and stereotypes, 47
radicalism, 108–11
Rasmussen, Cameron, 17–31
Re: Sim, 76–7
reckoning, 117–18
reconciliation, 121–2. See also Truth and Reconciliation of Canada
Red River, 55, 62, 67
reflection, 169, 172, 173–4
reform, 26–7, 197n22
Rehearsals for Living (Maynard and Simpson), 177
Reid, P. Nelson, 4–5

relationality, 121
reparations, 1
reparative justice, 26
residency based programs, 158
residential schools, 1, 59, 121, 218n4
resistance: and Black people, 52; decriminalization, 101, 128–9; and marginalization, 11; National Association of Black Social Workers, 196n4; and risk, 130–3; Scott's ideas, 195n46; teaching social workers, 126; as "unprofessional," 157. *See also* abolition of social work; abolitionism; community-based approaches
restitution, 141, 142–3, 147
restorative justice, 25, 143–4
Restorative Justice Conflict Resolution/Harm Reduction (RJHR), 129
retribution, 138, 140, 142–3, 147
The Revolution Will Not Be Funded (INCITE!), 8–9, 90
Richie, Beth, 11, 19–20
The Right Food: Right to Food campaign, 183
right-wing Christians, 96–7, 98–9
risk, 56, 58, 59, 71, 72, 78–9, 131–2
Risk-Drive Tracking Database, 42
River Run, 122
Roberts, Dorothy, 18
Rusza, Joan, 129
Rwigema, MJ, 1–15, 52

Said, Edward, 4
salvage accumulation, 116
saviour complex, 96, 98–101, 122
Schenwar, Maya, 19
schizophrenia, 33, 34
scientific racism, 32, 33–8, 43
Scott, James C., 195n46
secondary decision maker (SDM), 41
Seltzer, Carly, 70–81
settler colonialism: accountability, 119, 151–3, 173–7; Children's Aid Societies as, 160–1; colonial equivocation, 175–6; and eugenics, 33; Indigenous Peoples and justice, 135–6; and Indigenous Peoples dispossession, 10; and land, 148; and MMIWGT2SQ, 144; settler framing of, 34–5; as structure, 170. *See also* decolonization; Indigenous languages; Indigenous Peoples: and Eurocentric system
"The Settler Colonialism of Social Work" (Fortier and Wong), 10
settler nativism, 174
settler perpetrators, 150–1
sex workers, 92–102, 126, 127–8
Sexual Sterilization Act of Alberta (1928), 36
shadow carceral state, 45
Shahidi, Golta, 70–81
Sharma, Manoj, 49
Sharma, Nandita, 5
Shattered Bonds (Roberts), 18
shelters, 62, 157, 181
Shera, Wes, 4–5

Shotwell, Alexis, 119
Sim (NCR labelled), 76–7
Simpson, Leanne Betasamosake, 177
situation tables, 42–3
16x9 (TV program), 64–5
Sixties Scoop, 117, 121, 160
Skeete, Krystle, 82–91
skill sharing, 43
slavery, 9, 33–4
Smith, W. G., 34
social work: overview, 115, 116, 124–6, 217n3; abolition of (*see* abolition of social work); areas of, 3; and Christianity, 98; defining, 2–3, 170, 211–12n4; history of, 3, 4–5, 6–8, 51, 170, 175; individuals vs. institutions, 52; and protection, 18; as social justice, 6, 11, 12, 19, 89, 101, 126; and specialization, 4, 7; and third party reports, 41
social working: areas of, 4; defining, 2–3; as inferior, 7; Restorative Justice Conflict Resolution/Harm Reduction, 129–30; and social work, 4, 116. *See also* community-based approaches; mutual aid
solidarity, 126, 128, 131–2
solitary confinement, 107, 209–10n28
South African Truth and Reconciliation process, 141
Spade, Dean, 26–7
St. Stephen's Community House, 129
the state, 23, 27–30

Stella's, 101
sterilization, 36–8
stigmatization, 7, 53, 84, 128–9
Strawberry Ceremony, 142
street kids, 56–7, 62, 66, 67–8. *See also* Child and Family Services; "frequent flyers"
suicide, 60–1, 63, 64, 65
support meetings, 86–7
surveillance, 41, 42, 51, 57, 67, 87. *See also* antitrafficking
survivors, 24, 68–9, 143–4
systemic discrimination, 53
Szigeti, Anita, 79

Taft, Jessie, 36, 39
Tammaro, Catherine, v–vi
Tecle, Sam, 182–92
teepees, 179–80
temperance societies, 3
Tester, Frank, 6
Thomas-Bernard, Wanda, 53
threats, 41, 72–3, 78–9, 80, 94, 131
"Toronto 18" terror plot, 108
Toronto Aboriginal Research Project (TARP), 171, 172, 173
Toronto Birth Centre, 154
Toronto Indigenous Harm Reduction, 179–81
Toronto Urban Farms, 183
trans liberation, 24
transformative justice, 26, 28–9, 144
transparency, 157, 158
trauma: and burnout, 89–90; and foster care, 60–1; and health care providers, 163; infants and parents,

157–8; and injustice, 127; and language learning, 167–8; and Not Criminally Responsible, 75; and responsibility, 81; system as retraumatizing, 136–7; as weaponized, 57
Treurer, Anton, 167–8, 172–3
Trudeau, Justin, 151
Truth and Reconciliation of Canada (TRC), 1, 115, 139. See also *Calls to Action*
truth and reconciliation (other), 139, 141, 173
truths, 163–4
Tsing, Anna Lowenhaupt, 116
Tuck, Eve, 118, 119, 173, 174, 175, 176
Turcotte, Nolan, 103–8, 111–13

Udegbe, Onyinyechukwu, 52
unions, 5
unsettling, 121–2

van der Meulen, Emily, 95
violence: and distress, 73; in foster homes, 62, 65, 66–8; in language learning context, 176; police and Black people, 45, 48–9, 85; police and Indigenous people, 85; and restorative justice, 143–4; and slavery, 33–4; of the state, 28; and street kids, 56–7. See also law enforcement

Wahab, Stephanie, 95
Walcott, Rinaldo, 51
Wang, Jackie, 9
WAVAW, 102

Waypoint Hospital, 76, 209n23
Wayward Lives, Beautiful Experiments (Hartman), 7
Weapons of the Weak (Scott), 195n46
welfare state, 51
"welfare" checks, 43, 52
white farmers, 183–4
white saviour complex, 98–101, 117, 122
white supremacy, 19, 120, 183–4
Whitebird, Wanda, 142
whiteness: of Canadian nation, 34–5, 38–9; and citizenship, 109; defining, 199n14; and protecting women, 18; and racial equity commitment, 6
Williams, Krysta, 136, 138, 139, 145, 148, 150, 152; "Baby Bundle Project and Community Birth Work Journeys," 154–64
Wilson, Alex, 138, 139, 140, 143, 148, 152
Winnipeg, 55, 66–7. See also Child and Family Services
Withers, A. J., 6
Women's Coalition, 99–100
Wong, Edward Hon-Sing, 1–15, 32–43, 115–23
Wright, Cynthia, 5

Yang, K. Wayne, 118, 119, 174, 175, 176
Yatim, Sammy, 40
Yip, Harry, 38
York, Reginald, 4–5
Yu (sex worker), 92–3, 97
Yu, Nilan, 120

CRAIG FORTIER (they/them) is a Tkaronto/Toronto based scholar and community organizer. They have worked as a social worker in housing, youth organizing, and non-profit funding organizations while also organizing with migrant justice, queer/trans*, anti-capitalist, and Indigenous solidarity movements. Currently, they are an associate professor in Social Development Studies at Renison University College (University of Waterloo) and are the author of *Unsettling the Commons: Social Movements Within, Against, and Beyond Settler Colonialism*.

EDWARD HON-SING WONG (he/him) is based in Tkaronto/Toronto. With a background in mental health practice, labour organizing, and community organizing, his work and research centers on social work abolitionism in Canada and Hong Kong, mutual aid, social work and colonialism, institutional violence in the mental health field, and organizing in Chinese communities. He is currently a lecturer at York University's School of Social Work and a former chair of the Chinese Canadian National Council Toronto Chapter.

DR. MARIE-JOLIE (MJ) RWIGEMA (she/they) is assistant professor in Applied Human Sciences at Concordia University in Montreal. MJ's work draws from twenty years of community practice with Black, racialized, immigrant, and LGBTQ communities. Her work focuses on the interlinkages between resistance, political voice, and recovery from racial trauma. She is the co-director of a SSHRC-RGDI project titled Community-centered knowledges: fostering Black wellness in Montreal and the PI of a SSHRC-Connection project titled Resisting white supremacist violence against Black, Indigenous, and People of Color communities. MJ enjoys fiction, writing, meditating, and creating spaces of care in community.